KITTY LARSON WAS A TEEN-AGED PROSTITUTE WITH NOTHING LEFT TO LOSE — EXCEPT HER LIFE

She had already lost her innocence while barely into her teens, and soon her inhibitions about doing anything with any man for pay were gone.

Finally, the time came when her pay-off for depraved sexual degradation would not be cold cash but cold-blooded death. Her trick had her tied with a rope as he tried to convince her he would let her go if she pleasured him yet one more time.

But Robert Hansen had not reckoned on one thing when he picked Kitty as his latest victim. Kitty might be many things—but she was also the survivor who became the first live lead a stubborn Alaskan state trooper would have to the most shocking case of serial murder in the annals of sex turned savage. . . .

BUTCHER, BAKER

BUTCHER, BAKER

A TRUE ACCOUNT OF
A SERIAL MURDERER

WALTER GILMOUR & LELAND E. HALE

AN ONYX BOOK

ONYX
Published by the Penguin Group
Penguin Books USA Inc., 375 Hudson Street,
New York, New York 10014, U.S.A.
Penguin Books Ltd, 27 Wrights Lane,
London W8 5TZ, England
Penguin Books Australia Ltd, Ringwood,
Victoria, Australia
Penguin Books Canada Ltd, 10 Alcorn Avenue,
Toronto, Ontario, Canada M4V 3B2
Penguin Books (N.Z.) Ltd, 182–190 Wairau Road,
Auckland 10, New Zealand

Penguin Books Ltd, Registered Offices:
Harmondsworth, Middlesex, England

First published by Onyx,
an imprint of New American Library,
a divison of Penguin Books USA Inc.

First Printing, November, 1991
10 9 8 7 6 5 4 3 2 1

 REGISTERED TRADEMARK—MARCA REGISTRADA

Printed in the United States of America

ACKNOWLEDGMENTS

The authors would like to thank the following people for their support and assistance during the sometimes trying journey *Butcher, Baker* took from first draft to final publication: Marie Chevrier; Robert Lescher, our agent, and Mickey Choate, his assistant; Michaela Hamilton, our editor, and everyone at NAL/Dutton; Virginia Gilmour; Mark and Frances Hale; Martha Hale; Maxine Farrell; Glenn Flothe, Rollie Port, and everyone at the Alaska State Troopers; the Alaska Department of Public Safety; the Anchorage Public Library; the Chevrier sisters, Gail and Darlene; Marvin Wiseman; Ralph Hudek; Mr. and Mrs. Ken Richardson; Miss Myrtle Merryman; Kerry Conrad and the *Anchorage Times*; Nick Lamberto of the *Des Moines Register*; Joann Henning and her son, Darin Galle; and Ann Rule.

AUTHORS' NOTE

This is a work of nonfiction. While much of the dialogue in it is taken directly from court and police transcripts, there are numerous instances in which it has been reconstructed on the basis of the authors' interviews with relevant individuals. In addition, certain scenes have been dramatically recreated in order to portray more effectively the personalities involved in this story and the atmosphere surrounding the events upon which this book is based.

It should be emphasized that a police investigation produces conflicting versions of events. Where such conflict exists, the authors have sought to provide the version which in their opinion is the most credible.

The real names of the people involved in this story have been used, except for Kitty Larson, Robyn Patterson, and Melanie Michaels. The authors have chosen to disguise the identities of these people to preserve their privacy. Any similarity between the fictitious names used and those of living persons is, of course, entirely coincidental.

PART ONE

1

The baker snatched her off the street at Fifth and Denali. Right in the heart of town, where all the hookers hang out. He couldn't stop himself. Never could. When he wanted something, he took it.

This one's name was Kitty Larson. Known to her parents as Victoria Matthew. Like so many others, she was seventeen and pretty.

By the time she got to his house he had slapped handcuffs on her. Then he dragged her to his basement and raped her. She'd had strange sex before, but nothing like this. "Tell me you want it," he demanded. She started to cry, wishing she'd never gotten in this man's car. She should have known the two hundred bucks he'd offered was way too much for a lousy blow job.

"Tell me you want it, baby," he repeated.

"I want it, I want it," she muttered dumbly. It seemed to work: He came quickly. But Kitty had other things to worry about, like how to escape.

"Maybe if I go to the bathroom," she thought, "I can crawl through a window." She told him, "I have to go real bad. It hurts, I gotta go so bad." He nodded in agreement, but only after putting a thick nylon rope around her neck. He held it taut like a leash until she started to pee. When the rope suddenly went slack Kitty dashed to the bathroom window. It was nailed shut. "Shit."

The sound of heavy chains rattling in the den brought her back to the bathroom door. They made a sharp, ringing sound as they were dragged across the floor. She stood with her toes to the doorsill, silent as a church mouse. She was so paralyzed she was almost afraid to breathe. "He's gonna kill me," she thought. "After what he did, he has to kill me."

Kitty didn't wait to find out what he had planned next. No way was he going to trap her in the bathroom. The door nearly came off the hinges as she hurled it open. She stood before him stark naked. He looked her over with tight, beady eyes. "Go back in," he said, his voice flat and demanding.

Kitty had always been a rebel, the girl in the principal's office. Now she was the prisoner confronting her captor. "No," she said. "No."

"I said go back in," he repeated, his voice now edgy and mean. She stood her ground. Before she could move, however, she found herself grabbed and chained to a sturdy wooden post in the middle of the den. The baker fondled the shiny silver tow chain before winding it around her neck four times. It was an unsettling ritual, because he clearly enjoyed it.

"If you cooperate I won't hurt you," he said, tightening the chain around her neck. And then he was standing nose to nose with her, stealing her breath, violating her sight. His face was a lunar landscape of acne scars and what looked to her like facial warts. He was ugly, she decided, with horn-rimmed glasses and slick hair that gave him the look of a gawky adolescent who'd grown old but not up.

Almost as quickly she saw a gentler side of him. From somewhere he grabbed a brown, yellow, and orange afghan. He looked almost kind as he wrapped her in its comforting folds. "I'm tired," he told her. "I haven't slept in a long time. I'm gonna go to sleep on the couch. And d-d-d-don't wake me up," he stuttered, "or you'll m-make me mad. And you d-don't want to see me mad."

His face had regained its hardness, and his eyes were flinty and faraway. Most important, a gun was in his hand. Kitty tried to look compliant. He reacted by walking away without even changing his expression. Then he turned on the television. "Here," he said, trying to put her at ease again, "you can watch TV while I sleep."

While her keeper slept, Kitty's thoughts roamed everywhere. "How many more hours do I have left to live?" she wondered. She thought about her mother and father, and all the people she loved. "I'm not going to see them no more," she concluded. Looking around the den, dimly lit by the dusky rays of the Alaskan midnight sun, she noticed a clock—its hands never seemed to move—a computer, a rack of women's clothes, a pool table, a foosball table. What sent a chill through her, though, were all the hunting trophies.

On the floor was the bearskin rug where he had raped her. In the corner were piles and piles of wolf hides. Huge caribou and goat heads graced the paneled walls. Stuffed ducks and other game birds appeared to fly from their mountings. A stuffed fish rested on a coffee table. She got the message: This guy liked to kill things.

"I gotta get outa here," she told herself.

Just then she spied a pool cue leaning up against the pool table. "I got it," she told herself. "I'll grab it and hit him on the head." She soon realized it was a stupid idea. If she killed him, she'd be left to die. If she didn't kill him, he'd kill her in retaliation. So she made a vow. "If I get out of here, this motherfucker ain't gettin' away with it. No fuckin' way."

As though hearing her thoughts, the man on the couch suddenly awakened. In an instant he was by her side. She wanted to call him by name, put him at ease, but she wasn't sure what to call him. First he had said his name was Don. Then it was Bob. Whatever it was he sat in the chair and stared at her, him and his two names. Kitty thought he looked like a lizard with warts, and the sight of him made her cry.

"All I want is to go home to my mom," she pleaded. "I won't tell nobody. Just let me go home."

"Don't worry about it," he told her, doing his best to sound reassuring. "Everything's gonna be okay. I'm not going to hurt you."

"I hope . . . I hope not. . . . "

"Hey, I've brought seven other girls here. Usually I keep them a week. But, I really like you . . . so I'm gonna treat you special. . . . "

When he said that, she knew he had killed the other girls. After all, she thought, who would have let this man treat them so horribly? He had to have killed them.

"Why do you do this?" she asked, her voice plaintive.

"I used to work on the North Slope," he told

her matter-of-factly. "And I'd come down to Anchorage and spend two hundred dollars for a girl and go to a room for ten or fifteen minutes. Well, I'm gonna get my money's worth now. I'm gonna bring 'em to my house and do what I please." He paused and gathered his thoughts.

"But I like you so good," he said, "I'm gonna take you to my cabin and make love to you one more time. And then I'll have you back here around eleven o'clock in the morning."

"Okay, good, that's fine," Kitty replied, acting like she wanted to go. If she refused, she reasoned, he'd kill her right there in the house. Nobody would know. They were downstairs. It was quiet. Only the animals on the wall could see, and they had glass eyes. . . .

He was talking to her again. This time his voice was firm and filled with confidence. "And even if you do tell on me," he announced, "well, I'll have an alibi. My friends will say I went to the lake with them."

Despite his assurances, she thought he would kill her the moment he took off the chains. She jumped when he inserted the key in the padlock. "This is it," she thought. Instead he stood her up and made her get dressed.

"I got a plane over at Merrill Field," he told her. "I'm gonna fly you to my cabin."

Kitty planned to bolt immediately after they got outside. She carried her shoes in her hand: It was hard to run in pumps, and she wanted to dump them when she made her break. She'd wake up this slumbering middle-class neighborhood with bloodcurdling screams if she had to. It didn't even matter now if he shot her.

They didn't go outside, though. The car was waiting in the garage, away from prying eyes. He made her lie on the floor in the backseat, then gingerly laid a green army blanket on top of her. Soon they were driving through the half light, presumably on the way to downtown Anchorage.

In the car Kitty momentarily considered a surprise attack. She'd seen the gun and the rope in the front seat, next to her captor. What if she threw the blanket over him and covered his head so he couldn't see? Then she thought, "What if he crashes and kills us both?"

Kitty struggled to stay under control. As they drove on, another plan came to her. This one might work.

"We're going to Merrill Field," she told herself, "and I'm staying at the Big Timber Motel. It's just down the street." She could try a getaway when they got to the airfield. She'd run straight to the Big Timber. At the motel there were friends to protect her. She'd be safe.

At the airport the man parked near his plane, then went to the rear of the car and began pulling things out of the trunk. He started making a steady pilgrimage between the car and the plane. Were they going camping or something?

The driver's door had been left ajar and Kitty watched him go back and forth, waiting for her chance. "I'm gonna go for it, motherfucker," she told herself, building up her resolve. Peeking through the crack, she waited until she could see only his legs. "Now."

She sprang through the door like a startled doe and started to run frantically, driven by fear; barefoot in the gravel, handcuffed, tears swimming down her eyes.

She looked back just for a second. He was coming after her with a gun. "I'm gonna get you!" he yelled. His short legs were pounding as fast as they could.

"For God's sake, get moving!" she told herself. It seemed like hours before she finally raced into a used car lot. Not sure what to do next, she ducked behind one of the cars. No, that won't work, she told herself. The guy was right behind her.

Just as the assailant started to close in, Kitty spied a truck coming down the road. She dashed into the street and waved madly. But the guy in the truck didn't stop. Kitty screamed. Finally he slammed on his brakes.

"Are you all right?" he asked, as she leapt into the truck and slammed the door behind her.

"No. He's gonna kill me."

"Who's gonna kill you?"

Kitty didn't answer. The truck lumbered forward, slipping up through the gears. Kitty looked back at the man who was chasing them. She remembered what he had told her when he'd forced her onto the floor of his car: "Don't cause no problems," he had said, "because whoever sees you in my car, I'm gonna have to kill them and you."

"Take me to the Big Timber Motel," she blurted, as she turned back to the driver.

"I think we ought to go to the police station. That guy's got a gun."

"No, just stop!" Kitty yelled.

"No way," the man said, and kept on driving.

"Then just stop right here. Just stop and let me out, man!" Kitty yelled, as she saw her assailant turn around and jog back to the airport. She was safe. "Just stop, man!" she shouted.

The trucker pulled up at the Mush Inn Motel, right down the street from the Big Timber. A dazed Kitty Larson got out, went to the front desk, and had the desk clerk call her pimp, who came by cab a few minutes later. The driver of the truck, meanwhile, drove straight to the Anchorage Police Department and reported the incident.

Back at the Big Timber Motel, Kitty's pimp was having a hard time figuring out what to do with her. She was shaking with tears. She was hysterical. Between sobs, she demanded that he get the handcuffs off. The pimp wasn't having much success. He couldn't calm her down, and the handcuffs stubbornly resisted his best efforts to remove them.

"Stop it, please," he demanded. It was the voice he used to scold her, but this time there was an undercurrent of desperation. "Just stop crying," he begged. "Please."

"Okay," she whimpered.

But Kitty couldn't stop crying. The pimp grabbed her and slapped her. It didn't do any good. Finally, in frustration, he raced down the hall to his brother's room. When he came back he was waving a gun. "I'm gonna kill this motherfucker," he said. He left Kitty in handcuffs while he went to the airport.

2

The Anchorage police had known for three years that something was amiss in their fair city. The place was getting to be dangerous for prostitutes and topless dancers. Anchorage had always been a Wild West city, where men forever outnumbered women, and it was tricky going for these women in the best of times. All the same, Anchorage police detective Maxine Farrell had begun to notice an increasing number of missing persons reports involving topless dancers. Did it mean anything? Initially it was hard to be sure.

Alaska, a land of vast uninhabited expanses, experiences more than its share of missing persons. Trappers disappear in the untrekked outer reaches of the bush. Fishing boats are lost at sea, without even a life jacket to mark the spot where they went down. Miners, hikers, and hunters get caught in freak storms and become lost. Topless dancers and prostitutes also turn up missing, though for quite different reasons.

Women in "the life" are a restless bunch. Some are junkies, and when their habits start to cost too much they may leave town without warning so they can get cleaned up and start all over again. A greater proportion, though, work the circuit that stretches from San Francisco to Seattle to Anchorage and then Honolulu. When a woman gets tired of the pimps and pushers in one place, she can easily move on and get work elsewhere.

During the seventies and early eighties, moreover, there were many amateurs who came north to make a bundle of money servicing the pipeline workers. Their money made, they disappeared without a trace, returning to their hometowns in the lower forty-eight. Add to this list the women who just "upped and quit" and there were, at any given time, many women unaccounted for.

Farrell noticed a pattern, however. A topless dancer would make a date with a man she did not know. He offered her two or three hundred dollars for something innocuous, like nude photography or "lunch." The woman did not return from the date, and later a friend or lover would report her missing.

Then on September 12, 1982, two moose hunters found a partially clothed body in a shallow grave on a Knik River sandbar some twenty-five miles north of Anchorage. The hunters, who happened to be off-duty Anchorage police officers, were trying to see if they "could stir something up before dark" when they found the body. They were initially unsure about what they'd found, but became suspicious after finding a boot and jacket. At first daylight they went to the Palmer office of the Alaska State Troopers and reported their discovery.

The point man for the troopers who went to conduct a thorough crime investigation was Sergeant Rollie Port, a much-decorated Vietnam veteran who had an uncanny ability to find evidence that everyone else had overlooked. Before the body was even touched, Port had the grave site photographed from every angle. He also made certain that the body itself was carefully examined for any trace evidence that might lead either to the killer or to the identity of the victim. Equally important, Port personally made sure that every bit of gravel taken from the grave was sifted through a large wire screen. It was exhausting work, made unpleasant by the strong stench emanating from the decomposing body.

During the investigation several facts became evident. Although the grave was shallow the body definitely *had* been buried, indicating foul play. Second, the body had lain there for some time. Third, in sifting the gravel in and around the grave Sergeant Port turned up a valuable clue: the shell casing from a high-powered rifle. Presumably it had been ejected from the murder weapon.

Preliminary pathology reports showed the body to be that of a woman of undetermined age. She had been dead since the spring or early summer of 1982. Moreover, the troopers were having difficulty determining who she was, a problem compounded by the fact that, as one officer put it, "There are lots of missing persons of the same general description."

Not until September 27 was the woman identified. She was twenty-four-year-old Sherry Morrow. In a gruesome twist, she was also known as Sherry

Graves. She danced under the name of "Georgia" at the Wild Cherry Bar in downtown Anchorage and had vanished in November 1981, leaving all her worldly belongings behind. Publicly, troopers and the Anchorage Police said they doubted that Morrow's murder was related to the disappearance of at least three other dancers from Anchorage since 1980.

"There's nothing now to indicate that the disappearances are anything other than a coincidence," said Trooper Lieutenant John Shover when speaking to the news media. His remarks were echoed by others in the police establishment. "We don't believe that we have a mass murderer out there, some psycho knocking off girls," said Maxine Farrell, "but we have to cover every possibility."

It seemed as though the cops were playing it tight, maybe to keep the killer off-guard. After all, the troopers immediately began to search for more bodies on the willow scrub sandbars of the Knik River. Digging test holes in the gravel was a laborious process, and ultimately unsuccessful, but it had to be done. Trooper Homicide Investigator Sergeant Lyle Haugsven came closest to saying what was on the mind of police authorities when he said: "We've got to keep those other girls in the back of our minds."

Police knew a lot more than they were saying. Morrow was a topless dancer, and had been reported missing by her boyfriend when she failed to show up for a doctor's appointment. The night before she disappeared, moreover, she had told a girlfriend she had a date with a man who'd offered her three hundred dollars for a photo layout. She was supposed to meet him the next day at noon.

That was not all they knew. When the body had been exhumed from the grave, troopers found that Sherry's head had been wrapped in an Ace bandage. Presumably it had served as a blindfold. Had she been killed execution-style? The shell casing found in the grave turned out to be from a .223-caliber shell, normally used in high-powered semi-automatic rifles like M-16s, AR-15s, or Mini-14s. These were very deadly weapons, and seemed to suggest that the perpetrator was a Vietnam vet, a survivalist, or someone seriously deranged.

The remote grave site, in the shadows of magnificent Pioneer Peak, was accessible by motor vehicle, airplane, or river boat, meaning that anyone could have gotten to the scene of the crime. On the other hand, though, there was very little traffic through the area. It would be hard to find witnesses. It was, in fact, going to be impossible.

Based on the information they had, troopers and the Anchorage Police started to take a closer look at reported incidents between prostitutes and their johns. It proved to be fertile ground: When Kitty Larson was kidnapped, police had the names of fifteen men with whom prostitutes reported having strange encounters, this in a city of barely one hundred and fifty thousand people.

With the heavy influx and outflux of men through Anchorage—the boomers, the busters, the oil men, and *cheechakos* (the native Alaskan term for a newcomer)—police had to concede the possibility that the killer had already left the state. Maybe he had gone south to Seattle, where reports of the Green River Killer were receiving more and more attention. But the remote grave site made police think it might be a local, someone who knew his way around the bush country. Perhaps this man was using the bush as a way to commit his crimes with impunity.

When Anchorage Police Officer Gregg Baker, a ten-year veteran, arrived at the Big Timber Motel, he found Kitty Larson alone, in a state of shock, and still in handcuffs. He got the cuffs off first. When she was calm enough, she told her story. She also said she was afraid her assailant would come back and kill her. He told her they'd need her help to catch him.

"I really wanna help," she told him, "but am I gonna get in any trouble? I mean, because I'm a prostitute?"

"I don't think so." Baker knew about the disappearing dancers, and if this was the same guy then Kitty Larson could turn out to be an important witness against him.

"But if I don't help, I'm afraid he's gonna hurt somebody else," Kitty said. "He's killed other women. I just don't know what I should do."

Larson led Officer Baker to the southwest corner of Merrill Field and identified a blue-and-white Piper Super Cub aircraft with tail number N3089Z. Not long afterward they were approached by Brian Demers, a private security guard at the airfield. He told Baker that at five-fourteen that morning he had observed a white male, wearing a green coat and cap, running from the woods to a green vehicle with Alaska license number BJZ-775. When he saw Demers, however, he slowed his pace to a walk, entered the green car, and drove away.

A check with the flight tower showed that the plane was registered to Robert C. Hansen, who resided at 7223 Old Harbor Road. A further check with the Division of Motor Vehicles through APD dispatch showed that the car, too, was registered to Robert C. Hansen.

As several officers were dispatched to Old Harbor Road, Officer Baker took Kitty to Humana Hospital, where she completed a rape exam kit. As it happened she had been in the midst of her menstrual cycle, and thus had had a tampon in her vagina during her rape. The doctor found evidence of sperm on her tampon. He further observed that she had linear red abrasions on her wrists, which were consistent with handcuff marks.

Officers Hanson and Becker of APD, meanwhile, had arrived at Robert Hansen's home. He was not there when they came but drove up shortly after that. He seemed to match Kitty Larson's description: medium build, about 5'6" tall, about 170 pounds, short brown hair, with crossed front teeth and acne scars on his face. Wearing glasses, an army coat, jeans, and work boots. The police informed him of the nature of their investigation, and Hansen voluntarily agreed to accompany Officer Becker to headquarters, leaving Officer Hanson to secure the vehicle in the driveway.

When Officer Baker returned to APD headquarters from Humana Hospital, he joined the investigation. Hansen was read his Miranda Rights, and waived the right to have an attorney present. When told by Investigator Dennis that he was suspected of having raped a prostitute, Hansen cracked a joke.

"You can't rape a prostitute, can you?" he asked with a grin.

"In this state you can."

"Well, I didn't pick up any woman or prostitute last night."

"Can you prove that?"

"Yes, I can. From 5:00 P.M. until 11:30 P.M. last night I was at the home of John Sumrall, fixing an airplane seat. You can ask him. And then from there I went to the home of John Henning. I stayed there until about 5:00 this morning, talking about fishing. You can call him, too. After that I went to Merrill Field and put the seat in my airplane. From there I went straight home. When I got there I saw the police officers, who asked me to come to the station."

"Right now what I want from you, Mr. Hansen, is permission to search your residence and your plane," Dennis told him.

Hansen signed a written waiver of search for his green Buick sedan, his home, and the Super Cub airplane at Merrill Field.

Investigator Dennis and Officer Baker drove to Hansen's home. In Hansen's car they found a bundle of center-fire rifle cartridges under the front seat. Baker thought the cartridges looked like .30.06- or .223-caliber. On the dash they found a rolled-up Ace bandage, and Baker saw a pair of rubber surgical gloves on the back window shelf of the Buick.

Entering the garage the officers saw several animal traps with chains attached, but no ropes, chains, or towels. There was a padlock on the floor. On a workbench they saw several green wool army blankets. Also in the garage was a large amount of equipment for hand-loading firearm ammunition.

In the basement they found exactly the scene described by Kitty Larson: black bear rug, mounted game animals on the walls, foosball and pool tables, and an adjacent bathroom. On the south basement wall, behind a false panel, they also found a compartment containing many rifles, shotguns, and pistols. None matched the description that Larson had given.

Officer Baker also saw an unusual weapon: a Thompson Contender. A lightweight, single-shot pistol favored by marksmen, it was available with interchangeable barrels in many different calibers, including .30.30, .223, and .222. Looking around the rest of the basement Baker found a small hole in the support pillar, but no bolt or similar device attached. He also found another small hole in the pillar, like a bullet hole, just above the floor.

The officers then went to Merrill Field and searched Hansen's Super Cub. They found nothing of evidentiary value in the plane.

The next day, June 14, 1983, Investigator Dennis showed Kitty Larson a photographic lineup of unidentified males. She unhesitatingly picked out the photograph of Robert Hansen as her assailant.

Then, however, the building case against Hansen

suddenly met a dead end. When Dennis called John
Sumrall, he confirmed that Hansen had been with
him from 5:00 P.M. until 11:30 P.M., fixing an airplane seat. What's more, when Dennis called John
Henning he said Bob Hansen had been at his house
from about 11:30 P.M. until 5:00 in the morning.
They talked about fishing and ate pizza, he said.
Suddenly the stories of Kitty Larson and Bob Hansen were greatly at odds.

Two major facts emerged from Investigator Dennis's investigation. First, Hansen's alibi witnesses
would look good on the stand. John Sumrall, the
manager of one of the city's biggest insurance com-
panies, lived in a plush house up in the hills over-
looking Anchorage. A solid citizen with impeccable
credentials, his mere association with Hansen con-
ferred a certain respectability on the baker.

Henning was nearly as impressive. A private
contractor and professional boat-builder, he had
even built a custom boat for Bob. The cops had to
ask themselves the same question a prosecutor
would ask them: Whom would a jury believe?

The answer to that rhetorical question brought
the officers to a second conclusion: Bob Hansen
was apparently the upstanding member of the community he claimed to be. A computer check of his
criminal record, for instance, showed nothing (im-
portantly, however, the APD was changing to a
computer system at the time, and not all its records
were in the data bank). Hansen owned his own bakery, a home, several cars, and an airplane. He also
had a wife and two children, who were presently
in Arkansas visiting his wife's parents and on their

way to Europe after that. He was not only an upstanding citizen but a good provider. Who would
take the word of a prostitute against that of a respectable businessman?

Because of this, Kitty Larson was treated roughly
at the police station. The investigators thought she
was inventing a story and wanted her to take a
polygraph test. She refused. What was the use?
They didn't believe her anyway. To make matters
worse, the officers hadn't seized any evidence at
Hansen's house, the scene of the alleged crime.
They hadn't even taken any photographs.

Not surprisingly, when APD ran its case up the
flagpole at the prosecutor's office no one saluted.
Their case was completely lacking in probable
cause. The investigation was shut down and filed
away. But not before APD Investigator Maxine Farrell had passed along information about the incident to the Alaska State Troopers.

At the same time as Sergeant Lyle Haugsven was
handed the remains of the Kitty Larson case, he
was also assigned the Sherry Morrow case. This
was no stroke of luck for him. His fellow troopers
regarded the Morrow case as a hopeless one, and
the Larson case would prove no less difficult to put
together. Despite these odds, Haugsven was determined to see them through.

A competent, steady officer, Haugsven was a
quiet, hardworking family man who'd been all over
Alaska. One of his first steps had been to re-
interview the friends who'd reported Sherry missing, especially her boyfriend Dale Yonkoske. He
told Haugsven that Sherry always wore a gold ar-

rowhead necklace. He'd given it to her as a gift. It was an important piece of new information. Haugsven knew no such necklace had been found in Sherry's grave or anywhere in the vicinity. Could the killer have taken it as a memento?

Because the Morrow case entailed a great deal of work, the Kitty Larson case seemed like a nuisance. It was true that there was talk of Hansen as a possible suspect in the Morrow homicide—because of his actions in the Larson case—but he was seen merely as one of many suspects. Nevertheless Haugsven decided to take a closer look at Hansen, on the off chance there might be a link to the Morrow investigation.

Haugsven's first step was to find the cabin Hansen had mentioned to Kitty Larson. A search of property records, however, turned up nothing. Was the cabin in someone else's name? Did it even exist?

Simultaneously, Haugsven decided to begin having the Merrill Field tower report on Hansen's flights. The trooper sergeant knew that the best way to the spot on the Knik River where Sherry Morrow's body had been found was by airplane, and it was possible that Hansen could be linked to the Knik grave site merely by the flight information he reported to the tower.

Unfortunately for Haugsven, this led nowhere. Unknown to him, Bob Hansen did not abide by the rules. He had purposely painted tiny ID numbers on his aircraft so the tower would have trouble seeing them. He called the tower as needed, but because the tower always took a pilot at his word he gave them another aircraft number, typically one taken from an aircraft parked near his.

When taking off, Hansen made sure he was high in the air by the time he reached the tower. On some runways he could reach about a thousand feet before passing the tower. Someone would have needed binoculars to doublecheck his numbers, and at busy Merrill Field that was unlikely to happen, even if troopers were looking for him. Not only that, whenever Bob flew north to the Knik he immediately swung his plane in that direction and got out of the airspace over the field.

Bob took these devious measures for a simple reason: The FAA had denied him his pilot's license when they found out he was taking lithium for a manic-depressive condition. Determined to keep flying despite the FAA, Bob began lying to the tower and doing other little things to keep them at bay.

3

On September 2, 1983, another body was found on the Knik River. It was quite near where the body of Sherry Morrow had been found the previous September. By chance Sgt. Haugsven was on leave for two weeks. The troopers really had to scramble this time around.

So Sergeant Ed Stauber led the investigation this time. Getting to this site was more problematic, since even in the summer months it was accessible only by boat or light aircraft. Stauber came down by boat from the old Palmer Highway bridge.

At this part of the Knik River's five-mile run to the sea from its headwaters at Knik Glacier, the view is dominated by 6,398-ft. Pioneer Peak. Snow-covered the entire year, it stands like a cathedral over the river valley. It is beautiful country, and at that time of the year the aspens are just days away from the first of several autumn transformations. First they turn a bright yellow. Then a deep orange. Finally, a crimson red. The air that day was a crisp reminder of what was to come.

At the scene Stauber found the decomposed remains, buried in a very shallow grave on the sandy river bank. Apparently the murderer had been in great haste or had panicked. The body was still clothed. She was wearing unbuttoned and unzipped blue jeans, a striped sweater that had been cut in half in front, a bra that had also been cut in half, and tan boots.

After carefully noting and photographing the position and state of the body, troopers removed it from the grave for further analysis. No purse, no identification, and no jewelry were on the body or in the area.

The state of decomposition was such that fingerprints could not be taken. They did have an intact jawbone. If they got lucky they might identify this woman by matching the jawbone to her dental charts. That's if they could find a woman who'd been reported missing, who had dental records somewhere, whose jawbone matched the one found on the Knik. It was, at best, a time-consuming process, given the reality that the troopers were starting essentially from zero. There was no collection of dental records ready to be consulted at a moment's notice.

The sole positive finding of the investigation was a single .223-caliber expended shell casing found near the grave site. It was identical in caliber to the shell casing found in Sherry Morrow's grave, just upstream. Troopers would send them both to the FBI to see if they had been fired from the same rifle.

At the autopsy conducted the next day, several facts were determined. The female victim had been in her late twenties or early thirties. She had been killed by a single small-caliber gunshot wound to the sternum. The bullet had passed through her heart.

The troopers also knew something else: Anchorage had a serial murderer on the loose. He packed a high-powered rifle and had the ability to bring his victims to a remote, inaccessible portion of the scenic Knik River. For all the troopers knew he was still murdering the women of the city. But like his latest victim the killer's identity was still unknown.

PART TWO

4

"I walked around to her side of the car and got her up and out of the seat. Then I took her back around behind the wing strut—she's still handcuffed behind, you know—grabbed her by the arms and let her put her feet up on the step and walk herself on in and then she sits down. Once she's inside the plane—again, she's pretty much confined, can't move.

"Then I have to go back out and get in my car and just move it fifteen feet. I told her what I'm going to do, you know, that I'm going to be watching you, so please don't start getting out of the airplane, because I don't want to shoot a bunch of holes in the side of it. And she didn't even blink an eye. I got back in and started the airplane and taxied out.

"I got out there on the Knik River, you know, I landed there and it was all fine. Right away I reached in and got her loose. It was awful hard for me in the first place to get her out of the airplane when she was still handcuffed, so I just reached in there and unhooked her handcuffs so she can grab the back of the seat and window supports in front and step on out. I grabbed her after she stepped down.

"The spot where you land out there is all gravel, then there's some woods over here and a shack—it was a frame for a tent cabin; in other words, the walls are only about so high. And they have a meat shack out here, which is the same way. It's only half walls around, but then it has a roof on it and is screened in with a door on it. And there's a bar through the middle of it so they can hang moose meat and stuff in it so it can cool down without flies getting to it.

"Anyway, I got her out and got the handcuffs off and just took her by the arm. I said to her 'This is where we're going to spend the day.' Just as we was walking in here, a damn plane comes down the river, going down around and in big circles over. He made a pass around and I thought, 'Oh shit, that son of a bitch is going to stop.' I'm still holding her by the arm and I say, 'Don't say a goddamn word to him. If you raise hell and he starts for me, I'm going to have to shoot the son of a bitch, and if I've got to shoot him I'm going to shoot you, and you don't want that, do ya?'

" 'Oh, no, no, no, no.'

"I said 'All right, let's go in here,' and we went to the meat shack. Next to the screen door there was a nail that was bent over to hold the door shut. I twisted that down, got her inside, and I backed her up against an iron pipe running across the top of it where they could hang meat from. I said, 'Hey, I'm going to make sure the guy don't land, or if he does land, I'm going to make sure he don't come up here. You stay here and keep your mouth shut and we're going to have no problems whatsoever.'

"So I handcuffed her hands behind her, around that post, and as I walked back out to my airplane, this guy made one more pass—they were quite big turns, you know. And as he was coming around one more time he dipped his wings at me, and I just waved to him. He waved a couple more times and leveled off and went back down the river. That scared me a little bit there.

"But I had the .223 in my airplane, and I carried that back and I leaned that against the shack. Then I went back in to her in there and got her freed.

"Up until the time when that guy first flew over, everything was just right. As a matter of fact, when the plane came over the first time, I said, 'There comes a plane. Let's get out of sight.' And boy, you know, she just right away got behind some bushes and done everything she could to keep out of sight.

"But the problem was, I think, maybe I shouldn't have called it a meat shack to her. Maybe that's what got her thinking. I thought about it a lot of times, but I don't know the answer. All I know is when I started walking out of there with her, she started screaming.

" 'You're going to kill me, aren't you? You're going to kill me.'

"I said, 'No, I ain't going to kill you. The problem is over with. The guy is gone.'

" 'Oh, no, no, you're going to kill me.' She slapped me and started running. I caught up to her and stopped her. I said, 'Now look, it's over. There is no problem, the guy is gone.' But she had got hysterical and I couldn't get her calmed down. The more I tried to talk to her—and maybe it was because I was getting excited—the more hysterical she got and she broke away from me again and started to run.

"I took a couple steps back and grabbed the rifle. Then I ran and caught her again and I said, 'Now look, don't make a bad thing worse. Don't. Stop. It's okay.' But then I had a gun in my hand and she said, 'You're going to kill me right now.'

"Then she—it just went completely, things just went completely bad again. If that son of a bitch hadn't circled in there it would never have happened. 'Cause as a matter of fact I'd never had one that tried as hard to keep it under wraps, you know. But I think when she was by herself in the meat shack, she just—confined there—that's when things went bad.''

5

Five days after the second body was found on the
Knik, Lieutenant Bob Jent of the Alaska State
Troopers assigned Sergeant Glenn Flothe (pro-
nounced "Flowthie") to the Knik River murders.
At that time he'd been working on seventeen other
homicides. He'd solved all except one of them, but
most still needed follow-up. That meant Flothe was
stuck shepherding his cases through the judicial
system.

Jent changed all that. Flothe was to work full-
time on the Knik cases. His assignment was clearly
necessary, since Haugsven wasn't scheduled to return from leave until the following week. And
Flothe had some familiarity with the case, since
he'd sat in on the weekly Monday morning meetings where the investigators discussed their homicide cases. He'd heard Sgt. Haugsven recite the sad
litany of frustrations he'd encountered while investigating the Morrow homicide, including the lack
of promising suspects.

Flothe didn't look like your usual cop. Tall, slender, almost gawky, he was mild-mannered but intense, soft-spoken but intelligent. He looked like a

schoolteacher with his glasses, mousy brown hair, and rumpled suits, and in fact had almost become a teacher.

Certainly nothing in Glenn Flothe's background had prepared him to become a state trooper. At twenty-one he was poised to become a teacher when, on a whim, he enrolled in some Police Science classes at Anchorage Community College. He started to meet some of the top cops in the state. The best part came after class, when investigators went to a nearby bar to discuss real-life cases. On some of these occasions they asked Flothe to join them.

Flothe was the proverbial church mouse. He sat very quietly, listening intently, only occasionally offering questions. He understood the seriousness of these discussions—they were, after all, mentally trying to solve some exceedingly difficult cases. But he was also completely transfixed by what was said within this ad hoc group.

They talked about the murder of a woman who had escaped, half-naked, from her kidnapper only to freeze to death in a state park on Christmas Day three years earlier. Her murder was still unsolved. They also talked about a more recent case, the murder of a young airline employee whose mutilated body was found in a gravel pit by some kids. She had been raped, and one of her breasts severed. What kind of subhuman would commit that kind of act?

At the same time Flothe was also becoming better acquainted with Sergeant Walter Gilmour, one of the group, and the trooper occasionally gave him a ride home. Naturally enough they talked cop talk. And one night near the end of the term the sergeant gave Glenn Flothe a vital bit of encouragement. "Listen, Glenn, if you ever decide to become a trooper, get your wife and come down to the trooper academy in Anchorage."

Shortly after this conversation Flothe applied to the troopers. Of course they weren't exactly waiting for him. The months passed and he heard nothing. It was a good thing, he decided, that he was close to getting his teaching certificate.

He was just about to start teaching when he got a call from Major Harold Sydnam of the Alaska State Troopers. "I want you to be part of the new trooper class that starts in Anchorage in two weeks," the major told him. "I have to have your answer now."

At the academy Flothe told his superiors that he wanted to be a criminal investigator. They laughed. After graduation they sent him to work traffic. He began to think he'd never become an investigator.

Then out of the blue he was transferred to a training position in Investigations. He was twenty-three. He had been in the troopers all of eight months. He hadn't been so unrealistic after all.

While assigned to the General Investigation Unit, Flothe had done it all: conducted burglary and robbery investigations, assisted in homicide investigations. Then came the first of several transfers and promotions. In Fairbanks he investigated homicides and sex crimes and, eventually, pornography and sexual assaults involving young children. Back in Anchorage he was initially assigned to the Airport Narcotics Detail. By September 1983 he was with the Homicide Division of the Criminal Investigation Bureau, a special unit modeled after the Texas Rangers.

Flothe decided first to take a close look at the list of missing women. Maybe there was a pattern. Of course, Glenn Flothe wasn't the kind of guy who just took a casual look at a missing persons file. Flothe was an organizer. So he started a matrix of possible victims that included pictures of the women, their profiles, the dates they were last seen, and anything else he could come up with.

It was tedious work, sorting through these disrupted lives. There were women who had fought with abusive lovers and presumably left town for good, leaving nothing but a few darkened, one-minute photos behind. There were teenage runaways, some missing one night and found the next, many more cast adrift to become who knows what. From this tragic assemblage Flothe was able to compile seven similar cases.

Paula Goulding, thirty, from Hawaii—reported missing April, 1983. Kathy Disher, twenty-three—disappeared late 1982. Delynn Frey, twenty— reported missing September, 1983, but may have vanished in March of that year. Karen Baumsguard, twenty-four, of Portland, Oregon. Sue Luna, twenty-three, of Washington State. Tamara Pederson, twenty-one, of Washington State. Teresa Watson, twenty-two, of Sacramento, California. And Angela Feddern, twenty-six, of Seattle, Washington.

The list was tentative, to be sure, but with one

exception these women were all in their twenties, all between 5'4" and 5'7", weighing from 120 to 125 pounds and slim, usually busty, according to sources. All had at one time or another worked as topless dancers in Anchorage. All had made big-money dates with a stranger before disappearing. And all were presumed dead at the hand of the Anchorage killer.

The importance of Flothe's list was not academic. Troopers still hadn't identified the body found on the Knik—it is never easy to identify decomposed remains. Although pathologists had an intact jawbone, they couldn't just match it willy-nilly with the hundreds of women who were missing. Narrowing the list of possibilities was, therefore, essential to identifying the victim hastily buried in the shadows of Pioneer Peak.

While Flothe was immersing himself in the case files, he also started to read some of the literature on serial killers. He found the subject fascinating, and was especially intrigued by the books about Ted Bundy. Most interesting, as far as Flothe was concerned, was the episode in Colorado when Bundy handcuffed and kidnapped a young woman, trying to take her away in his Volkswagen. The young woman escaped, fingered Bundy for attempted kidnapping, and was instrumental in putting him in jail for the first time.

Thus when Flothe read the Kitty Larson case for the first time on September 13, it was an almost incandescent experience. It was just like in the Bundy case. "If this is the guy who killed those women up on the Knik, then this could be the key to putting him in jail,'' Flothe decided. He was so excited about his discovery that he read the passage from the Bundy book to his wife that night, then told her about Kitty Larson.

It wasn't just the parallel between the two stories that convinced Flothe that Bob Hansen deserved a closer look. Kitty Larson matched up strongly with the missing persons matrix: her age, her height, her weight. All the missing women had been offered big money by somebody before they disappeared. And Kitty Larson claimed she'd been offered two hundred dollars for a blow job, then handcuffed and taken at gunpoint to his house, where she was raped. ''He's gonna kill me,'' she told the officer who investigated the incident. She was still scared for her life after she got away.

That fear, more than anything else, was what impressed Flothe. Chained to that post in his basement she had known terror, known that the guy would murder her. ''This woman is telling the truth,'' he told himself over and over as he read her statement. ''I have to talk to this woman. She's the clue.''

Flothe was realistic about his mission. He knew it wasn't going to be easy to find her. The street is a place that swallows people whole, where rumors are worth more than the truth, a place with its own rules and regulations. If he was lucky Kitty was still in town, working at one of the topless clubs or massage parlors. Even then he couldn't be sure that those who knew her would tell him where to find her.

His preliminary investigation gave him cause to

worry. The word was that Kitty had fled the state and gone back home to Seattle. That meant he would have to leave Alaska to find her, a more daunting task.

While pondering what to do next, Flothe weighed the data before him. The good news was that Kitty Larson had identified her attacker; the bad news was that no one had taken her seriously. Yet even that didn't dampen Flothe's enthusiasm, because there was still something about Hansen that just didn't seem right to him. Flothe felt a faint glow of excitement every time he contemplated what he'd found in the case files.

By Tuesday afternoon Major Gilmour had heard that Flothe was telling other investigators about his suspicions. So he stuck his nose into Flothe's office. He was only being conversational when he asked the sergeant how he was doing in his new assignment, but Flothe figured something was up. It wasn't every day that a major stuck his nose in his office.

"Just came across something that looks interesting."

"Oh, yeah?" Gilmour replied. "What'd you find?"

"A gal named Kitty Larson came to Anchorage PD with a story about how some guy kidnapped her at gunpoint, put her in handcuffs, took her to his house, and raped her. Just like in the Ted Bundy case. And listen to this: When he finished raping her, he tried to take her to a cabin in his airplane. The girl was absolutely certain he would kill her."

"How'd she get away?"

"Just took off and ran. Some concerned citizen picked her up. He confirms the story that some guy was chasing after her with a gun."

"So why do you think this might be the guy?"

"He's got an airplane, first of all. Whoever killed those women up on the Knik had to have an airplane to get in there. And she fits the profile."

At that moment Gilmour eyed Flothe's matrix stretched across the wall behind him. There were eight-by-ten glossies of some of the missing women, with a grid a foot wide and four feet long for each.

"Is she a dancer?"

"A hooker. Works Fifth and Denali."

"And she's identified a suspect?"

"Yessir. A guy named Robert Hansen."

Gilmour looked up sharply. " 'Bad Bob Hansen'? Kind of a short, dippy guy? Stutters? Wears glasses? Some kind of a baker or something?"

"I don't know. That sounds like him."

"Did this guy have some prior arrests, like for kidnapping, rape, assault with a dangerous weapon, say about—God, it was about 1971, so that'd be twelve years ago. . . ."

"I checked him out on the computer and the only thing that came up was a 1977 arrest and conviction for larceny in a building. He tried to steal a chain saw from ol' Freddy Meyer."

Major Gilmour was now brimming with excitement, although Flothe wasn't sure why. "Well, if you can't get the records here," Gilmour continued, "you better contact Juneau. Because I'll tell you one thing: If this is the same Robert Hansen, he's got an arrest record as long as the Aleutian chain. And it ain't just larceny in a building. He's been messing with girls in this town since he got here, the dimple-dicked little shit.''

''Are you telling me that . . . ?''

''What I'm telling you is that Hansen is your man. You're absolutely right, Glenn, your assessment is right on target. The son of a bitch is a killer. A little chicken-killer.''

The way Gilmour derisively said ''Hansen'' told Flothe volumes. In fact, the sergeant was slightly taken aback. Sure, he had a strong feeling that Hansen was up to more than kidnapping and rape, bad as that was, but it was nothing more than a hunch. With Gilmour, apparently, hunches had gone out the window at high speed. When he said it was Hansen, he meant it.

Gilmour's face had taken on a determined seriousness that Flothe had often noted while working for the man. The sergeant could almost hear the snap, crackle, and pop of the veteran investigator's brain at work. The irony was that they'd taken him off investigations and sent him to California to buy the troopers a computer system. He'd learned the language of bytes so he could create a state-of-the-art system to automate trooper records. Yet for an investigator it was an all glory and no guts type of job.

''Did you say 1971, sir?'' Flothe asked.

''Yeah. December of 1971. As I recall he was arrested for some kind of assault charge involving a secretary or somebody he was trying to rape. I don't know the details, but I'll ask Ron Rice over

at APD It was his case. Anyway, while he was
waiting to go to trial on the assault, he went out
and kidnapped a woman who happened to be working the streets. Took her all the way to the Kenai
at gunpoint. Threatened to kill her. Told her he'd
killed people before and got away with it.'' All
6'4" and 200 pounds of Major Gilmour showed his
irritation. ''Know how that happened?'' Gilmour
demanded.

''No, sir,'' Flothe offered, almost sheepishly.

''We took it to the DA's office and the DA told
Hansen they'd drop the kidnapping charge if he
pleaded no contest to the assault. He took the deal.
And the sonofabitch didn't serve hardly any time
on it, either.''

''Geez, you know,'' Flothe responded, ''just
looking at this guy on the surface, he looks pretty
skookum. Successful businessman. Got some well-
respected members of the community to vouch for
him.''

''Hansen is *thought* to be well liked in the community,'' Gilmour said, a trace of a sneer on his
face. ''He's a worm.''

Flothe's conversation with Gilmour opened another door, one with a commandment written on
it: Know Thy Suspect. Flothe wanted everything
he could on the man: parole and probation records;
trooper and APD files regarding past offenses; files
on any police contacts or field interviews involving
Hansen; information about motor vehicle accidents
and work history; psychiatric court testimony; any
out-of-state arrests or convictions; tapes of sentencing hearings. Whatever there was, he wanted it.

As it turned out, the only readily available document was the trooper case file on Hansen's 1977 larceny in a building conviction. He couldn't get anything from APD "What's the case number?" they asked him.

"I don't know the case number," Flothe responded.

"We need the case number," they told him.

Flothe contacted the archives in Juneau instead, and they told him they'd send him everything they had. They assured him that they would include the APD cases as well.

"I need it ASAP," he told them.

Flothe also wanted to tell Juneau to keep their lips sealed about this, but knew he didn't have to. The entire enterprise had to be carried out with as little noise as possible. The last thing Flothe wanted was for Hansen to know the police were on to him. Killers can do some pretty strange things when they know too much.

Even the documents Flothe already had supplied a tantalizing look into Hansen's psyche. One of the documents that caught his eye was from the Alaska Supreme Court, dated August 11, 1978.

"(On) November 3, 1976," the justices wrote, "a security guard observed (Robert Hansen) 'acting suspiciously' in the store's sporting goods section. He watched Hansen place an old sales receipt on a chain saw box and leave the store with it. The guard apprehended Hansen in the store parking lot. Hansen described his thoughts leading up to the shoplifting as follows:

" 'I looked at them and remembered about five

weeks previous my father and I had been cutting wood for our fireplace and his remarking three or four times how much he would like to have one (my folks live in Oregon and were visiting us for four weeks), to use when he and my mother go camping along the coast. I told my father that he would be more than welcome to take mine but he refused.

" 'I thought of this and all the presents my parents had given me through the years and how wonderful it would be if I could give him a chain saw for Christmas. I also thought of course about my wife, and I had just bought this summer a new home and put everything we have saved for more than nine years into.

" 'I guess many, many thoughts went through my mind as I looked at the saws. I wanted almost more than anything to please my father, and could just imagine the expression on his face on Christmas day. If I could give him that saw.

" 'I walked around the store some more and out the front door. Outside a native man had just had a heart attack. The police, fire department, and paramedics were there to give him treatment. My father is sixty-nine and has had one heart attack and is very overweight. Again I thought of the chain saw, and how pleased he would be to receive it at Christmas. I walked back into the store, again to the saws.

" 'I thought there was a young man watching me, but then he seemed to disappear. On the one box that I picked up there was a sales receipt. I guess this is when I first really seriously thought about taking the saw. It seemed like nobody would know if I paid for the saw or not, if they saw a sales receipt on the box. I took the saw and walked out the door when I was apprehended and arrested.

" 'I know what I did was wrong and I am very sorry for doing it.'

"Hansen was thirty-seven years old at the time of the offense," the justices wrote. "He was the first child born to his parents and spent his youth working for his father in the family bakery as well as attending school. Following his father's example, Hansen was trained as a baker. Hansen depicts an ambivalent relationship with his father, whom he describes as very demanding and never satisfied with Hansen's work despite the great effort Hansen exerted to please him."

Major Gilmour had a good reason for remembering Bob Hansen. In one way or another Hansen's name had been turning up for the past twelve years. The first time had been during the Vietnam War era. Gilmour had been a former paratrooper turned investigation supervisor with the troopers. As sergeant he was responsible for investigating homicides, rapes, robberies, major burglaries, and gathering data on organized crime.

Then on Christmas Day, 1971, an eighteen-year-old woman froze to death in McHugh Creek State Park. When she was discovered she was naked from the waist down and her wrists were tied behind her back with speaker wire. She had been sexually assaulted, and her chest slashed with a knife. Somehow before her death she had managed to escape her assailant. She literally ran for her life.

Her first fall was fifty feet from the presumed location of the murderer's car. With her hands bound behind her and in snow three feet deep on a dizzying slope, it would have taken a superhuman effort to regain her feet and continue the descent into what must have seemed a black hole. She got within ten to fifteen feet of a frozen waterfall, but somehow turned away at the last minute.

Incredibly, she found a hiding place behind a bush. But her abductor was still looking for her: Troopers found "doughnut-shaped tire tracks" throughout the parking lot. And with temperatures going down to minus 5° F that night, her best hope was for him to find her. He didn't.

The case went fairly well at first. The woman was quickly identified as Melanie Michaels. Last seen December 22, at 9:00 in the evening. She had been on the way to the store. Her brothers didn't report her missing until the next day, however. They assumed she had gone to a baby-sitting job instead.

The person for whom she was to baby-sit became the first suspect. Gilmour became suspicious when the young man, a friend of the family, told officers he had come by to see her the night she disappeared. The victim's brothers, who were home that night, insisted the suspect hadn't been there. That meant someone was lying.

"You can't lie in a murder investigation and be innocent," Gilmour told himself and anybody who'd listen.

What they really had, though, was a case with too many suspects. The victim had had many boyfriends. She'd just broken off an engagement to one of them when he went to Vietnam. There were other broken hearts spread out in a trail behind her.

Some of Gilmour's men thought it was a hitchhike-type case. Certainly all the elements were in place: They had a pretty girl out on the streets at night, a busy thoroughfare, the hint of drug use among some who knew her, brothers who looked like hippies as far as the cops were concerned. It was the dark side of the Age of Aquarius.

The day after news of the murder hit the papers, Gilmour got a phone call. On the line was a senior officer in the Alaska State Troopers, John Patterson. "Hey look," he said, "I've been hearing about that dead girl down to McHugh Creek. I think I got an informant that may be able to help you."

"We need all the help we can get," Gilmour told him.

"The thing is," Patterson continued, "she doesn't want to be identified. She doesn't really know the person, but thinks he may be your killer. Also, she might have been working the street."

Gilmour's reaction to the last revelation was blunt. "I'll take anything you have to give me," he said. "But what the hell am I going to do with the third-hand story of a street girl?"

There was an icy silence, but then Patterson promised to talk to the informant and, hopefully, bring her in to talk to Gilmour. When Patterson called back he had news that the woman would talk. He also had a request. "I'd appreciate it if you'd keep this out of the newspapers." He cleared his throat nervously before he continued.

"You see, this girl is my daughter, and you know me and her mom are pretty active in our church. I have talked to her about what she's doing. She knows we love her, and she can always come home. Maybe this will help her find her way. At the same time her mother and me are not proud of what she's done. We love her and will stand by her in this, so I will have her come by and see you."

Gilmour fumbled for words. "Jesus, J.P.," he attempted. "I didn't know. I sure hope I wasn't too offensive when you called. I had no idea you were talking about your daughter."

"It's okay," J.P. said. "There was no way you could know."

The story Robyn Patterson told Gilmour that gloomy night in December was strikingly similar to the brief account Flothe had given him about Kitty Larson. Both were teenage prostitutes, working the streets. Both were kidnapped and raped. Both had their wrists bound by some type of restraint. Both had feared for their life.

Gilmour had strong memories of Robyn Patterson. To begin with, she was the most beautiful woman he had ever seen. She was as poised and confident as a fashion model. And she described a suspect who was a white male, 5'8" or 5'9". He was slender, she said, with blond hair cut fairly short. His face was kind of lumpy from acne scars, she thought. The man she was describing was Robert Hansen. Her story was a tale of terror.

She had been kidnapped at gunpoint from the parking lot of a sleazy café frequented by street people. Bound with her hands behind her back by big, leather shoelaces, she was driven to a remote spot, where her john asked if he could rip her bra off. She then was made to strip down to bra and panties so she couldn't escape. They drove deep into the Kenai, where they found a motel and had sex. "His penis was shaped funny," Robyn told Gilmour. "Like it was deformed or something. It was short, but very large around."

He promised to take her back to Anchorage, but he didn't. Instead he drove her deeper into the bush. He stopped his big Pontiac at the side of a steep bank that rolled on forever. "Nobody will even find me," Robyn thought. "I'll roll right off the face of the earth."

She asked him why they'd stopped. Her heart, she said, was trembling. "I—I saw somethin' in the trees," he said.

He paused a moment, then turned to look directly at her. There was nothing reassuring in those bluish-green eyes.

"I can't . . . can't take you back to town," he murmured. "N-not anymore. You'll t-t-tell on me, or g-go to the police."

"I won't tell anyone," Robyn purred. "Honest. I hate cops. They're the last people on earth I'd tell anything. As far as I'm concerned, none of this even happened. If anybody asks, I've never seen you before."

Somehow, some way, Robyn convinced Hansen she was no threat. Miraculously, he untied her hands and started driving back to Anchorage. When he let her out of the car a block from where he'd picked her up, he said, "I wish we could have met under different circumstances."

Remembering Robyn Patterson in this new light, Gilmour recalled one thing she had told him more than any other. "You know," she said, after identifying Hansen's mug shot, "I may be doing something that some people don't think is totally acceptable, and it may not be. But that isn't why I'm here. I'm here," she said, "because that guy, that Bob Hansen guy, is probably a premeditated, cold-blooded killer. And he has killed before. He said he killed before, and everything else he said was absolutely true. Everything he said he would do to me came true, everything he said he would do, he did. Every threat he made, I believed. And if he says he's killed people, I believe he's killed people. And if you've got a young girl who was killed around the same time and in the same area, then I believe it was Hansen who killed her."

Robyn has paused and caught her breath. "And I believe he'll kill me, too."

If Robyn Patterson was a prophet, hardly anyone believed her at the time. The troopers, for example, had taken the case away from Gilmour and given it to another officer. The main suspect in the McHugh Creek murder remained the young friend of the family. He looked guilty as hell until he took a polygraph and passed, and even then he looked guilty as hell. Gilmour still considered him the prime suspect. But twelve years had passed and no one had ever been charged with the murder.

Could Hansen have been responsible? Gilmour had treated him like a suspect then, but he was only

one of several. And when Gilmour interviewed
Hansen about the Melanie Michaels murder Hansen had some type of alibi, one that Flothe's research would have to help him remember.

Meanwhile Gilmour decided to call Captain Ron
Rice of the Anchorage Police. Rice was an old
friend of Gilmour's, a highly respected member of
the police community. As the man who had arrested Bob Hansen more than once, he was someone who could be counted on to remember him.
Sometimes, Gilmour decided, living memories are
the best.

6

"Yeah, I remember Bob Hansen," Rice told Gilmour. "He's a mad dog. He's so dangerous he should be put away forever."

"So, do you remember the case? What happened, anyway?"

"He followed some secretary home, and got into her house by making up some story about how he needed to use her phone. He left, but a half hour later he walked right in the house—didn't bother to knock or anything—and asked her for a date. She flat-ass turned him down. About a week later he came back with a gun and tried to kidnap her at gunpoint. She screamed, he ran, and we caught him."

"And that was the assault charge?"

"Yeah. Listen, Walt," the ace homicide detective continued, "I was there when we brought him in on that charge. Here was a guy who had hidden a gun under the wheel well of a car, and his statement was something to the effect that he had been out bow-hunting. What a dumb dipshit."

Rice was getting more disgusted with each sentence, and Gilmour could imagine his cheeks and neck flushed with excitement. His sentences had become short and staccato.

"Let me tell you something else. I went to Hansen's house to arrest him. On that deal with Robyn Patterson. I saw a roll of wire in his basement. Looked just like the wire used to bind Melanie Michaels' wrists."

"Why didn't you seize it?"

"It was Trooper Hughes' case, Major. And he wouldn't let me. I guess other things seemed more important at the time."

Gilmour remembered how they'd dragged Interpol into the case in a vain effort to identify that wire. The best they could do was tell him it was made by a gypo manufacturer "somewhere in Asia."

"You remember anything else?" Gilmour asked.

"When Robyn Patterson was shown the lineup photos, she went straight to the guy. And when Hughes took her back over the kidnap route, she remembered everything. I mean *everything.*"

"So you really think he was a killer way back then, huh?" Gilmour said, playing devil's advocate.

"You have to remember, Walt, that this guy threatened Robyn's life and the life of her kid. When Robyn Patterson said she believed he'd kill her, I knew she wasn't making it up. No way was she making it up. And I'll tell you one goddamned thing, Walt," he said, his voice rising in anger, "we taught him to kill. When we didn't put him away for a long time, we taught him to kill. We not only taught him to kill, we taught him who to kill.

Way back in '72. We told him it's all right to kill whores. 'Cause nobody gives a shit about whores.''

Gilmour knew Rice's "editorial" voice. He had heard it often, not always believing it. Maybe he should have. It was still too early to tell, and Gilmour was still not quite ready to suspend his disbelief. Rice, meanwhile, continued talking.

"You know, I told the DA at the time that we should go balls-to-the-wall on the Robyn Patterson thing. It was a strong case. She was an excellent witness. And we put together a pretty good list of witnesses who'd seen them. We had people all the way down the Kenai who'd seen them. You'll remember that I went to my boss, telling him that we should go for it. I even went to you. And ended up writing a report on the damn case, trying to get people to listen. The DA just gave me the cold shoulder. He was more interested in making deals with Hansen's attorney. So what else is new? It's a little club down there."

Gilmour had to laugh. *He's a cop,* he thought, *for the same reason that I am. He's a cop because, every once in a while, he gets to put a bad guy away. Forever.*

After talking to Rice, Gilmour's memories of the Robyn Patterson case flooded in on him. He was still burned that his supervisor had taken the case away and given it to Sergeant Hughes. And as it turned out, Hughes was involved in a calamity that may well have sabotaged the case in the eyes of the district attorney.

It seemed that, during Robyn's ordeal, Hansen had gone through her purse and found the court documents giving custody of her son to her parents. He wrote her father's name and address on a piece of paper. "Now I know where they live," he told her. "If you say anything to anybody, I'll have to kill them."

When Hughes and Rice interviewed Hansen, Rice asked for a handwriting sample. Hughes had already retrieved the registration card from the motel where Hansen raped Robyn, and they wanted something to compare it with. Rice had him empty his wallet on the table, and spied the triangular piece of paper with John Patterson's name and address.

"Who's this?" Rice asked, his voice hardening.

"I don't know," Hansen replied.

"Then what's it doing in your wallet?" Rice wanted to know.

"I don't know how it got in my wallet," Hansen said.

"We'll see about that," Rice responded. "Because we're going to take this little piece of paper into evidence."

"Now wait a minute, Ron," Hughes interrupted. "We're gonna need a search warrant." Rice protested, but lost the argument.

Hansen was later taken to the Alaska State Jail, where a correctional officer conducted a strip search before booking him. A rookie officer, it turned out, was at the desk. He took Hansen's wallet from the plastic evidence bag and emptied the contents onto the desk, counted the money, and completed an inventory. That done, he returned the contents to the wallet and laid it on the desk. It was here that

Hansen mumbled something: "Maybe there's some more money hidden inside my wallet."

The correctional officer then made two rookie mistakes: He handed the wallet to Hansen, and instead of keeping his eye on him he turned his back, becoming occupied with something else. Out of the corner of his eye, though, he thought he saw Hansen take a slip of paper out of his wallet and hide it in his hand.

"You better shake him down again," the desk officer said, when his co-worker returned to take Hansen for fingerprinting. "I think he took something outa his wallet."

A thorough search of Hansen's pockets uncovered a wadded-up piece of white paper in his back pocket. "Now, what's this piece of paper doing in there, Mr. Hansen?"

"It's the name and address of the person who is going to raise bail for me tomorrow," Hansen replied. "I need that piece of paper."

The correctional officer got another sheet of paper and copied what was written on the piece found in Hansen's pocket. But he returned the original to Hansen and took the copy to the front desk. Neither officer knew it then, but they'd just been had. The delicate link between victim and rapist was irretrievably broken. There was nothing Rice or Hughes could do but shake their heads. For his part, Gilmour was disgusted. Years later, he was still disgusted.

Looking back on it all with the benefit of hindsight, Major Gilmour had to admit that the loss of that slip of paper was somehow inevitable. It was part of a chain of dead ends and lost hopes that had started with a dead girl at McHugh Creek and brought Bob Hansen before Walt Gilmour to make a written statement:

> Went to work at 4:45 a.m., Wed Dec 22 1971. Got through work at 2:00 p.m. went home to 327 Thomas Ct. Spent rest of the afternoon from 2:00 p.m. till 5:00 p.m. with my wife and sister-in-law and daughter then went to Lonny Brisker's home on 6th Street for pizza supper. Left there about 10:30 went home with my wife and daughter. Went to bed about 11:00 p.m. got up again about 4:30 dressed and arrived at work about 4:45 a.m. Thursday and worked until 2:00 p.m.

Twelve years later they were getting another chance at Hansen, and maybe a small measure of vindication if they could pull it off. Yet it would still be a Pyrrhic victory. Flothe already had a list with seven potential victims, and it was growing.

In twelve years this man had had too many opportunities to kill women. Too damn many. The troopers could only hope that their luck was changing—and Gilmour knew they wouldn't be able to depend on luck with someone as wily as Robert Hansen. "If he can get out of this," Gilmour thought aloud, "he'll kill forever."

Gilmour didn't notice how glum Flothe looked when he burst in, bearing glad tidings from Captain Rice and intent on being a cheerleader.

"I've got some news for you, Glenn," he said. "I just talked to Ron Rice and he said Hansen's 'a mad dog.' Swears he's been killing women since '71. He told me that we had him on two cases that should have put him away for a long time, but didn't. One case was a real-estate receptionist he chased at gunpoint. She screamed. He took off. APD caught him. About a month later we got him for taking a young woman off the streets at gunpoint, a young woman who just happened to be a trooper's daughter. I'm telling you, Glenn, I'm positive Hansen is the guy we want. He's just the kind of creep who'd do something like this. Did you get the records on him, by the way?''

"Just got the 1976 larceny in a building case. I had to call Juneau for everything else. They're sending it up. I couldn't even get anything out of APD on him. I think they lost his stuff.''

"I'd sure like to take a look at it when it comes, if you don't mind. I remember those cases, but it's been a long time. By the way, how's your other case going?''

"You mean Larson?''

"The one who got away.''

"I think we're gonna have problems on it, Major.''

"Why's that?'' Gilmour asked, noticing that Flothe's dour expression had not deserted him during the whole of their conversation in his cramped and crowded office. The place was strewn with manila case files. Odd batches of xerox copies surrounded his coffee cup. Flothe had to draw a breath before he could speak.

"Well, to begin with, this is a circumstantial case. Nobody's seen him killing people. If I look at his past it tells me he's capable of this, but that's all. I mean *I* know he did it, okay? But I can't even get my partner to believe that Hansen's the one.

And if that isn't bad enough, I talked to Bill Dennis from APD. He told me Larson is crazy. That she made the story up. That she refused to take a polygraph. And he says the DA wouldn't touch the case. He says Steve Branchflower told him that it didn't appear they had proof beyond a reasonable doubt. And Hansen has an alibi witness for the time Larson says he was with her.''

"And . . . ?''

"That's all.''

"That isn't so much to worry about,'' Gilmour explained. "First, just because Hansen has an alibi witness doesn't mean the guy's telling the truth. And secondly, just because the Assistant District Attorney doesn't want to take it doesn't mean it isn't a good case. Nobody confesses on the street, Glenn. Nobody. You gotta bring 'em in and put a little heat on 'em. And I tell you, this Hansen's got a lot of explaining to do.''

"Well the thing is, Major, I'm not sure how good a witness this Kitty Larson will make.''

"Not because she's a hooker . . . ?''

"Because she's seventeen. And what if she really is crazy?''

"You believed her statement, didn't you?''

"Yeah. I still believe her. She's my case, Major. She's the one who's gonna get Hansen off the streets.''

"Have you talked to her yet?''

"No. Not yet. I will, Major. Trouble is, I think she's in Seattle. She hasn't been leaving any forwarding addresses, evidently.''

A busy week would get much busier. The next

day Haugsven returned from leave. Flothe hastily filled him in on what he'd been learning. Haugsven was willing to go for it. It wouldn't hurt to take a closer look at this guy.

They decided to start by finishing the job APD had started. They drove to Merrill Field, armed with a camera to take pictures of Hansen's Super Cub. Then they drove to Hansen's Bakery, which was a little storefront in a concrete block structure on Ingra Street. As they took photos they noticed a pizza joint next door, right on the main drag into Anchorage from the south and only blocks from where the hookers hung out.

When they got back to trooper headquarters, Flothe found a message from Sergeant Sam Barnard in Fairbanks. Glenn had known him since his first police classes back in the mid-seventies. In fact he was one of the men who had influenced his decision to become a trooper. Barnard told him he'd just talked to Major Gilmour, and that Gilmour had told him Bob Hansen's name came up on the Anchorage serial killings. Barnard just happened to know a 1975 case involving—guess what?—the kidnapping and rape of a topless dancer.

In this case Hansen had pulled a gun on a woman, driven her to Chugach State Park, raped her, performed cunnilingus on her, and forced her to perform fellatio. "If you don't do what I say, I'll kill you," he had told her. He'd bound her wrists, then told her that he worked the pipeline, that he was raping women in the Anchorage area, and that he had a friend who worked on the pipeline who also was raping women. "You won't be a good witness against me anyway,'' he told her, ''because you're a nude dancer and a prostitute.''

The woman memorized the license plate number on what she described as a ''red foreign station wagon.'' Barnard's follow-up investigation showed it was registered to Bob Hansen, and he observed a red Volvo station wagon parked in Hansen's driveway. The problem, according to Barnard, was that none of this information was coming from the victim herself.

The victim was giving police the information through a third party, Sheryl Messer of the Anchorage Rape and Assault Center. She was afraid for her life. She'd sworn Messer to secrecy about her name.

When Barnard interviewed Hansen, he denied abducting or raping any woman. He said he knew a tall, dark-haired girl he'd met at the Kit Kat Club in Anchorage the previous summer, when his wife was out of town. According to Hansen they struck up a conversation and then agreed to go to her place. As they drove to her house, he said, she told him the visit would cost him one hundred dollars. This upset him, so he said he drove her back to the Kit Kat Club. She became angry and started calling him names, but he denied doing anything to her.

''What about the gun?'' Barnard asked.

''I'm a convicted felon,'' Hansen replied. ''I can't own a gun. Besides, I was in Seward that day. Fishing.''

Barnard didn't believe Hansen or his alibi. He got an unmarked photograph of Hansen and gave it to Sheryl Messer. Shortly afterward Messer called him back and told him the victim had positively identified the photograph as that of her assailant. But she still refused to be identified to police or to talk to them directly, out of fear for her life.

The trooper later learned there was another, less profound reason for her reluctance. She was a schoolteacher from the lower forty-eight, and was afraid that cooperating with the police would lead to a trial and make public her involvement. Understandably, she feared her school district almost as much as she feared Robert C. Hansen.

No charges were filed against Hansen, nor could they be. The DA wasn't ready to let innuendo become a probable cause for arrest. Barnard didn't give up. He contacted Dwayne Burgess, Hansen's parole officer, hoping that he'd take some action to revoke Hansen's parole. But Burgess didn't do a thing, Barnard said. Not one thing.

Flothe soon learned why Hansen's parole officer had not taken action. Leafing through the records on Hansen's 1976 arrest for stealing a chain saw, the trooper found the proceedings from Hansen's April 5, 1977, disposition hearing. Dwayne Burgess had testified in the state's behalf at the sentencing, and the 1975 rape was a topic of discussion.

"I confronted him with it," Burgess said, "and he didn't deny raping her. He said he'd seen the woman several times and that one night she suddenly asked him for money. He said he never did use a weapon."

"What did you do?" the judge asked.

"I suggested he return to psychiatric counseling. He felt he did not need counseling."

"Did you look for a weapon?" Hansen's defense counsel asked.

"No."

"Did you suggest that Hansen's parole be revoked?" the DA asked.

"No charges were ever filed. The lady was in fear for her life and left the state."

"Did you consider him a good parolee?" the judge asked.

"Not after the rape," Burgess answered.

"Did he give you any problems?" Hansen's counsel asked.

"I believe he had mental problems, but he was hardworking. He had two jobs," Burgess said. "And there were no problems with drugs or alcohol. Just the problem with the rape. And I found him in some of the downtown bars during the late hours."

"Did that change your relationship with him?" the judge asked.

"No."

"Do you think the defendant needs counseling?" Hansen's attorney asked.

"The defendant needs counseling, most definitely."

And there it was. Hansen was sentenced to five years in prison on March 24, 1972, for assault with a dangerous weapon. His parole ended in 1976, according to a court officer at the disposition hearing. The rape incident had no bearing on the outcome of the parole hearing or, for that matter, on his sentencing for the stolen chain saw. It was simply filed away, left to gather dust, except in the minds of a few troopers.

7

In what was now becoming a twelve-hour-a-day job, Sgts. Flothe and Haugsven trekked out to the suburb of Muldoon, where they photographed the Hansen home. It was a ranch-style house in an attractive, woody setting on a dead-end street. There was a big garage, with moose antlers on the roof. From the outside you could see the windows of a daylight basement. The house neatly matched Kitty Larson's description.

Back at the office they found a truckload of reports from Juneau. The package included the report detailing the kidnapping and rape of Robyn Patterson. There was the report on Hansen's attempted kidnapping of the eighteen-year-old real-estate receptionist, whom he had jumped in the shadows of a carport in the predawn darkness; the one who had not been afraid to scream, whose scream doubtless had saved her life. And then there was the report from 1979, when he'd kidnapped a topless dancer, who was stark naked by the time she managed to escape. Already Flothe was starting to see a pattern in Hansen's explanation of the incidents.

Hansen's explanation for the 1979 kidnapping was typical. He denied having bound or abducted the dancer. He said he had met the woman several months before at The Embers, but only offered to give her a ride home after she got off work. He said that during the ride she put her hand on his leg and asked him if he wanted to stop somewhere. Hansen stopped the truck, he said, and they got in the back of the camper.

According to him the dancer stripped off her clothes and performed oral sex on him. When she'd finished she demanded seventy-five dollars. Hansen refused to pay, he said, because no one had mentioned money. The dancer got upset. Hansen panicked and threw her out the back door of his camper.

What Flothe couldn't figure out from the report was why the investigating officer hadn't asked Hansen to explain the broken window of his truck, or the glass that must have been at the scene. According to the topless dancer, just before she escaped Hansen smashed his fist through the driver's window in an attempt to grab her. No wonder she ran naked through the streets.

Coincidentally the state of Iowa also called to inform Flothe and Haugsven of Hansen's 1961 arson conviction in that state. Reports of the conviction would follow. Gilmour was right, Flothe thought. This man has an extensive record. "The light came on," Flothe would later say. "Hansen was no longer the gentleman businessman who ran a bakery downtown. His past was starting to catch up with him."

Yet there was one remarkable fact that struck
Flothe. Despite his nefarious activities, Hansen had
done very little time for his crimes. Some com-
plaints had disappeared after the initial investigation. The authorities hadn't done much more even
when he was convicted of crimes.

In the assault on the real-estate receptionist,
Hansen pleaded no contest. He was sentenced in
March 1972, transferred to a halfway house three
months later (where he was placed on work-
release), and paroled in November 1973, just
twenty months after his conviction. In the stolen
chain saw incident Hansen was convicted of larceny in a building in Superior Court on April 5,
1977, and sentenced to five years in prison. He ap-
pealed his sentence as excessive in a brief to the
State Supreme Court, a right guaranteed to him under Alaska case law whenever the sentence is longer than one year. On August 21, 1978, the
Supreme Court reversed the sentence and re-
manded it to the Superior Court with directions to
place Hansen on probation "as expeditiously as
possible." This time he had served all of sixteen
months in prison. This man, Flothe decided, was
as slippery as a seal on ice.

As the case reports chronicling Hansen's past
started to roll in, there seemed less and less question whether the man was capable of murder. And
if Bob Hansen was capable of murder, and those
were his victims up on the Knik River, then probably more bodies were strewn among the willow
sandbars. On Tuesday, therefore, just two days after Haugsven had returned from leave, he and

Flothe took a trip north to the Knik to search for more bodies. "Negative results," Flothe's report said.

Associated Press writer Paul Jenkins, getting wind of the unusual Saturday search on the Knik, made some inquiries the following Monday. The resulting story, which appeared on the 20th, was titled, "Authorities Fear List of Dead Women May Grow." All seven women named as possible victims in Jenkins's story were on Flothe's tentative list. Jenkins reported that, although investigators said there might be more than one killer, they suspected one man perhaps had murdered them all.

"He's still here," said Maxine Farrell of APD. "The publicity may have pushed him under a little, but he's here.

"They're going off with somebody they trust," Farrell added. "I believe he's in his late thirties, early forties, probably clean-cut and soft-spoken to where the girls feel really safe with him. He may be affluent. If not, he pretends to be.

"These girls aren't stupid," she said. "He's got to be able to show he can pay. I don't think they just ran away. These girls are leaving behind things they would not normally leave."

Haugsven, meanwhile, told Jenkins that troopers were trying to assemble a psychological profile of the killer. He said one man, possibly from the Anchorage area, might have been responsible for killing the two women whose bodies were found on the Knik River. "The graves were so similar— shallow," he said. "No great effort was made to bury them, but there may not have been time. Just to know the area where he took the girls—yeah, it's a local.''

Haugsven also told Jenkins that troopers had made checks with other states for similar crimes, but had found nothing. The names on their list of possible victims, meanwhile, were being fed into a computer, in hopes of ''finding another thread.''

''It's extremely frustrating,'' Haugsven said. ''You think you've got a lot of things going, then 'Boom!' you're back to square one. If it is a mass killer, maybe he's on a mission or something.''

Almost by accident Glenn Flothe had become the lead investigator in the Sherry Morrow and Kitty Larson cases, which were now part of who knew how many more cases. At least that was how Flothe felt. He still had to convince his fellow officers— except Gilmour and sometimes Haugsven—that Bob Hansen was the one whodunnit. More important, he had to convince the DA.

What he needed, Flothe decided, was the most extensive package he could put together—a kind of criminal collage. The package was to have a bit of everything in it: the Kitty Larson case—the corner- stone—a recent case with a live (if unfound) wit- ness; the four earlier cases involving women he'd kidnapped; and anything else he could find.

Reading the reports on the 1976 larceny in a building charge, for instance, he became con- vinced that Hansen stole continually. The psychi- atric report labeled him a kleptomaniac. Flothe figured the man's geographical range had to be incredible. He'd driven all the way to the Kenai with Robyn Patterson. He had his own plane. Flothe decided to start culling out all the cabin robberies of the past twelve years, especially those that had involved a plane.

Flothe called the Palmer-Wassilla trooper post, up by the Knik River where the bodies had been found. He called Soldotna post, deep in the Kenai. He got records from the Anchorage post, too. Simultaneously he put out a Police Operational Line System (POLS) message to all police agencies in south-central and southeastern Alaska, asking them to forward any unsolved missing persons cases, or strange murders, from the past twelve or so years.

The plan also included a decision to talk to people who'd hunted with Hansen and who could verify his knowledge of the tangled willow scrubs on the Knik where the bodies had been found. Flothe knew he had to be very circumspect; he could talk only to people he trusted, a hard item to come by in any circumstance. He would have to swear them to secrecy lest they tip off Hansen, wittingly or unwittingly.

Yet even a trial run proved useful. Flothe learned, for example, that Hansen held several world's bow-and-arrow records. He had the world's top mark for a Dall sheep taken by bow, set in 1971 when he killed a ram with forty-two-inch horns in the Chugach Mountains. The second-ranked caribou in the world was also his, according to the Pope & Young Club, the official judge of trophies taken by bow. Hansen had killed that animal in 1971, along the Susitna River on the northern edge of Cook Inlet. There was more. The twelfth-ranked mountain goat, the thirteenth-ranked Dall sheep, the thirty-fourth-ranked black bear. This man is a true hunter, Flothe thought. *His hands are always in blood.*

8

Whenever Bob got in trouble with the law, friends were quick to come forward and testify on his behalf. The link between them, often as not, was provided by Darla Hansen, Bob's wife. Darla was active not only in her church but her community. And Darla's friends were Bob's friends. Among these friends were the Gerald Goldschmidt family, whom Darla knew through church. Another stalwart friend was John Sumrall, an insurance company executive. John and Bob were often inseparable. They flew together, went hunting and fishing together.

Both Sumrall and Goldschmidt testified in Bob's behalf in 1972. What they told the court showed the way they felt about their friend. John Sumrall told the judge he was a good friend of Bob's and said he believed Bob should be permitted to return to the community. Goldschmidt, a public health sanitarian, told the court he'd had a close relationship with Bob since he'd come north in 1967. He said he knew about Bob's previous arson charge but recommended they allow Bob to work in the community and get psychotherapy.

And in one respect Bob didn't let his friends down: He never got into trouble while he was incarcerated. Maybe it had something to do with the fact that he could work as a baker while doing his time. Maybe it had something to do with his wish to do his time and get out of jail as soon as he could. Even the halfway house was better than jail. In the halfway house he could at least see his wife and kids with some regularity.

In fact he wasn't seeing them much less than when he was working in the bakery. Bob had always been a restless soul, disappearing for entire weekends at a time. What his wife didn't realize was how he spent all of his free time.

When Darla Henrichsen had first met Bob Hansen they were both working at a Minnesota lake resort owned by Bob's parents. Darla was working as a maid on summer vacation from college. Bob was fresh out of jail on an arson charge. He was helping his parents with painting, boat repair, and whatever else they needed, as well as acting as a guide for guests on fishing trips.

The two of them soon discovered that they were from the same small town in Iowa. Not only had they gone to the same school but the same church. Bob was four years older than Darla, however, and they'd never met before.

Their romance bloomed. They took rowboat trips out onto Leech Lake, where at night they could see a million stars. What moved Darla the most were Bob's stories of his childhood.

"When I was in school," he said, "I used to stutter so bad that I wouldn't answer a question, even if the teacher called on me. It didn't matter if I knew the answer or not. People used to make fun of me all the time," he said. "I used to run away from people, and avoid them rather than try to have a conversation."

That's one reason why Darla fell in love with him: She instinctively wanted to help other people. Then, too, he was the first man ever to pay her much attention. Darla had forever been the tall girl at the school dance. She was the one who always stood stoop-shouldered on the sidelines, a full head taller than any of the boys, awaiting the invitation to dance that never comes. Never one of the pretty girls, or one of the popular girls (an honor reserved for her sister), it only made it worse that Darla was smart.

As their idyllic summer came to an end, Bob asked Darla to marry him. Always the sensible one, Darla told him that she wanted to wait until she finished school. So Bob went to Chicago for a three-week course in cake-decorating at the Wilton School and Darla returned to the University of Iowa. They wrote endless letters; it was difficult to be separated.

When Bob finished the cake-decoration course, he returned to work at his parents' resort. He even drove down to Iowa City to visit Darla. It was a long, exhausting drive on roads that could turn treacherous with ice and snow at a moment's notice, and Bob made the trip several times before he grew impatient. As Bob put it, they decided that "doggone it, we can get married." The wedding took place that fall in Pocahontas, Iowa, where Darla's parents lived.

Darla dropped out of college when they got married, and Bob took jobs wherever he could get them, mostly in bakeries. They moved throughout the Midwest in those years. From Minot, North Dakota, up near the Canadian border, to Rapid City, South Dakota, where the mountains meet the plains, and finally to Minneapolis. There, Darla enrolled at the University of Minnesota to finish what she had begun.

There was no irony in the fact that she became a schoolteacher. Or that her area of concentration was special education. Her husband had learning disabilities and speech problems similar to those of the children she worked with.

Almost immediately after Darla earned her BA, Bob suggested they move to Alaska. That faraway land of ice and snow had a mystical appeal to Bob, who'd read stories about the fantastic hunting and fishing since he was a child. It would be like moving to another country while still living in the United States. It was a place to start over, away from his parents and in-laws and the memories of his troubled Iowa past.

Bob had no difficulty talking Darla into going along. He thought her venturesome, but she probably would have followed him anyway. They moved north almost immediately, despite the disapproval of both sets of parents.

Many people dream of living in Alaska. Just as many do not stick it out. Even in boom times there aren't enough jobs to go around. But the Hansens had the one requirement necessary to make a go of it on the last frontier: readily marketable skills. Teachers and bakers are always in demand.

Darla's teaching career in Alaska proceeded on a steady course. She worked in both public and private schools. To earn extra income she sometimes tutored children with special difficulties. She had also taken many courses in her field. Darla had dedicated her life to aiding those with learning disabilities. In a way she lived in her husband's world each day with her students. And so it was that Christian charity and career were interwoven in Darla's life like a prayer.

Not that Darla's marriage to Bob Hansen was an easy one. He had a way of constantly disrupting her life: When he went to jail in 1972 their first child was about to turn two; when he went to jail in 1977 their second was two and a half. Bob also was a demanding person, given to inexplicable fits of rage. When he was in the heat of anger, there was no reasoning with Bob Hansen.

Darla's only refuge from Bob was Christ and the church. Her strong faith was the one thing she brought with her from the Midwest. And it was her faith that held them together for those twenty years. Because Darla was a good Christian woman, she always obeyed her husband. That much was in the Bible.

9

Glenn Flothe soon found that his nights belonged to the prostitutes. They were the victims, he reasoned, so they should know something. But if he was going to use them he had to work their hours. They weren't going to work his.

They also weren't willingly going to talk to the cops. Take the case of Sue Luna. From the missing persons file Flothe knew she had been a dancer at the Good Times bar. Her sister had reported her missing on May 30, 1982, and her roommate, also a dancer at the Good Times, supplied the details.

According to the roommate Sue made a date with a man she'd just met at the bar. He offered her three hundred dollars for an hour's worth of sex. She agreed to meet him on May 26 at Alice's 210 Restaurant. Sue left their apartment at noon, but the roommate said she did not appear for work that night. Neither the roommate nor Sue's sister had seen her since.

Since more than a year had passed, Flothe felt it was a safe bet that Sue Luna had met with foul play. That put him on the avenues, looking for Tanya, Sue Luna's roommate. If he could find her

maybe she could recall, however faintly, the identity of the man who had made the lunch date.

Alice's 210 Restaurant, however, became a met-
aphor for the whole adventure. This was Alice as
in *Alice in Wonderland*. And Tanya was the rabbit,
disappearing down a hole.

"I'm looking for Tanya," Flothe announced each
time he went into one of the topless clubs.

"Tanya who?" was the invariable reply.

There were lots of Tanyas, as it turned out. Teenage runaways with wholesome names like "Carol,"
"Mary," or "Barbara" become "Tanya" the second they hit the street. Secretaries on the run from
boredom printed TANYA on their dressing room door
the minute they put on a G-string. There was a
"Tanya" everywhere Flothe went. Not one was the
right one. The rabbit had gotten away.

On Thursday, September 22, 1983, Flothe received an unusual visitor: Officer Gregg Baker of
the Anchorage Police Department. Baker had made
the first call on Kitty Larson, and he was troubled
by what had happened since that time.

Later Flothe would realize how courageous Baker
had been to come in and talk, because what he had
to say was not complimentary to the Anchorage
Police Department. As far as Baker was concerned,
APD had blown the investigation of the Larson incident.

They'd talked to Hansen, all right, and gone to
his house, but Baker was convinced they could have
done a much better job. Baker had seen at least two
potentially incriminating items. One was some surgical gloves in Hansen's car. The other was a

Thompson Contender pistol, which he knew came with interchangeable barrels, including a .223-caliber barrel. The Thompson Contender seemed particularly important, because a .223-caliber weapon had killed both women on the Knik River. But the APD had done nothing about it.

To make matters worse, Baker told Flothe, the APD had as much as told Kitty Larson she was a liar. Yet as far as Baker was concerned Kitty had been telling the truth. Not only that, but he was convinced that Bob Hansen was the man responsible for killing the two dancers up on the Knik, and who knew how many more. He'd come to Flothe because he felt something had to be done to get the Kitty Larson case going again.

Bolstered by this opinion so close to his own, Flothe decided he had to find Kitty Larson, even if he had to fly down to Seattle. He asked his boss for permission to go south. "Do what you have to do," Lt. Jent told him.

The problem was, Kitty could be anywhere. "The life" was a fluid through which people free-floated and got lost. Flothe had no reason to think Kitty's case would be any different.

The sergeant also knew that only someone who understood the mean streets of Anchorage could guide him to the young woman. Only two categories of people fit that description: pimps and vice cops. Pimps were out, so that left him only one choice: Go to APD and find the sharpest street cop around.

Word had it that a vice cop named Gentile was the man Flothe should talk to. Since night was approaching, Flothe had to take to the streets to find him. Street cops are night cops because street people are night people.

The trooper finally found Gentile in the heart of the city's red-light district: a collection of seedy taverns, pawnshops, and topless bars sandwiched between the Alaska Railroad right-of-way and the "respectable" hotels up on Fifth Avenue. It was a zone where a person could buy drugs, proposition women, and get stinking drunk.

It was a man's world. The bars were for efficient drinking and little else. The one-way streets through the five-block area were perfect for cruising. Native men overflowed the beer-and-wine joints and fell into nearby doorways. Pimps with Cadillacs and Lincolns parked nearby.

"So you want me to help you find this girl, huh?" Gentile asked as they walked. "What'd you say her name was?"

"Larson. Kitty Larson." They stepped around a group of native men drunkenly arguing about which bar to go to next. Flothe could already tell that Gentile knew this world; he moved through it with confidence, even élan.

"Excuse me a second, okay, Sergeant?" Gentile said as he approached a young woman with bright red hair. "Hey now, you know I can't let you stay here," he said gently. He tugged on her long rabbit-fur coat. "You're gonna have to get moving."

Flothe noticed that the cop cocked his head as he talked. He was animated, used his hands a lot.

"I'm just waiting for my ride, Sergeant," she whispered.

"Well, okay. We'll see. You know how the game works. This time it's just a warning." Gentile raised three fingers on his right hand, like an umpire calling a baseball game. "Three strikes and you're out, right? Right?"

"Right."

And then they were off down the street again, Gentile's eyes sentinels scanning the horizon. Without missing a beat he was back to Flothe. "Don't think I know this Kitty Larson. But I'll check around. Know her pimp's name?"

"Reggie Roosevelt."

"He's also a coke dealer."

It was an old game: Pimps used drugs to gain control over the women in their "stable."

"Big-time coke dealer?" Flothe asked.

"Not that big. You said you thought this girl might be in Seattle? Why Seattle? Family?"

"Where else do you go when you've been picked up off the street at gunpoint?"

"I'd get an indoors job. The streets are too goddamned dangerous."

Flothe liked what he was hearing. This guy knew the streets. Here's my connection right here, he told himself.

Ahead of them, a riproaringly drunk fisherman cursed the sidewalk under his feet. He'd been tossed from one of the taverns and served a slice of frontier justice. He was so drunk he swayed on the sidewalk as if it was a ship's deck.

At the next corner stood another working woman. Blond and eighteen, she was trying to look like she was waiting for the light to turn green. Though the streets were a march of people out on the night, Gentile snaked his way straight to her, never varying his pace, walking with an easygoing but firm stride. When he reached her he acted like they were old buddies.

"Well, sorry, honey," he said, his manner fatherly and almost apologetic. "But this is it. You gotta go. I told you three times, you know."

"Okay, officer," she said with mock solemnity.

Back at the station, where they took the young woman and booked her for soliciting, Flothe asked Gentile why she'd been so cooperative. Gentile shrugged his shoulders. "This pimp beat her up. I put his ass in jail." No wonder the hookers loved him.

Two days later Gentile called Flothe back. "I found Kitty," he said. "She's in a massage parlor right here in town. She's back."

"Great.'

"Not only that," Gentile said: "I even know her. You know her as Kitty Larson, right? And I know her as Vicky Matthew. Small world, ain't it?"

"You think she'll let me talk to her?"

"She better. She owes me a favor. A while back I got her off on a theft charge she should've done time on. She and her pimp rolled some pillar of the community. You know the scene: He comes to us, says all he wants is his gold watch and checkbook back. Says he doesn't want to press no charges. So I tell Vicky-Kitty, whatever you wanna call her— 'Just give me the watch and the checkbook and I'll see if we can make this guy forget about it.' I told her I'd try to talk the guy out of it. Which I did. Yeah, she'll talk to you.''

"I'd like to meet with her right away.''

"I understand.''

The first meeting was in one of those hotels where the plaster is cracked and rust-stained from leaking steam radiators. It looked like big pools of tea were on the ceiling, and the hallways smelled of drugs and stale semen. It was the kind of place where the desk clerk raised a momentary eyebrow and then forgot about you.

Gentile arranged for a room and the three had coffee. Gentile did most of the talking.

"Glenn is a straight-arrow guy, Kitty,'' Gentile said. "He'll treat you right. And if I tell you that's right, that's right, right?''

"Right.''

"Now, you know what I'm talking about, right? Have I ever steered you wrong? Of course I haven't, right?''

"Right.''

"Okay. Now Glenn tells me that you had a little trouble with some guy, and he wants to help you out. And you know what, Kitty? I think he really wants to help you out. Hard to believe, ain't it? But Glenn's a good guy, Kitty. And look, you don't have to tell him anything right now if you don't want to. I just want you to think about it, maybe get to know him a little better first. Glenn's good people, Kitty.''

They met again a few days later, in a homey cafe chosen for its ability to provide them some anonymity. Gentile built up Flothe. Again. Before they left, Flothe felt confident enough to ask Kitty if she'd mind coming down to the trooper office and examining the statement she'd given the APD. She agreed.

In the full light of his office at trooper headquarters, Flothe got his first good look at Kitty Larson. She was a gaudy tramp weighed down by a tangle of costume jewelry and a cheap fur coat. Underneath the makeup, though, was a child trying to look like a woman. She was, Flothe decided, a good-looking girl despite it all. She had dark hair and small features—a small mouth, a small nose. A big-busted girl, she stood about 5'5" and weighed about 135 pounds. She also seemed vulnerable beneath her tough exterior, and looked like she could show either face on a moment's notice.

Though anxious to get Kitty's story, Flothe was a gentle interviewer. His voice never varied from a soft tone, the kind of voice a therapist uses, with all the threat washed away. Each question flowed naturally from the conversation.

Kitty started off with a torrent, unleashing a steady, chronological monologue that captured all the terror of her experience at the hands of Bob Hansen. It was a horrifying tale, and by the time she'd finished she was in tears. Flothe stopped the interview, got her some Kleenex, and gave her time to compose herself.

"Do you feel he was going to hurt you?" Flothe asked when they went back on record.

"You know, I didn't feel nothing, 'cause I knew I wasn't going to live. I mean, the man, what he did to me, he had to kill me."

Then Kitty's story circled back to the beginning. She told how Hansen had first driven by and made a date for the next day, which she missed when she overslept. She told about how he appeared the next day, a Sunday. "He said, 'How about two hundred dollars for a blow job in the car?' 'cause I wouldn't go to his place. 'Sure, no problem,' I said.' "

"Two hundred dollars is a lot of money. . . . ''

"Hey, for a blow job in the car? Hell, yeah." For a second Kitty sounded like the tough street-walker again.

Kitty confessed to Flothe that she hadn't wanted to go to Hansen's house, because she was new to Alaska and didn't want to go to anybody's house. She ended up at his house anyway. And from there on out, her story was far more graphic than anything she'd told the APD.

"Every time the gun was in my face I knew I was in trouble," she said. She barely paused for breath. "He said to take my shirt off. I did. Shit, with a gun in your face you would, too. After he raped me on the bearskin rug I was handcuffed, and as he was taking the rope off my neck he put chains on me. And I stayed there for five hours while he slept."

When he woke up, Kitty said, he told her that he would take her to his cabin. "And like, you know, I told him, 'Okay, fine, that's good.' I acted like I wanted to go, you know."

"What if you had acted differently, what would have happened?" Flothe asked.

"I don't think he would have took me."

"What would he have done?"

"Probably would have killed me there in the house."

After listening to Kitty's story and seeing her emotional response, Flothe had little doubt that she had been the victim of a dangerous man. A killer.

He also decided the case would take a lot more work than he'd originally thought. It would take time, and Flothe decided to place Hansen under twenty-four-hour surveillance. Going to the colonel of the troopers to get permission to do it was a major commitment. But from the way Kitty described him, it was obvious Hansen could kill again. At any time.

10

To beat this guy, Flothe figured he had to get inside his head. Luckily for him, others had been there before. Psychiatrists had been brought in at almost every step of Hansen's criminal career.

Bob's first psychiatric session had been in 1961, at the Men's Reformatory in Anamosa, Iowa. He had been sentenced there after he burned down the bus barn in his hometown of Pocahontas. "He has an infantile personality," said the shrink. "I wonder if he has a mental disease?" Then he answered his own question, concluding that "It might be social in nature."

Hansen's next session came after his 1971 assault of a young real-estate secretary. He laid the groundwork for the examination by denying all knowledge of the incident. He told the police it "seemed like a bad dream" and asked for psychiatric help. In early 1972 his lawyer had him examined by Dr. J. Ray Langdon, a psychiatrist at the Alaska Clinic in Anchorage.

Langdon's psychiatric report said Bob had a dissociative mental illness accompanied by loss of memory, and suggested his criminal activity stemmed from that illness. The doctor added that he exhibited a compulsive personality with thought disorder, perhaps with periodic schizophrenic episodes in which he dissociated in a psychotic rather than neurotic fashion.

"His compulsive actions have psychological causes," Langdon said, adding that Hansen "walked on an Army firing range" while he was in the Reserves during the late 1950s. Hansen also told Langdon that as a teenager "he fantasized about doing all sorts of harmful things to girls who rejected him."

At Bob's sentencing, Dr. Langdon told the judge that the "proper sentence to impose on Mr. Hansen—and I'm not trying to take the judge's prerogative—would be close supervision for a long period of time, two or three years, with psychiatric consultation once or twice a week." In his evaluation, however, Langdon concluded that, assuming his diagnosis was correct, Hansen's mental illness would be very difficult to treat successfully.

In October 1972, seven months after he had been sentenced to prison for the assault, Bob was examined by another psychiatrist, Dr. Allen H. Parker. Dr. Parker indicated that Hansen had made enough improvement through therapy to warrant release on parole. He was paroled one year after this evaluation.

In 1976 Bob saw Dr. Parker again, a visit prompted by his attempted theft of a chain saw. Parker's examination this time showed what the doctor described as an "episodic stealing problem." "His stealing is probably obsessive," he wrote, "because Hansen has an inability to resist it and a feeling of being forced."

After the examination by Dr. Parker, Bob began therapy with Dr. Robert McManmon, also a psychiatrist. McManmon ultimately testified in his behalf during his March 22, 1977, sentencing on the larceny in a building charge.

"Mr. Hansen has a bipolar affective disorder," said McManmon, "which is a variant of a manic-depressive disorder." Bipolar disorders are distinguished from unipolar ones, he explained, because a unipolar condition is all depressive, while a bipolar disorder is all manic. "The defendant does not have a low, depressive area," he said. "In his behavior speech is fast, ideas are not related, and attention span is not very long." He also said Hansen's impulses were "poorly controlled during the mood and energy upswings of this disorder."

According to the psychiatrist, during manic episodes sufferers of this disease "develop an abnormal preoccupation (mania) toward some activity." Kleptomania, or the urge to steal without economic need, was a manifestation of this illness, he pointed out. "Mr. Hansen reaches levels of mania above the norms of society." He also noted that he'd been told Hansen's previous assault with a dangerous weapon charge "was really a sexual assault."

In his discussion of Hansen's therapy, McManmon said that the defendant was on thorazine therapy, which had proven effective. "Lithium takes longer to be effective," the doctor said, "and I'd be reluctant to stop medicine at this time." McManmon wanted Hansen to return quarterly to

"keep in touch," but added that this disorder was
not something that would haunt him throughout his
life.

"It's a problem that psychiatrists are able to control," he said, "and manic episodes tend to dimin-
ish with age." Noting that Hansen "would be
controlled by society if he were incarcerated, but
would not get treatment," Dr. McManmon recommended to the Court that Hansen continue treatment, even if that meant he didn't go to jail.

Under cross-examination by the prosecution, Dr.
McManmon testified that "by treating the manic
episodes" he was "also treating the kleptomania."
He said Hansen had told him, "I get on one subject," and the doctor noted that the defendant did
this "with hunting, going to great lengths to get a
certain type of animal."

In additional testimony he said Hansen had
"talked about problems with his wife," but that
"she was not a major part of his therapy." He said
he also presumed "that his arson and sexual assault
were an outgrowth of his illness." He ended by
saying that he thought Hansen's problem was "a
long-term one, and he should always be under medical attention. I don't know what will happen if he
doesn't have medical attention."

Obviously Hansen hadn't received much attention of any kind, Flothe decided. The judges had
taken whatever the psychiatrists were saying about
Bob Hansen seriously, but still something had gone
terribly wrong. A man this dangerous, he reasoned, should have spent a lot more time in jail.
He quickly turned to the judicial record.

First off was the sentencing for the 1971 assault with a dangerous weapon. The judge was James M. Fitzgerald.

> THE COURT: Mr. Hansen, is there anything you wish to tell me before I pass sentence, judgement, or make a sentence this afternoon, either tending to show why I should not now do so or otherwise in your behalf?
>
> THE DEFENDANT: No, Your Honor.
>
> THE COURT: I find you guilty of the crime of assault with a dangerous weapon in accordance with your plea. These are the factors I take into consideration: You've been once convicted of the offense of arson, I'm told it was ten years ago. From all reports I have here, apparently you are able to get along well and are able to associate with others, who have come here to testify their high regard for you. I'm told that you're a capable and willing worker.
>
> I believe you have a serious mental illness and one which makes you, under certain circumstances, extremely dangerous to others in the community. I think this condition requires psychiatric therapy and I'm told by the doctor that it's the condition which he has apparently diagnosed or . . . your condition is one that may be treatable. I believe that this offense was committed, as the doctor tells us, during a period of dissociation which he states is a condition arising from your mental condition.
>
> I'm going to sentence you to five years in prison, but I'm going to make some other conditions because I think that they are appropriate. First of all, I don't know how long the psychotherapy is going to take place, but it must be given to you because, if it's not given to you, in my opinion, you'll be released from the penitentiary and perhaps in an even more dangerous condition.
>
> I'm going to make you eligible for parole at the discretion of the parole board, because if the progress in treatment is satisfactory or at a later point the psychiatrist can give a reasonable assurance that you are no longer a danger at large in the community, I think you

should be released and I want to make it possible for
the parole board to do this.

I think that you must have psychotherapy, or you
must have psychiatric treatment, and I strongly recommend it and I recommend as well that you be allowed a release to follow your employment or your
work, because I'm told that you are a good worker and
I believe that you're not a danger to the community as
long as you're subject to close supervision and so long
as that supervision is afforded you I think that the danger to the community and to the others in the community will be minimized.

Flothe knew what had happened on this one. The
psychiatrists came to his rescue. But what about the
next one?

For the 1976 larceny in a building charge, Hansen had come before Superior Court Judge James
K. Singleton. Before pronouncing the sentence, the
judge said he had "had a great deal of difficulty
with this case. . . . And I was frankly unable to
make up my mind as to an appropriate sentence in
this case until very, very recently. In fact, I was
not even completely sure as to where I was going
until I'd heard argument in this case. And frankly
that is rare. . . . I am greatly troubled."

"Mr. Hansen is dangerous," the judge said. "I
think Dr. McManmon made that clear, that during
the manic phase of his condition he is capable of
committing crimes, of acting out. His behavior,
whatever his capacity to control it, is largely un-
controlled. . . . Dr. McManmon indicates that the
counseling and the lithium treatment would not be
curative but would only suppress the symptoms. In
other words, would suppress the illness but would
not cure it.

"So if we assume that the condition is ongoing, then we can assume that Mr. Hansen presents a real danger to the community, not only a danger of committing larcenies but of committing the other kinds of crimes that he previously has committed. So he does present a substantial danger and there is a substantial incentive to incarcerate him in order to isolate him and preclude criminal activity during the period of isolation."

Because Hansen was a third-time felon, the judge felt it important that a sentence be imposed to deter others. "His sentence should be near the maximum range permitted for this crime," the judge said, "since he is not a first-time offender and is not entitled to the consideration that first-time offenders are usually given. To suspend imposition of sentence or to provide straight probation would in my opinion unduly deprecate the seriousness of the crime."

Before imposing his sentence on Hansen, Judge Singleton asked the defendant if there was anything he wanted to say. In the past Hansen had declined the opportunity to make a comment to the judge; like pleading guilty, it was something he did to spare himself and his family the agony of exposure. This time, however, there seemed to be a lot on the line, and Hansen broke his customary silence.

"Your Honor," he said, "there is no doubt I committed the crime. But I would like you to consider my wife and two small children. I am the sole supporter of my family. I have a home, I own my own home, but now I will lose it.

"Since seeing Dr. McManmon," he continued,

"there has been no problem. I'm now in the lith- ium program, and I'm able to talk without stutter- ing. Your Honor, there will be no future problems. I have had enough problems. They have been hard on my family.

"I have been seeing Dr. Parker, and talked to him regarding my problem. It was a sex-related problem, but now that's cleared up. For the first time I can handle my problem now. Now I don't feel I have to take something out of a store. I am ashamed of being here. I'm just asking for restric- tions to help me keep things right."

"Well, just as your attorney has made a very eloquent presentation on your behalf," Judge Sin- gleton said, "you also have spoken eloquently on your own behalf. And I can say without hesitation that were this the first offense, there would be no question but that I would grant you probation for the reasons that you've outlined. . . .

"However, this is not a first offense. This is not the first time, Mr. Hansen, that you have appeared before a judge. This is not the first time that you have had the opportunity to say to a judge, as you have said to me, that this is the last time I will be before a judge. . . . It will therefore be the sen- tence of this court that you be sentenced to a period of incarceration of five years. That during that time you should receive psychiatric treatment and under no circumstances should you be admitted to parole without first having established for you a program of psychiatric counseling and therapy to ease your transition into the community."

Hansen was classified to the Juneau Correction

Center. Just as quickly he turned to the State Supreme Court, appealing his sentence as too severe for a non-serious property offense. This is what the State Supreme Court wrote in its decision:

"Hansen's prior convictions were five and fifteen years before the current offense," the justices noted. "During that time Hansen has otherwise conducted his life in a normal and respectable manner. He has maintained steady employment, has been a good provider for his family, and has earned the reputation of a hard worker and a respectable member of the community. It is quite possible that the instant offense and the earlier convictions stemmed as much from psychological aberration as from a general criminal propensity. . . .

"We agree that Hansen's prior record did compel some term of incarceration rather than straight probation. However, the particulars of this case—the clearly diagnosed mental illness; Hansen's amenability to treatment; the linkage of the mental illness to past antisocial behavior; the definite, prescribed course of treatment to mitigate the possibility of future criminal behavior; the stable home and work environment; and the factor that the monetary value of the property stolen was relatively low—lead us to conclude that the court below was clearly mistaken in imposing a five-year sentence. Hansen has already served a year in prison. We believe his sentence should now be revised to provide for imprisonment for the period of time he has served, but that he be placed upon probation for the remainder of his term."

11

The body of the second Knik River victim was finally identified. A month had passed since her body was found by hunters, but now, through dental charts, troopers confirmed she was Paula Goulding, a thirty-one-year-old woman from Kona, Hawaii. Though Flothe was convinced Hansen was responsible for Goulding and Sherry Morrow's deaths, if only because both bodies were in almost the same spot, his fellow troopers were hedging their bets. The news reports about the identification of Goulding said that ''investigators are not sure whether one person is responsible for the slayings or whether they are being committed by more than one person.'' Flothe just hoped the FBI would hurry up and identify the shell casings found at each of the grave sites. Maybe then his peers would feel the way he did about Bob Hansen.

From the missing persons reports, Flothe knew that Goulding's disappearance had been much like Sherry Morrow's. She was reported missing in April 1983 by a friend, who told APD that Paula hadn't been seen since the 24th of the month. The friend, a woman who was Paula's roommate, told

APD that Goulding was a Caucasian female, 30 years of age, about 5'7" inches tall, weighing about 125 pounds, with short, curly hair. She said that both of them were dancers at the Great Alaska Bush Company in Anchorage.

The roommate told the investigating officer that Goulding had met an unidentified male at the Bush Company, and that he'd offered her two hundred dollars to meet him for lunch. His only stipulation was that she come in a cab. On Sunday the 24th, Goulding called a cab and departed her home. Her roommate hadn't seen her since. She told APD that when Paula left the house she was wearing blue jeans, a red-and-white-striped T-shirt, and a gold nugget pendant shaped as two hearts.

Paula Goulding was inexperienced at prostitution, a factor that may have contributed to her demise. Before coming down to Anchorage to get a dancing job she had worked as a secretary in Fairbanks. She had never danced before. It was her good looks and eagerness that got her work.

Still, dancing nude did not come easily to her. For the first week she danced only topless. She was a beautiful woman, however, and the woman who managed the club was patient with her. Then she finally got up the nerve to dance bottomless. She knew that the girls who did made more money than the girls who didn't. Ironically, that was the night she made a date with the mystery man, a date she should have refused.

Only a short time after Goulding's body was identified, the FBI Laboratory in Washington, D.C., informed the troopers that the .223-caliber cartridge casings found near Paula Goulding and Sherry Morrow's graves had been fired from the same weapon. Both casings had been manufactured at the Lake City Ordnance Plant.

The FBI further reported that the fragments found in the chest cavity of Sherry Morrow were from a copper-jacketed bullet of .223 caliber. There were enough markings on the casings to match them to a particular weapon, if such a weapon was found. The FBI also reported that the .223-caliber shell casing found in Sherry Morrow's grave had the characteristics of a reloaded cartridge.

From Flothe's point of view, all this was good news. The FBI report now linked Sherry Morrow and Paula Goulding to the same murder weapon. Not only that, but one of the shell casings looked like a reloaded cartridge. Flothe knew Hansen had the equipment necessary to reload his own cartridges. More important, there was enough evidence to match the casings to a particular weapon, which could prove crucial in any courtroom test of Hansen's guilt—if they found the weapon. Even if they found the weapon, however, Flothe knew it was less than the ideal match: Shell casings don't kill people, bullets do. That limit notwithstanding, Flothe still could feel the noose starting to tighten around Bob Hansen's neck.

The missing women were, in all likelihood, dead. And putting Hansen behind bars was all the more important, because Flothe's list of Hansen's presumed victims had now reached a total of twenty-two names.

He couldn't be certain, of course. There were

certain controversial entries, such as a woman known only as "Eklutna Annie." She didn't seem to fit the profile. She had been stabbed to death, and the other victims had been shot. But the circumstances of her death—including the fact that her body was found in a remote spot just north of Anchorage—convinced Flothe that he should keep her name on the list.

Another was a victim known to investigators as "the Bear Lady." It was an old case, from the summer of 1980, and it had never been solved. A woman's body, later identified as that of Joanna Messina, a former nurse, had been found in a remote spot on the Kenai Peninsula. When troopers got to the site, they were told that a bear had been in the vicinity earlier. When Chief Investigator John Lucking reached the site he found that parts of the body had been eaten by the hungry carnivore. As he began his scene investigation, moreover, the bear returned.

Anyone who has been the object of a five-hundred-pound black bear's attention, especially one intent on protecting its food, knows that these beasts can be troublesome. Although some experts believe black bears are less dangerous than grizzlies, that's not true in Alaska, and even less true when they're feeding. As Lucking and his fellow investigators stared down the possibility of becoming another link in the food chain, they determined that they had better scare the bear away.

Scare tactics didn't work, and the bear became yet more menacing and protective. Lucking couldn't let the bear destroy their evidence, though, so the only logical course of action was to destroy the bear. The problem with that was that black bear are a protected species, and killing one is tantamount to homicide. The hue and cry raised in response to Lucking's destruction of a hapless bear almost became a major distraction.

Despite this, troopers almost solved the case when a suspect failed a polygraph test, but no arrests were ever made. The case was dropped.

When Chuck Miller, an investigator who had worked the case, saw that Flothe had put Joanna Messina on his list of probable victims, he couldn't believe it.

"Glenn, why do you have her up there? We know who did it, because the guy failed the polygraph," Miller told him.

"Well," Flothe replied, "I've got her up there because of where the body was found, and the way she'd been shot, and her lifestyle sort of told me she was a potential victim."

"We're fairly sure we've closed the case, Glenn," Miller said. "We can't prove it, but we're fairly sure that our main suspect did it."

"She stays on the list," Flothe replied.

Whether every name on his list was really a Hansen victim was less important, though, than the fact that Flothe had to start closing in on Hansen. Almost immediately he contacted Officer Dennis of the APD and got his permission to get the Larson evidence. Just as quickly, the CIB sent someone down to transfer the evidence to the troopers. Flothe also contacted the examining doctor at Humana Hospital and seized Kitty's rape examination kit. It included a frozen tampon and a filter paper stain. With everything he had, he figured he had a strong case against the baker from Iowa.

Flothe knew he couldn't go to the DA's office empty-handed. He needed a lot more than the Kitty Larson case to get a search warrant and warrant for Hansen's arrest. Fortunately, his plan to get Hansen on everything he could had started to bear fruit.

A major break came with a routine review of the APD files on Hansen. Buried in that stack of paper was a burglary report Hansen himself had filed. He'd called the police, it seems, to report a break-in at his house. Thirteen thousand dollars worth of furs and trophy mounts had been stolen, including some of his world-record trophies. APD had gone to the scene and found that one of the locks had been jimmied. They took photos of the bald spots on Hansen's wall where the trophies once had been.

Within months, Flothe learned, Hansen had received a check for thirteen thousand dollars from State Farm Insurance. Shortly after that he bought a brand-new Super Cub airplane. Right away Flothe suspected insurance fraud.

The investigation of the burglary reports from trooper posts throughout south-central Alaska, however, was proving to be much slower going. Flothe was most interested in cabin burglaries in remote areas of the bush, since he figured that Hansen would favor a crime that allowed him to use his plane. Flothe did find quite a few reports of this kind, but the details of these cases were often sketchy at best—because of limited manpower and money, troopers usually took such reports over the telephone, and no scene investigation was ever done. That meant that Flothe had to call each burglary victim individually. Were there any details that pointed to a particular suspect, or would help the troopers identify a suspect? he asked.

It was slow, tedious work. Often as not Flothe found out that an airplane had not been used, even in the more remote spots, or that details of the burglary were completely lacking beyond a knowledge that the cabin had been broken into and certain items stolen. Undaunted, he kept plugging away, call by miserable call.

Although Flothe would have liked more on Hansen, by the time he was ready to talk to the DA he figured he had a whole package to present. He was confident that even if he couldn't pin all the murders on him he could at least get him off the street.

He had him for the rape and kidnapping of Kitty Larson. (Flothe even wanted to charge him with attempted murder, although he relented when it was pointed out that it would be difficult to prove that he intended to kill her.) He had a hunch, moreover, that once charges were filed on the Larson case, Hansen's key alibi witness would "roll over." From reading Henning's statement, Flothe decided he was just an upstanding citizen of the redneck variety protecting his buddy from the embarrassment of a run-in with a prostitute who'd gone to the cops and maybe wanted to blackmail him.

That wasn't all he had. There was also the insurance fraud. A home burglary of hunting trophies had turned into an insurance settlement, and then the purchase of a new airplane, with uncanny speed. It just didn't seem like a coincidence. Hansen's past was predicting the future, as far as Flothe was concerned.

Flothe also had a long list of incidents in which Hansen's name came up, incidents all too similar to those described by Kitty Larson. Hansen's behavior had a pattern to it, Flothe would argue. He had a habit of taking the women of Anchorage off the street and doing with them what he pleased. Sometimes the results were deadly.

Looking at the wide array of evidence he had on the man, Flothe was certain the combination was enough to put Hansen away for a long time. Once he was locked up they could start worrying about murder.

What Flothe wanted was a search warrant that would let him look not only for the insurance fraud items and the items associated with Kitty Larson's kidnapping and rape, but anything linking Hansen to the murdered and missing women. Flothe realized it would be complicated, and that he was asking a lot.

How was he going to convince a judge, much less a DA, that the specifics of Hansen's past made him a killer in the present? Flothe's "proof" came from his reading of the man's criminal history, and clearly it met the standard tests of criminal investigations: Bob Hansen had access to the victims and the crime sites (he had an airplane); he had the ability (he was a world-champion hunter and outdoorsman); he had a history of kidnapping and raping women; and the .223 shell and elastic bandage seen in Hansen's car by Officer Baker linked him to Paula Goulding and Sherry Morrow. The question was: Would the DA buy it?

Lieutenant Jent arranged a meeting with the DA's office, and Flothe took it as a favorable portent that both the head DA and his assistant appeared at trooper headquarters. Flothe, for his part, was prepared: He'd put together huge paper wall charts on each case, listing the witnesses that could testify, what they would say, and what property troopers expected to find in a search warrant. These were the cases Flothe knew he could get Hansen on.

He also had a wall-sized chart of the missing women, with all their background information, and time-frame charts linking the incidents with Hansen's known whereabouts at the time. From Hansen's parole records they knew he had been in Seward, Alaska, for the Fourth of July in both 1973 and 1975. A woman named Megan Emerick, it turned out, had been reported missing in Seward on July 7, 1973. A woman named Mary K. Thill, it turned out, had been reported missing in Seward on July 5, 1975.

Unfortunately, Flothe overwhelmed the DA and his assistant with the complexity of what he wanted. He was trying to tie a murder to Hansen through his past, with just a few fits and pieces of the present. The DA said that it "could maybe be done" but it would take a lot of work.

"What about just a search warrant for the insurance fraud, or for the Larson case?" Flothe asked, hoping to at least get Hansen off the street. Having the man under twenty-four-hour surveillance was beginning to take a toll. The unit doing the surveillance was the colonel's narcotics team, and they weren't doing any narcotics work. The CIB investigators also were spending an increasing amount of time on the case. They were looking everywhere for the key that would put Hansen away, but it was costing them time, energy, and money. How much longer could the troopers sustain their collective effort?

"You got a problem even with the Larson case," Flothe heard the DA say.

"Why's that?"

"It's because APD already dropped the case, and they didn't even believe the witness. They wanted to polygraph her. And you want me to get you a search warrant based on what she said three months ago? It's stale. Not only is it stale, you don't even have a credible witness."

"Fine," Flothe said. "Listen to this tape." He dutifully played the tape recording of the statement she'd given him during the re-interview. The DA and his assistant listened politely. "It doesn't change things," the DA finally said. "It's still stale."

"Look," Flothe offered, "I have a living witness. What if Kitty goes before a judge to tell him that we have a live, viable witness? When he hears her story, he'll know that she was a victim of this man."

The DA just shook his head. "I want you to do some more work on this case. See if you can't firm up that insurance fraud case. See if you can find somebody to contradict the alibi witness. See if you can solidify this case."

Major Gilmour came in to hear the results. "The DA flat turned down my request for a search warrant. Said the case was flimsy."

"Look, Glenn, let me tell you something," Gilmour said. "Just because the DA doesn't take this case doesn't mean it isn't a good one. I'm telling you, Hansen is your man, and if you can get him off the street you've got a chance with him.'Cause nobody confesses on the street."

"If I can't get a search warrant, Major, I can't do anything," Flothe replied.

"Well, as I recall, Vic Krumm isn't the only DA around. I mean, you don't need Vic Krumm to help you write a search warrant, do you?"

After Gilmour left, Flothe resolved immediately to do three things: Contact his friend Pat Doogan, an Assistant DA in Fairbanks who'd already given him valuable advice on the case; contact the FBI in Quantico, Virginia, and ask for their help; and contact Glenn Larson of State Farm Insurance, to ask him about the burglary at Hansen's house and the resulting thirteen-thousand-dollar insurance claim.

Pat Doogan and Glenn Flothe had become close friends over the years. Sure, they had worked some tough cases when they were both in Fairbanks, but it was a raft trip they took five hundred miles down the Yukon River that forged an unbreakable bond between the two men. Flothe could still picture Doogan sitting at the front of their raft, wearing a pair of old GI pants and a faded cotton shirt, smoking his pipe as they floated downstream. In the weeks of that idyllic summer, Flothe had learned a great deal about his friend. He'd learned that Doogan was a man who didn't ask for much, who could take pleasure in the simple things in life, although he was a very successful district attorney. All Pat Doogan wanted from other people was a little bit of respect and honesty.

To Flothe's mind, Pat Doogan had a way of seeing people for what they were. He neatly avoided the hard-driven, vindictive personality all too characteristic of up-and-coming district attorneys. Doogan's attitude to his job told it all: He took the view that people were capable of doing bad, but could make mistakes without necessarily becoming "bad persons."

Flothe had consulted Doogan early on in the Hansen case. Doogan had helped him formulate a package for the Anchorage DA, one he thought he would accept. Doogan had even flown down from Fairbanks to help lay out the pertinent facts in Flothe's dog-and-pony show for the district attorney. When that plan failed, Flothe knew who to call.

"Well, Pat," he said, "they didn't buy it."

"If you want a warrant, Glenn," he said, "I think we can put one together."

"No, no, no," Flothe said. "I'll tell you what: I'll make one last stand. I'll go to the lieutenant, and we'll get the colonel to set up another appointment with the DA. And if you don't mind I'll use your name. If they tell me that they don't have an attorney to write the search warrant, then I'll tell them that we already have one lined up. You."

Doogan was more than willing to accept the proposal. What Flothe didn't tell him, however, was that he still had a lot of legwork to do if his "last stand" was going to mean anything. That was why he was on the phone to Lieutenant Jent almost before he got off the phone with Doogan.

"What's the chance," he asked, "of our working with the FBI guys down at Quantico? You know, maybe one of them will come up here and help us put this together."

The Behavioral Sciences Division of the FBI in Quantico, Virginia, was the top research lab in the country on serial killers, and one of the first. Flothe wanted an idea of what he could expect to find with a search warrant, and something of the killer's state of mind. He figured if anyone could help him, Quantico could. Lieutenant Jent was more realistic.

"I don't know, Glenn," he said. "That's a pretty tall order. Don't expect them to come up here and work this case."

Call it dumb luck, but the man Flothe got when he called the FBI at Quantico was Roy Hazelwood, one of the men instrumental in starting the Behavioral Sciences Division. Hazelwood was extremely receptive as Glenn started to tell him about his suspect. "He's got an extensive history of kidnapping and raping women," Flothe started, "and . . ."

"Don't tell me anything more about the guy," Hazelwood interrupted. "I want you to tell me more about the crime scenes. I'll see if I can tell *you* about the guy."

Flothe started his list. Remote sites. Women buried in shallow graves. Killed with a high-powered rifle. Often fully clothed, probably sexually assaulted. Brass from the murder weapon found in the grave with the body.

"Any arrests?"

"Yeah. Arson, assault with a dangerous weapon, and larceny in a building."

"What about his victims?"

"Prostitutes or topless dancers."

"Okay," Hazelwood said after a brief pause. "I'd say this guy is probably an avid hunter. He's probably into guns and hunting and being an outdoorsman. Is he married?"

"Yes," Flothe responded. "Yes."

"I wouldn't be surprised if his wife was very, very religious. More than likely she's not aware, or not aware of the extent, of what he's doing. I mean, he's been in jail before, so obviously she knows that he's not quite together. But as far as going out and killing women—more than likely she's not totally aware. As for age, I'd say he was between thirty-three and forty-four, and I'd say that there's a good possibility he's a prominent member of the community. I don't mean that he's the mayor or anything, but he's probably someone who's known throughout the community as a good, upstanding citizen, a hardworking guy, that kind of thing. And he may be involved in a business."

"This is my guy!" Flothe blurted out over the phone. "If I send you all his stuff, can you tell me more?"

"Sure. We're busy, but we can take a look at it for you. And hey, if you want our help, go to the FBI boss in Anchorage. Have him put in a request

for us to come up and give you a hand on this thing.
We'd love to."

When Flothe got to Lieutenant Jent's office, he
was confident again.

"Lieutenant," Flothe said, "I talked to Quantico. They want me to send them a package of Hansen's stuff, so that they can take a look at it. And
they said we can request their help through the local FBI guy. Hey, these guys are gonna come up
here. I mean, all we gotta do is convince the FBI
here in town that we've got a good enough case."

That afternoon Jent and Flothe visited FBI
Agent-In-Charge Larry Nelson to request help from
the FBI's Behavioral Sciences Division. Nelson
didn't need much convincing. He immediately put
in a request to Quantico for a profile of the Anchorage serial killer. The troopers needed a profile
that would not only put the finger on Robert Hansen but add weight to any argument made in a court
of law.

Later that same afternoon Flothe called Glenn
Larson, the agent with State Farm Insurance. He
wanted to know what he could find out about a
certain burglary at the Hansen property out in Muldoon, and the later payment of a thirteen-thousand-
dollar insurance claim.

Larson managed to dig through the files and find
two separate sets of color photos. One Hansen had
taken before the burglary, showing all his trophies
on the wall of his den. The other set had been taken
by the Anchorage Police, showing bare spots along
the same walls.

"Don't lose them," Flothe cautioned.

If a search warrant showed that the missing trophies had magically reappeared on Hansen's walls, they had him on insurance fraud. It wasn't a lot, but it was something.

Flothe kept thinking about what Gilmour had said about "nobody confessing on the street." They had to get him off the street. And from that standpoint Friday, September 30, 1983, was a good day for Glenn Flothe.

12

An early signal that Bob Hansen had taken a wrong turn somewhere was his arrest and conviction for arson in Iowa during the early 1960s. It had happened, predictably enough, right after Bob got back to Pocahontas, Iowa, from six months of basic training in the Army Reserves at Fort Dix, New Jersey. His Army experience had made him a man.

Not only had he walked onto a firing range at Fort Dix, but he'd managed to earn a one-day pass to New York as the USO's "Soldier of the Week." It was in New York that Bob had his first sexual experience. He tagged along with another soldier who had been so honored and they went downtown to "get a piece of ass."

They met some girls and went to their hotel. It was a disappointing experience for Bob. They jumped in bed and jumped right back out. "I got to feel it, but that was about it," he complained. "Everything was strictly 'Slam-bam, thank you, ma'am.' "

The young man who returned from basic training was a troubled one. Pocahontas Police Chief Marvin Wiseman, who had once promoted Bob to a position as Junior Police Instructor, eased him out of the organization after Bob's return from the Army. Wiseman probably knew Bob Hansen better than anyone.

Bob Hansen's dad owned a bakery, and Wiseman was in the shop for an hour or so every day it was open. He remembers Bob showing off his skill with a bow and arrow by shooting at targets he'd placed on cardboard boxes at the rear of his father's bakery. Once, almost ominously, Bob shot an arrow into the target, then turned to Wiseman.

"You can't hardly hear that, can you?" he said.

Later Bob whipped out a knife and threw it into the wall in front of the police chief. "You can't hardly hear that, either," he said.

And after he'd returned from the Army he became the ringleader of a younger group of kids. They didn't have much use for the "Poky" Police Department. They were a bunch of rural smart-asses, full of mischief and capable of almost anything.

In the months before the arson fire, according to Wiseman, Bob and his friends were suspected of blowing up a tractor in the town of Rolfe, just north of Pocahontas. They were apparently practicing for an attempt on the Pocahontas water tower, and had used a single stick of dynamite in their rehearsal run. Only a fire in a bus barn intervened to thwart their attempt on the water tower.

Bob planned the arson of the Pocahontas Community School bus barn several days beforehand, at the back of his father's bakery. His accomplices were two sixteen-year-olds who also worked for his father. On the night of the arson they were to give their parents some excuse and come to the bakery instead. Once there, they would paint the ovens so they would have an alibi.

On the morning of December 7, 1960, while one of his cohorts was at work in the bakery, Bob passed the word. "Tonight is the night," he said. "We'll meet at the bakery as planned."

At 6:00 Bob drove to the house of his other accomplice. The family was eating supper. His friend came out to the car, which Bob had parked in front of the house, and talked to him there. Bob told his friend to meet him at the bakery at seven. Tonight the school bus barn would burn. Bob pointed with pride to a five-gallon can at the rear of the car.

Only one of Bob's cohorts bothered to appear at the bakery at the appointed hour. The other one took a drive into the country with his parents. The guy who did show up got there before Bob did, and rode around town with another friend until Bob finally came slightly after seven o'clock.

Inside the bakery they began painting the ovens, setting up their alibis. At seven-thirty they got into Bob's car and drove to a spot behind an abandoned Pontiac garage. They parked, and Bob gave the order for his accomplice to carry the gasoline.

As they scrambled to the bus barn Bob's friend slipped on a small incline and spilled some gasoline. "Gimme the can," Bob demanded, "before you spill it all."

Soon they had crossed the school playground and were standing at the foot of the ladder leading to the loft of the dusty old building. It was Bob who clambered up the ladder with the can of gas. His friend stayed behind with a flashlight and pointed the way of his return. The gas made a splashing sound as Bob doused the loft.

"Don't light the gas from the loft," the friend warned. "It'll blow up."

The next thing he heard was a great rush of fire. Bob's friend immediately ran out of the bus barn and across the playground, instinctively returning to the spot where the car was parked. Bob was right behind him.

They drove to the bakery and got there just as the fire siren sounded. Bob hastily threw the gas can into the back of the bakery, then drove the two of them back to the fire. As a member of the Volunteer Fire Department it was Bob's duty to fight the fire, even if he was the one who had started it.

At the fire his friend borrowed a dollar, wanting to go to the Pocahontas Catholic High School basketball game. Picking the night of the big basketball game had been a stroke of inspiration, for Pocahontas surely was preoccupied that cold December evening. The fire was first discovered by Ronald Walker, a vocational agriculture instructor who was getting ready for his regular farmers' night school class. The building, built of army "surplus" materials shortly after World War II, rapidly became a torch. Three of the school's seven buses were declared "total losses" and the bus barn itself, valued at eleven thousand dollars, was thoroughly destroyed.

Injured while driving one of the buses out of the burning building was Pocahontas fireman Dutch Leonard. He received burns and cuts when the gas tank of the bus exploded. A face respirator he was wearing at the time of the explosion was credited with saving him from more serious injuries.

The spectacle of the arsonist returning to watch his fire is a well-known one. The volunteer fireman as arsonist is hardly a new twist either. The primitive power of a fire that is savagely out of control is truly mesmerizing—even with the possibility of criminal charges looming in the background.

The act itself was in its purest sense nothing more than thrill-seeking. Yet the episode had far more disquieting meanings. Bob had told his buddies he wanted to torch the barn because he wanted to see if he could get away with it—as he surely would—and because he hated School Superintendent Waldo Mick, who just happened to be a close friend of his father.

The post-fire investigation eliminated faulty wiring as the source of the fire. It pointed instead to a combustible substance. It was arson, not an accident. That's about all that was established. No arrests were forthcoming.

Simultaneously, there were persistent rumors that somehow the Hansen boy had been involved. Police Chief Wiseman, who'd heard the rumors, couldn't help but think of the bus barn fire when, some months later, the Farm Bureau was broken into, or when he found the front seats of his police car slashed with a knife. Was it Bob Hansen and his buddies who were responsible?

Bob, meanwhile, had started his first romance. It was with Phebe Padgett, daughter of Dr. Padgett, the town chiropractor.

Dr. Padgett was widely regarded as being a non-social person, and his daughter shared some of those characteristics. Not very attractive, she was a loner, definitely not part of the "in-crowd." One of her few "pals" was Rosemary Shaw, the gifted daughter of Frank Shaw, one of Pocahontas County's more capable attorneys. Phebe and Bob seemed to be well matched: they were two loners who had found each other. As if proof of that assertion, it wasn't long into 1961 before the couple announced their wedding engagement.

By the end of March 1961, however, the jig was up. One of Bob's high school buddies, a GI on leave back in Pocahontas, happened to hear about the arson at a party attended by some of the teenagers who were hanging around Bob Hansen. The teens only intention had been to show off for the GI, but he went to the authorities with the story. Under questioning Bob's accomplice admitted his role, and on March 29, 1961, Deputy State Fire Marshall D.S. Hutchinson brought arson charges against Bob Hansen.

All hell broke loose in Pocahontas. Chris Hansen reacted with typical passion. "Bobby?" he angrily replied when Chief Wiseman brought the news. "No, no, not my Bobby! It better not be my goddamned Bobby!"

"Yes, it is your Bobby," Chief Wiseman told the senior Hansen. "He's under arrest."

Chris Hansen came unglued. A string of harsh Danish words erupted from his slight form. And then he found his English. "You framed him!" he raged. "You framed him!"

"A lie detector will tell if I framed him, Chris."

From that point on Pocahontas was divided over the issue of Bob's innocence or guilt. Chris Hansen made a point of hiring the best attorney in town, Frank Shaw.

No one loomed larger in Bob Hansen's life than his domineering father. His mother, Edna, was a frail, soft-spoken women whom everyone considered the dutiful model wife. She usually took a backseat to her headstrong husband.

As a parent Chris Hansen was very strict, and a man full of definite ideas. For example, his son was born left-handed but Chris forced him to use his right hand instead. A psychologist later told his parents that might have caused him to have language disabilities.

The son's first training as a baker came, quite naturally, at the father's hands, and started almost from the time Chris Hansen bought the bakery in Pocahontas. But Chris Hansen was never satisfied with Bob's work. Worse yet, Bob's dad often described him as "worthless."

After a while Bob began to think his father was right. As a result Bob was full of trouble and would do almost anything. He had learned, however, never to go directly against authority. That was a sure way to get caught and, given his father's temper, that was something he wanted to avoid.

Though his father wanted to pass the bakery on to him and Bob didn't want anything to do with it, Bob simply avoided the issue, never showing his true feelings. By being sneaky he could be as rebellious as he wanted and still avoid paying the price. For strong as his need was to act out his violent, rebellious fantasies, somehow Bob still didn't want to disappoint his father.

That helped explain the widespread belief among Bob's supporters that he'd been railroaded on the arson charge. Bob's reticence, however, made it necessary to waive his preliminary hearing and bind him over to the grand jury. There was not much Shaw could do.

At the Padgett household there was a debate as to whether the marriage should go forward as planned. Phebe believed Bob was innocent, and decided to marry him despite her father's opposition. But Phebe also issued a warning: She'd divorce Bob if she ever found out he was lying.

Had the Padgetts known the results of Bob's polygraph test, they might not have given in to Phebe's wishes. When the polygraph operator had finished administering the test, he nearly ran out of the testing room.

"Which one of you is Wiseman?" he asked.

"I am," Chief Wiseman volunteered.

"Man, you better watch it," the operator said, his voice strong and serious. "That boy is hot on you. You've been living in danger."

"Yeah? What kind of danger?"

"That kid was planning on blowing up your house."

The minister at Bob and Phebe's wedding as much as challenged Bob to proclaim his innocence. Bob so proclaimed. Now he was married.

Some town cynics dismissed it as a move designed to win him clemency at his sentencing. Still Bob had his supporters, mostly the town businessmen, who seemed to honor each other. Because of their mutual admiration they felt they could do no wrong, and neither could their offspring. In this group the feeling was strong that Bob Hansen was in jail because of Chief Wiseman's railroad.

Things took a turn for the worst at the September grand jury proceedings. There were three primary witnesses against Bob: the sixteen-year-old who was with him, a seventeen-year-old to whom Hansen and his accomplice had admitted their involvement, and the now seventeen-year-old bakery employee who had been invited but didn't go along.

As a result of the grand jury proceeding, formal charges were brought against Hansen. He was charged with willfully and maliciously setting fire to, and burning, a motor vehicle and other personal property belonging to the Pocahontas Community School District.

Instead of facing the publicity of a trial, Bob decided to plead guilty. He was essentially throwing himself on the mercy of the court, because he steadfastly maintained he'd been framed. At least Phebe and Bob's father were able to buy this explanation.

On October 9, 1961, however, Judge Joseph P. Hand sentenced Bob to the State Reformatory at Anamosa, Iowa, for a term of not more than three years. Almost immediately Chris Hansen was making the rounds of the town with a petition. It declared that Bob had been framed for the bus barn arson and demanded that he be freed from jail.

Six months into his jail term Bob admitted his

part in the arson. Phebe Padgett divorced him immediately. Chris Hansen was devastated by Bob's confession. As quickly as he could he sold the bakery and bought a resort at Leech Lake, Minnesota, the same spot where, some two years later, Hansen would meet his second wife, Darla Henrichsen.

Whenever Bob talked about Pocahontas, he emphasized the unhappiness of his years there. "If you look real close at my face," he said, "you'll see that I used to have a tremendous amount of pimples on my face. All through high school, and even all through service, it embarrassed me no end to even be around people. My speech was another thing—my gosh, I looked like a freak, and I sounded like one. I never had many girls that were interested in me. When they can go out with some guy that can at least talk to them halfway intelligently and not be with a pimple-face, they would sure rather do that. I can probably count on one hand the number of dates I had through high school."

Hansen was a social outcast in Pocahontas, and he desperately wanted to get back at those who had mocked him. "I was always so embarrassed and upset by people making fun of me that I hated the word 'school.' I guess that is why I burned down the bus barn. I just hated that place with a divine passion. I would do anything and everything I could think of to get back at that monster school that I convinced myself was out to do Bob Hansen personal wrong."

13

Wednesday, October 5, 1983

Flothe's request for FBI help was approved within days. Two FBI officers from Quantico would arrive in Anchorage on October 11th. Flothe was temporarily ecstatic. All the same, Flothe was worried he didn't have enough on Hansen. He needed more witnesses, for one. More criminal charges, for another.

To correct that situation Flothe met with a black topless dancer who had reported being kidnapped by Hansen in October 1979. The trooper met the woman at a rundown café, where even the coffee cups were worn. The dancer smoked one Kool cigarette after another and the air turned gunmetal blue during their interview.

The woman's face twitched involuntarily as she told Flothe how her assailant had pulled a .357 magnum on her, forced her to take her clothes off at the back of his camper, then tied her hands and feet with guitar wire. He kept his own clothes on, she said, and locked her in the back while he drove to an unknown location. She managed to free herself, she said, but Hansen noticed; he slammed on the brakes and came around the back of the camper with his gun.

This was her chance, she reported. She climbed into the cab through the open window connecting it with the camper. She locked herself in and started pulling at the wires, madly trying to get the car started. Furious, Hansen came back to the cab and smashed the window with his fist. The dancer escaped by jumping out the passenger side, still naked. She fled to the nearest house. Hansen sped away.

When the dancer had finished her story, Flothe pulled out a photographic lineup with six pictures. The woman immediately pointed to the photo of Hansen. "He's the one," she said softly. Still looking at his picture in the lineup, she began to update her story.

"What's weird, you know," she said, "is that just a couple months ago I went to Hansen's Bakery to apply for a job? And the lady, she gave me an application to fill out, which I did. But then I seen him and I said, 'Unh-unh, I'm gettin' my ass outa here.' I never even looked back."

"Did you talk to him, or did you just see him and leave?" Flothe wanted to know.

"I talked to him," she said. " 'Cause, see, I didn't recognize him at first. But when he was talkin' about the job and stuff, then I knew it was him.'Cause he stuttered a lot. I don't know if he recognized me or not, but it was him. No doubt about it. Like I said, I got my ass outa there."

The essential point to emerge from the interview, however, was the woman's willingness to testify in court. Even at that Flothe had to wonder how important it would really be, given that 1979 was ancient history.

Still, the dancer's lack of hesitancy to testify was proof enough of an undercurrent of truth in Flothe's basic logic. Robert Hansen had a pattern of abducting and raping women, and here was a woman who was still terrified of this man four years after the incident.

More important to his cause, however, was the Kitty Larson case. Perhaps Kitty herself wouldn't make such a good impression, but her supporting witnesses would. These were people like Robert Yount, the good Samaritan who had stopped his truck to pick Kitty up as she ran from her assailant. And Louis Bennet, the desk clerk at the Mush Inn Motel, where Yount had finally dropped her off so she could run to her pimp.

One by one Flothe got these people into his cramped office at trooper headquarters, where he re-interviewed them on tape. Clearly Yount was one of the better witnesses, although he could not positively identify Hansen in a lineup. But he had seen a man with a gun and had picked up Kitty Larson as she ran from that man, of that there was no doubt. Would it help? Was this time-consuming, almost redundant activity really going to help Flothe solidify his case? Or was it just a straw-clutching exercise?

The puzzle that this case had become was too delicate—he had eggshell evidence, gingerly glued together. He had to get more.

Flothe's persistence did start to pay off. In the

ensuing days he managed to contact a doctor whose cabin had been burglarized. The doctor, in turn, led him to an associate who'd also been burglarized, who told a fantastic tale of sleuthing in the far north.

"There were several cabins broken into," said the man. "Mine, the doc's, another guy's. And every single one of them was broken into by someone in an airplane. This was in the wintertime, see, and it left some ski marks out there, going right up to the cabins. Well, when the troopers shut down our cases, we decided we were going to find that airplane ourselves. 'Cause to tell you the truth, we were pissed."

The men divvied up all the airports in and around the Anchorage area: Merrill Field, Lake Hood, Birchwood, Hillside, Inlet, Eagle River. They had one thing going for them: The ski on the suspect aircraft was quite unusual. The skegs looked like they were either homemade or some type of a conversion done for a Super Cub.

"Now we searched and searched," said the mountain of a man, "and of all the planes we looked at, only one plane matched the description."

"And?" Flothe asked. The man kept him waiting. "What was it?"

"A plane belonging to a guy named Bob Hansen." The way the guy said it told Flothe volumes. The man not only knew the suspect, but there was no love lost between them.

"Sounds like you know him," the sergeant ventured.

"We used to be in the same bow-hunting association," the man said disgustedly. "Yeah, I know him."

"He's a pretty good hunter, from what I hear," Flothe responded.

"Yeah, you know he has all them world's records," the man said. "But some of us in the bow association wonder if maybe he shouldn't. See, that-there Dall sheep that he got—that number one sheep? That sheep had a bullet lodged in one of the horns. A fresh bullet. So whether he connived or cheated on that record, I don't know."

"So how come they accepted it into the books?" Flothe asked. "Or did they?"

"Hansen's friend John Sumrall came out and said he was with Bob when they bagged the sheep, and swore he never heard a shot. And that was that, because John Sumrall is a standup kind of guy."

The man had passed the test. Flothe decided to take him into his confidence. "It may be important for you to tell a judge the story you just told me," Flothe told him. "I've got reason to believe that Hansen is a murderer. I may need your help in getting him off the street until we can pin him for murder."

"No problem," the man said without flinching.

In addition the man gave Flothe another witness, this a man who'd recently been at Hansen's house and reportedly had seen his trophies.

Flothe contacted him immediately. "I was just at Hansen's place," the witness told him. "He took me downstairs and showed me his hunting trophy mounts. You know, the world's records?"

"Including the Dall sheep?"

"Yeah. I think so. . . . "

"If I got some photos, could you identify the ones you saw?"

"Yeah."

Now Flothe was excited. This man probably had seen the Dall sheep that Hansen had reported stolen. If that head was back on the wall it was insurance fraud, pure and simple. Flothe's pulse quickened even more the next day, when the witness told him that the stolen heads now were hanging on Hansen's wall.

The minute patches of Hansen's guilt were starting to form a mosaic of Hansen's criminal pattern. Flothe was finding it easier and easier to contemplate another bout with the District Attorney's office. What the hell—this time he'd have the FBI behind him.

Just the thought of the FBI tripped another circuit in Flothe's brain. Wasn't there something he still had to send them on the Larson case?

He checked off a mental list. Had he sent the file materials? Check. Had he sent the stuff on a half-dozen other cases. Check. Then he realized that he'd failed to send them the frozen tampon, frozen filter paper stain, and stained underpants Kitty had been wearing the night Hansen raped her. The FBI at Quantico was waiting for it. And where was it? Still in the trooper lab. Why hadn't he sent the stuff straight to the FBI? Why had he given in to the argument that it would be quicker to do the lab work locally? Sometimes there was just too much to think about.

On the same day, Tuesday, October 11, 1983, that Flothe finally shipped off the Kitty Larson evidence, FBI agents James Horn and John Douglas arrived in Anchorage from Quantico, Virginia. The feds got right down to brass tracks.

"From the stuff you sent us," they told him, "we were able to confirm Agent Hazelwood's analysis. The man you want probably stutters. Is likely an excellent hunter. His wife is probably religious, and not totally aware of her husband's activities. He's known as a good provider and hardworking businessman. He's successful, or at least we wouldn't be surprised if he is."

"So far so good," Flothe said. "The profile fits." Was it a coincidence or just plain old good police work? Whatever it was, Flothe approved.

"What I need to know now," Flothe told the agents, "is what I can expect to find in a search warrant. As soon as we can put a profile together, I want to put it in front of the District Attorney's Office."

"No problem," one of the agents said. "We think that the killer may keep a murder kit—disguises, that type of thing—so he is anonymous when he picks these women up."

"He probably stashes things," said the other. "Like maybe rings or jewelry or driver's licenses or maybe clothing."

"He likes to keep it close to him, so he can view it in private," the first agent continued. "He takes it out and relives the killings. It's a movie in his brain, and he's turned on by the objects he's taken from the scene."

"If he's really into it," the other agent said, "the killings are all he thinks about twenty-four hours a day. Everything else is just a motion to him. His work, his normal routine, are just a motion. Everything is wrapped up with murder. His whole life, his whole thinking. He probably plans the kills far in advance. . . . "

"What am I going to do to catch him?" Flothe asked.

"You've got a couple of choices," the other agent continued. "If you can get a warrant, fine. If not . . ."

"If not you may have to catch him in the act. Do you have him under surveillance?" asked the first agent.

"Sure do. Twenty-four hours a day. But we're using the narcs, and I don't know how much longer we'll be able to keep them."

"It's what you gotta do, though," the agent responded.

If there was any strong message communicated to Flothe in this exchange, it was that of urgency. It had been there all along, but now it was razor-sharp: *He couldn't afford to lose the mementos.* They were almost everything now. That and the murder weapon, or murder weapons. He had to get a search warrant.

"One way to get him to make a mistake is to do something to force his hand," one of the agents suggested.

"For instance, you can get a picture of one of his victims and blow it up real big. Tape it to the window of his car and roll the window down. When

he rolls the window back up, there she is,'' said
the other agent.

''It really freaks 'em out,'' the first agent said.

Flothe didn't know whether the agents were serious or not. It was hard for him to take their last
suggestion seriously. If he did what they suggested
Hansen would freak, all right. He would freak and
start destroying evidence. Better to get the search
warrants before the baker destroyed his sordid trea-
sures, he reasoned.

Flothe wasn't going to risk the DA again without
having all his ducks in a row. He'd taken the DA's
wish list and he'd completed it. This time he had
to be successful. If not Flothe would be reduced to
desperate measures, like playing ''Blow-Up'' with
pictures on car windows. Come on, he told himself. There's got to be a better way.

What he needed now, he decided, was a Plan
B, an alternate to go to in case everything else
failed. His first visit would be with Lt. Jent. Not
only was Jent duck number one, but without him
Flothe felt utterly alone when it came to dealing
with the cold anonymity of the criminal justice
bureaucracy.

''Lieutenant, there's a couple of things,'' Flothe
said, taking his superior aside for a quick chat in
the dimly lit hallway of trooper headquarters. ''The
FBI is behind us one hundred percent. They're putting a profile of Hansen together, and they say it's
urgent that we get a search warrant. We need to
have another meeting with the DA's office, Lieutenant. I've got an idea, too. Have the colonel call
them. Have him tell them it's absolutely necessary.

That the FBI's here and we're certain we've got the Anchorage serial killer.''

"Are we ready for the colonel?'' Jent asked.

"Yeah. We gotta let'em know we're ready. Oh, and another thing. If they don't go for it, I'm bringing Pat Doogan down to help me write the warrant,'' Flothe said. There it was. Plan B. He'd just announced it.

Jent could only shake his head. Flothe felt like he was all alone and out on a limb on this thing. Maybe he didn't realize that he was sharing that limb with others. That included the colonel, who after all was the man responsible for the twenty-four-hour watch on Bob Hansen and who knew better than anyone the strain it was putting on trooper resources.

"No problem, Glenn,'' Jent finally said. "I'll get the colonel immediately. I don't think there'll be any problem with him. Anything you want to get this killer off the street, he's willing to go with it. Just so you know.''

Less than an hour later Col. Kolovosky, Jent, and Flothe had set up an appointment for the next afternoon with Vic Krumm, the Anchorage District Attorney.

14

Wednesday, October 12, 1983

The meeting took place in Col. Kolovosky's office—a sound psychological move. All around the room were emblems of Kolovosky's authority at the top of the trooper organization. Flothe still couldn't escape thinking of it as a spectacle: Here he was in an office crammed with the symbols of power, and as far as he was concerned his boss almost was going to beg the DA's office for an attorney to help him write a search warrant.

"The FBI did a profile for us, Mr. Krumm," Flothe started. "Here's a copy for you to look at. Their analysis of the crime scenes and the victim tell them that we're looking for an avid hunter, an expert outdoorsman, a man who is a respected member of this community, probably a successful businessman. That profile fits Robert Hansen to a T.

"As I told you the last time we met," Flothe continued, "we have a recent victim, Kitty Larson, who was kidnapped and taken to Hansen's private torture chamber. He was planning to fly her off to her death but she got away. And I've talked to another victim, a topless dancer, who tells much the

same story. She was kidnapped by a man she positively identified as Robert Hansen, and she too
feared for her life. She had every reason to. I am
convinced, and so is the FBI, that this man is responsible for the murder of the two women we
found up on the Knik River—and who knows how
many others.''

Krumm cleared his throat. He appeared perpet-
ually tired, with hollowed-out cheeks, but underneath that was a man who knew how to use his
resources to their best advantage. ''So the FBI
thinks this Hansen is the killer, too, is that right?''
he said in a dusty voice.

''Yes, sir,'' Flothe replied, sitting rigidly in his
chair.

''Have you developed any new evidence?''
Krumm shot back, maintaining an even tone.

''I've tightened up the Larson case consider-
ably,'' Flothe said. ''I've got photos of his house,
bakery, and airplane. I also have statements from
the guy who picked her up in his truck, and from
the desk clerk at the motel where he took her. And
I've also developed two other cases against him—
I've got him on some cabin burglaries and a suspected insurance fraud—either of which might be
reason enough to get a search warrant for his house.
And that insurance scam is no small potatoes—he
faked the burglary of his world-record hunting trophies, collected thirteen thousand dollars, and
bought himself a new airplane.''

''Now wait a minute, Sarge,'' Krumm interrupted. ''You're telling me that you want to get into
his house based on an insurance fraud and some

cabin burglaries, but that you want to use that search warrant to get him for murder? I've still got problems with it, FBI or no FBI.''

''What the hell do I have to do?'' Flothe exploded, surprising even himself. ''I've tracked down every lead there is in this case. I've talked to every witness I could find. Even brought the guys from the FBI in to consult with us—and they're the top people in the country when it comes to serial murders!''

The colonel immediately jumped in to rescue the situation, using the diplomatic skills that had helped him get to his position in the first place. Then in his early forties Kolovosky had been the heavyweight boxing champ of Alaska. A six-foot, two-hundred-pound, jovial man, he understood the subtle politics of law enforcement. He worked his charm on Vic Krumm.

''What you've got to appreciate, Vic, is that Glenn has worked on this case night and day, day and night. And he keeps coming back to this one guy. Nobody else. And the thing is, when you really look at Hansen's entire history, he does look like a man who would kill over and over. We need your help on this, Vic. We're interested, and I'm sure you are, too, in putting these killings to an end.''

''Cooperation is a two-way street, Colonel,'' Krumm said. ''You say you need our help? We need your help, too. Let me give you an example. For months now we've been trying to get the troopers to work with us on a sexual assault kit. We think it's important—vital—to stop these kinds of killings before they get started. What type of cooperation have we gotten from the troopers on this, this crucial criminal prosecution package? Colonel, it's been pathetic.''

"We're not insensitive to the need for rape prosecutions, Vic. Let me tell you, anything my office can do to help you put something like that together, just give me a call." The colonel stretched like a prizefighter in his corner. He smiled. "Seriously, Vic."

"I have to tell you," Krumm said, getting back to the subject at hand, "that I'm still really nervous about the way Sergeant Flothe wants to work this thing. There's always a chance—even a poor chance—that a court's going to say we seized evidence illegally, because they may feel we went on a fishing expedition."

"We've got to get him into jail somehow," Flothe said, his face still flushed. "This man is still killing people, for all we know."

"Maybe," Krumm replied. "But what will you do if all your evidence is thrown out? Then what will you have?"

"Just give us an attorney. I've got enough right here to put together a search warrant," Flothe responded. "All I need is someone to write the warrant. Let a judge decide, Mr. Krumm. Let a judge decide."

"Two things come to mind," Krumm said, leaning forward in his chair. "First, we still don't have any spare attorneys available. That situation is unchanged. And even if we get you an attorney and you get a search warrant written, I'm still worried about the integrity of anything you can come up with. You talk about the history of this guy, but that's just the problem. All this stuff you have against him is old stuff.''

"Look,'' Flothe said, his fear and frustration rising again, "if you don't have a district attorney you can give us, that's not a problem. We've already got one who'll work on the search warrant.'' Flothe had dropped the bomb.

"Who?'' Krumm asked.

"Pat Doogan, up in Fairbanks.'' Flothe was straight-faced and serious. Colonel Kolovosky cocked one eyebrow.

"Look, Vic,'' the colonel interrupted, "I'm sure we can work something out here. We're not opposed to helping you out with the sexual assault kits. In fact we'd love to help.''

"That's not a problem,'' Krumm told Kolovosky. Then he turned to Flothe. "We may be able to get you someone,'' he said. "We're very busy, but I think we can spare someone pretty soon.''

"Real soon,'' Flothe blurted. "Right now.''

"I can't promise you,'' Krumm said. Flothe felt like he was being tortured. Any minute now, Hansen could get away from them. Flothe felt as if he was the only one who cared.

"It would really help if you could get us someone right away,'' Lieutenant Jent interjected. "This guy is slippery. The FBI tells us that he may have mementos from his kills, and the longer we continue this thing the greater the chance there is that he'll destroy that evidence. And we need all the evidence we can get. This is, as you know, a real circumstantial case.''

"I think we can free somebody up," Krumm offered. "We'll see if Gail Voitlander can't come over and help." The stage was now set. The DA was committed to the prosecution.

Reflecting on everything, Flothe had to acknowledge it had been an event-filled week. Tuesday with the FBI. Wednesday with the DA. And he was already sending Trooper "Rhino" Von Clasen to interview Ronnie Lee, a claims adjuster with State Farms Insurance, regarding the possibility his company had been defrauded by Bob Hansen.

The first person to hear of Flothe's good news was Pat Doogan. "The DA gave us an attorney," Flothe announced. "They finally bought the package. It was like pulling teeth."

"Who'd they give you?" Doogan wanted to know.

"Gail Voitlander," Flothe said.

"Starting when?"

"Saturday."

Gail Voitlander arrived right on time at Flothe's office at trooper headquarters, just ahead of Pat Doogan. Flothe handled the introductions, noticing the look of total surprise on Voitlander's face. Doogan acted immediately to put her at ease.

"Hey, what can I do for you?" Doogan said. "Whatever I can do for you, let me know."

They had a ton of material to go through, most of it case files. The guts of the search warrant, however, would be a rough chronology of Hansen's "career," starting in late 1971. It included: the real-estate receptionist, assault with a dangerous weapon, 1971. Robyn Patterson, kidnapping and rape, 1971. Unidentified victim, kidnapping and rape, 1975. The topless dancer, attempted kidnapping, 1979. Sherry Morrow, murder, 1982. Paula Goulding, murder, 1983. Kitty Larson, kidnapping, rape, and attempted murder, 1983.

And there was considerable background material on the suspect, plus many missing persons reports. Just organizing the material into some manageable order was a tall task, and the three of them spent all morning doing just that.

At noon they all took a break and went to Arby's for a hamburger. It was a quick meal. They went right back to Flothe's office so they could get back to work. Later that afternoon, however, Gail Voitlander began to feel ill and decided to go home.

Doogan and Flothe didn't see her the rest of the weekend. They worked that Saturday until 2:00 in the morning. Flothe's wife Cherry brought them dinner at trooper headquarters so they could work through the night. When Flothe finally got home he drank a beer and went straight to sleep. He was back at the office with Doogan by 8:00.

By Sunday morning the two men had arrived at a working method, though an outsider might find it difficult to comprehend. Flothe was in one room, writing from memory the key points in each case. Doogan was in the next room, taking the information from Flothe plus the case files and putting together the search warrant at the typewriter. As fast as Flothe could write Doogan was organizing and typing it, based on the outline they'd already put together.

The men shuffled constantly between the two rooms, putting together the evidence, the witnesses, the identification of Hansen. There were files throughout the office.

The Larson case, for example, was spread out on one desk; another case was spread out on a credenza; yet another was lying on an unused typing stand. All the desk tops were covered, and Flothe moved from desk to desk as they progressed, writing like mad on a yellow legal pad. Doogan banged away at the typewriter.

Sunday evening Cherry Flothe brought dinner again. It felt like the hair-raising night before the final exam to Flothe, not only because time was running out but because Doogan had to fly back to Fairbanks the next morning. Fortunately, their plan was working. They knew exactly what they wanted to do. There was no need to sit and argue about anything, and they didn't.

By Monday morning they'd written a forty-plus-page, legal-sized affidavit. It took until right up to the moment Doogan was scheduled to fly back to Fairbanks to finish. But they made it.

Every question on the exam had been answered by the time Doogan got on the plane. With him were copies of Hansen's past psychiatric evaluations, which he planned to give to Dr. Irwin Rothrock for further analysis. Rothrock was Alaska's leading expert on the psychiatric evaluation of murderers. His insights might prove a priceless addition to the affidavit Flothe and Doogan had so painstakingly prepared.

While Doogan and Flothe were absorbed in writing the affidavit, Bob Hansen was keeping the troopers busy. That Saturday troopers followed Hansen to Merrill Field; accompanying Hansen was his son, Johnny. They were going on a father-and-son outing.

When Hansen and his son took to the air at seven that morning, Officer Stewart Felberg of Fish and Wildlife was right behind them in his own plane. It was a hairy flight, by Felberg's description. The winds were so fierce the officer turned back, but not before he'd observed Hansen fly to Montague Island, just southeast of Seward in Prince William Sound, and land on its southeast corner. In Felberg's opinion Hansen was not only quite familiar with the route he took but was also a crackerjack pilot. He had showed himself an ace pilot under very trying conditions.

Felberg returned to Anchorage and stationed himself next to a plane with a "For Sale" sign conveniently parked next to Hansen's stall. When Hansen returned to Merrill Field, Felberg struck up a conversation on the general topic of planes.

"I've flown fourteen thousand hours myself," Hansen bragged.

"I see you have some nice rifles there, too," Felberg commented.

"Yeah," Hansen replied. "I got a .270 I use for hunting. And a Model 70 Winchester. It was built before 1964, so it's a good one. And I have a .17-caliber rifle."

"Sort of hard to get ammo for that one, isn't it?" Felbert asked.

"I reload my own ammunition," Hansen replied.

"You must have a lot of guns if you do that," Felberg said.

"I do have a lot of guns," Hansen said, smiling. "Yeah, I sure do."

"Which one do you like the best?" Felberg asked ingenously. "With all those guns, you must have a favorite."

"What I like best are small-caliber, high-velocity bullets."

"So where do you fly around here?" Felberg asked, changing the subject.

"Oh, there's some nice flying up by the Knik River. I go up there and practice 'touch-and-goes' on the gravel bars. And just for scenery, maybe Lake George or around there somewhere near Knik Glacier."

As Hansen busied himself with cleaning out the plane, Felberg watched him remove a portable rear seat from the plane. He also saw a small camera, maybe a 35-millimeter. Felberg took the opportunity to ask Johnny Hansen a question.

"This your dad's first airplane?"

"No, this is his third airplane," the boy said proudly. Soon he was in the car with his father, and Felberg watched them drive away.

On Thursday, when Dr. Rothrock called Flothe with his evaluation of the psychiatric materials delivered by Pat Doogan, he carefully chose every word.

"It is my opinion that Robert Hansen fits the pattern of a type of person who might be involved with the missing dancers,'' he said. ''Let me tell you why. First, Hansen appears to be impulsive, as reflected in his shoplifting behavior. Second, he was involved in arson at an early age. Third, he seems to pick victims he views as inferior to himself. Lastly, Hansen's an avid hunter, and serial murderers are oftentimes avid hunters.''

''So you think he's our guy?''

''He could be. Let me tell you, too, that oftentimes in cases such as this mementoes are kept. And since Hansen has a family, it wouldn't surprise me if he kept such mementos at his place of business.''

''Did you notice in the reports that it said he took thorazine and should be on lithium therapy? Would that make a difference?'' Flothe asked.

''Yes. But only a low percentage of people continue thorazine and lithium on a voluntary basis.''

With the Rothrock information, Flothe needed to make some additions to the affidavit. With the timely help of Gail Voitlander he did just that, adding not only the Rothrock interview but the Felberg information about Hansen's flight. He then added information gleaned in an interview with one of Hansen's past acquaintances, Lonny Brisker. It was Brisker who had supplied Hansen with an alibi in the 1971 murder of Melanie Michaels at McHugh Creek State Park.

''We were neighbors during the seventies,'' Brisker said. ''And on several occasions we went hunting, mostly for sheep, out of Seward, Moose Pass, and in the Jim Creek area, just . . . let's see . . . just northeast of the old Knik River bridge.''

''Did you ever go anywhere else with Hansen?'' Flothe wanted to know.

"Occasionally we used Bob's river boat and hunted the Knik River islands and sandbars right around the Eklutna powerhouse."

"Can you show me on a map?"

When Flothe brought out a map of the Knik River, Brisker pointed at the place where the bodies of Paula Goulding and Sherry Morrow had been found. "Right in here," he said.

"What kind of sportsman would you say Bob was?" Flothe asked.

"An avid sportsman. And he owned many handguns and rifles. He was even into reloading his own ammunition. Now that's a fanatic."

"When did he get into reloading? Do you know?" Flothe asked.

"In the early seventies. Bob already owned reloading equipment at that time."

"When was the last time you saw Bob Hansen, Lonny?"

"The last time I met with him was for dinner at his house, possibly in 1975 or 1976. And afterwards I remember we drove out to the Birchwood Airport in Chugiak and he showed me his airplane."

So there it was. Bob had been going to the Knik River since the early seventies. Probably knew the place like the palm of his hand. And according to Brisker, he'd been flying up there almost that long. The puzzle was starting to look more like a picture all the time.

By Friday a little more than a week had passed since an attorney had been assigned to the case. Flothe was getting antsy and called the DA's office. He wound up in a meeting with Vic Krumm.

"Well, I don't know," Krumm said on seeing what Flothe, Doogan, and Voitlander had wrought. "What I want you to do is get this thing roughed out, then fine-tune it. And then I want the Office of Special Prosecutions and Appeals to go through and review it, just to see if this thing's going to be appealable on the search warrant."

Flothe couldn't believe it. It seemed like more stalling. Already they were approaching another weekend, and nothing had changed.

Hansen was still under twenty-four-hour surveillance, and still there was no search warrant. Wasn't it now inevitable that he would kill again? And if so, how long would it be? A day? An hour? So Flothe made sure that the Office of Special Prosecution and Appeals (known as OSPA) got a copy of the affidavit. He wondered how it would survive their microscope.

Monday morning Flothe was on the phone to OSPA. They promised him they'd take a look at it. He called again that afternoon. Same promise.

Tuesday morning it was the very same thing all again. With apologies. They were busy in court with other cases, they said. But there was more to it than that, they said. Quite a bit more. They also had a trial going on. Close to desperation, Flothe got Gail Voitlander and together they went to OSPA. Their intent was to grab someone and get them to take a quick look at their handiwork. How long could that take, a couple of minutes?

It was October 26th, a Wednesday, when Glenn Flothe and Gail Voitlander made their trek to OSPA. They corralled a staff member into taking a look at the affidavit. It got tedious. The attorney looked at a section, mentioned a court case that might have a bearing on the question, then moved to the next section and did the same thing. There were Supreme Court decisions they should take a look at, they were told, and other questions they should research.

Generally, though, the attorney said they had a warrant good enough to take to a judge. Finally.

That very day they took their warrant to Judge Victor Carlson. At their request they met in chambers. Flothe didn't want anyone learning about the search warrant early, and would ask that the search warrant be sealed by the judge.

Judge Carlson, one of Alaska's leading jurists, is a scholarly man who brings gravity, wit, and an incisive intelligence to the bench. He read the forty-eight-page affidavit quickly but with great deliberation. And then he was ready to make his pronouncement. "I don't have any problem granting you this warrant," he said soberly.

"He gets to work early, Your Honor," Flothe said. "And we will probably want to serve it early tomorrow morning."

"That's fine," the judge said.

Sergeant Flothe almost vaulted out of his chair. Both the judge and the assistant DA gave him a quizzical look, but he didn't care. Because if he was going to start the next morning, it would take some fast motoring.

15

Nearly two months had passed since Glenn Flothe was first assigned to the case of the missing dancers. During that time, each passing day had brought only greater surety that Hansen would act out his fantasies once again. Days and nights had blended endlessly into one another, as Flothe rarely seemed finished with his day's work and his wife and children had nearly become strangers. Times of frustration, when no one seemed to care, had steadily dwindled as he painstakingly assembled a portrait of the worst killer in the history of Alaska. Now he was ready to trap the master hunter.

Flothe, Jent, and Lieutenant Pat Kasnick devised a strategy to mobilize the Criminal Investigation Bureau, organizing every step in commando-like fashion. They would be everywhere: Hansen's house, Hansen's bakery, John Henning's house, waiting at trooper headquarters to interview Robert Hansen himself.

This would be the culmination of Flothe's efforts. Once troopers picked up Hansen at his bakery on that morning, Flothe intended that he would never again walk the streets as a free man.

Yet even as he awaited the interview with Robert Hansen, Flothe knew he was going into it with one hand tied behind his back. The DA had made it quite clear they couldn't talk about the Kitty Larson case without fear of jeopardizing everything, because during the initial investigation of the Larson case Hansen had hired an attorney. Any mention of Kitty Larson meant bringing in defense attorney Fred Dewey. Flothe wanted to talk to Hansen, not his lawyer.

Since the burglary and insurance fraud cases were separate—and new—charges, Hansen didn't have an attorney of record for them. He didn't have to get an attorney when he talked to them about these cases, as long as he waived his right to an attorney. Flothe knew Hansen had done so in past interviews with the police. Would he do it again?

The bakery on the southwest corner of Ninth and Ingra was one story high and built in brown concrete block, the type of building that went up quickly and sold just as fast.

As Sgt. Gerald Smith and Trooper Forrest Bullington pulled into the parking lot, they noticed this was a busy location. Ingra Street runs oneway northbound, one of the few main roads into Anchorage from the south. Because of this thousands of people drive up the street on their way to work. Hansen had picked the location for that very reason.

As the troopers watched customers file in and out of the bakery, they no doubt noticed something else. The bakery was near both Merrill Field and the strip where the hookers and topless clubs were concentrated. Hansen had built a little world where he could follow his deadly pursuits away from the glare of home life. It was an old saw, as far as cops were concerned. People commit crimes in their own area, within their own comfort zone. Hansen was no exception.

While Bullington and Smith waited in the parking lot for Hansen to finish work, Sgts. James Mc-Cann and Chris Stockard made their way to the southern edge of Anchorage to find John Henning. He was Hansen's most important alibi witness and his statement had closed the door on the Larson investigation. Flothe intended to bring Henning in for questioning. He remembered Major Gilmour's admonition that nobody confesses on the street. Now Flothe had to hope that the man would roll over when confronted with police suspicions.

As 8:30 approached, Bullington and Smith were ready to pick up their man. Smith looked at his watch and nodded his head. "Let's go," he said.

Outside the car they reflexively straightened their ties and hitched up their pants. Then they strode deliberately across the asphalt pavement and into the store. Inside they found a display case running almost the width of the store, a cramped waiting area with a coffee machine, a few tables, and some uncomfortable-looking metal chairs. This was not a bakery designed for lingering. They also noticed a pass-through, which allowed them to see the working part of the bakery: the long wooden tables for working the dough, the large, stainless-steel mixing bowls, the ceiling-high coolers, the giant, multilevel ovens, the bakers dressed in white.

"Can I help you?" the young clerk asked.

"Yes, ma'am," Smith said. "We'd like to talk to Mr. Hansen."

Dutifully, pleasantly, she went to fetch her boss. A short, wiry man returned.

"Y-y-yes?" Hansen stuttered.

"Sergeant Smith, Alaska State Troopers." Smith pulled out his badge and showed it to Hansen. "We'd like you to come down to trooper headquarters with us. There's a few questions we'd like to ask."

"Oh-oh-okay," Hansen replied. He took off his apron and quietly followed Smith and Bullington to their car.

Just down the street other troopers were closing on an important locus for evidence. Hansen's plane had to figure as the means of transport in the crimes. If so a search might yield hair and fiber samples that would match those of the victims. Flothe knew that the FBI agents he was working with had already busted Wayne Williams in Atlanta using similar kinds of evidence.

There was also the chance that jewelry might have fallen off during transport. Through inadvertence or lack of housekeeping, it might be within the confines of the aircraft. Hansen might even have hidden mementos from other kills in the plane. There he could view them in safety, away from prying eyes at home. Flothe was hoping they'd find two other important pieces of evidence as well. First, he was hoping to find any ammunition left in the plane. It would be of definite evidentiary value. They could compare and match it with the shell

casings recovered at the grave sites. There was
some likelihood they'd find some ammunition, too.
Pilots commonly used .223 caliber shells in their
survival weapons.

Just as important, Flothe wanted to seize any
flight plans and maps. These items could establish
whether the aircraft was airworthy on the dates
when known victims had disappeared. They might
also establish the location of the cabin that Hansen
had so often mentioned to his victims. In truth,
however, anything they could find would be a score.

In Muldoon, meanwhile, troopers were at the
door of Hansen's house on Old Harbor Road.
"Darla Hansen?" Sgt. Haugsven asked. There was
no way Darla could know that in fact these people
felt great sympathy for her. They would later describe their task as one of the hardest things they'd
ever had to do.

"Yes," she said meekly.

"We have a warrant to search your house, Mrs.
Hansen," Haugsven announced, handing her a
weighty document. Darla was nonplussed. Though
she looked at the document, it didn't seem like she
understood its meaning.

"Sure," she replied, moving aside to let them
come inside.

"We are going to have to ask that you get everyone out of the house, Mrs. Hansen," Haugsven
continued, seeing that she wasn't alone. "And once
that's done, we want you to come down to trooper
headquarters to talk to us."

When Hansen got to the interview room he found
it was already set up in the most elaborate fashion.

Flothe led him into the room and sat him at a desk alone for a while. He wanted him to absorb everything.

On the desk were piles and piles of file folders, some with the names of hunting and fishing associates on them, another open to the page where his wife's picture was pasted, with the legend DARLA HANSEN written across the top. Next to them were photographs of some of the victims, arranged so that they faced him when he sat down.

Tacked on the wall was a gigantic map of the Knik River area. On it had been drawn a big red circle, with two X-marks penciled inside it. Sergeant Darrell Galyan had written in big red letters on the perimeter of the circle: HANSEN IDENTIFIED IN THIS AREA.

By the time the interview began some fifteen minutes later at 9:01 A.M., they figured Hansen had had enough time to take in the scenery.

Sergeant Galyan, an affable but persistent cop, started the questioning. Flothe operated the tape recorder and kept tabs on what was happening with the various searches.

Galyan began with seemingly innocuous topics, like Hansen's bakery, the baking business, the fact that Hansen owned a plane and was a hunter. The whole approach seemed, on the whole, biographical. Then, a little more than five minutes into the interview, Galyan started to draw the loop of questions a bit tighter.

"Bob, back in high school, you went into the military and you got back out of the military, ah, you got yourself into a little problem back there,"

Galyan said, his voice and demeanor even and calm.

"Um-hum," Hansen said, noncommittal, looking away.

"Okay. There was a little minor arson, is that correct?"

"Uh-huh," Hansen said, his voice dropping to near a whisper.

"And at that time you were married to Phebe Padgett?"

"Uh-huh."

"That was her maiden name. And apparently while you were incarcerated, at this time your marriage broke up, am I correct?"

"That's right," Hansen said. Hansen sure didn't seem to be a man of many words. Flothe had heard from his sources that Hansen could be quite a talker, but he was beginning to wonder if the man ever said more than two words at a time.

"Okay. Could you expound on that for me?" Galyan asked. "Was it [because of] the fact that you got yourself in trouble that Phebe left you?"

"Yes," came the monosyllabic reply.

"Okay. Some people can handle it real well, some other people can't," Galyan continued, just trying to keep some sense of conversation going.

"Um-hum" was all Hansen said in response. Would he ever open up? Galyan kept at him, gentle but prodding.

"And yet there could have been underlying problems there that, ah, had nothing to do with it," Galyan gamely ventured. "Would you talk to me about it, that incident that happened? Because I'm not real clear on it. How did you wind up getting in trouble over an arson?''

Hansen cleared his throat and sat forward in his chair. The harsh lights cast his acne-scarred face in stark relief. He seemed determined to leave a good impression. Then he spoke, in a tired but apologetic voice. ''Okay,'' he said. ''Ah, it um—something I guess, it just got more or less out of hand.''

''What exactly was it that you had done?''

''All right,'' Hansen said, a bit of irritation showing through. ''There was an old bus barn out behind the school there in town. And the fellow that worked with me there in the bakery—we more or less talked about, ah, we'd like to raise some excitement around town there. Ah, more or less a dare.''

Hansen was shaking his head, a smile on his face. He was laughing at the memory, or pretending to. ''I'm sorry,'' he said. ''I'm laughing, but it's not funny. . . . ''

''Well, apparently you went out and did it,'' Galyan pointed out.

''Ah, yeah. Well, I don't think either one of us had the thought in mind of actually doing it. But then we got there and this little barn was there and we thought, well, it would be some excitement. We would, ah, light a fire to it. And, ah—''

''You say 'we.' Was your friend with you at the time?''

''Yes. Uh-huh.''

''So you guys, ah, you set fire to this old bus barn?'' Galyan asked.

"Right."

"And what happened after that?" Galyan wanted to know.

"Well, in relation to the barn—" Hansen began.

"Right," Galyan interjected.

"—the damn thing burned down."

This admission gained, Galyan plowed right on. Everything about his manner continued to be well modulated. He was the "good cop" in this routine.

"Okay," he said. "And my understanding is that, ah, one of your co-workers or friends there said that you did it. And so you wound up—"

"Yeah."

"—going to trial over it and wound up being incarcerated for a period of time."

"That's right."

"And then you were released. What did you do with your life after that?"

Flothe and Galyan were about to learn an important lesson: Once Hansen felt like talking, he could continue incessantly. His thoughts roamed over topics and he remembered every rock, every tree. And for the next twenty minutes or so, he did.

He told the officers how he got out of jail and went to his parents' resort in Minnesota. How he met Darla, fell in love, and married, almost impulsively. How he and his wife traveled like gypsies across the Midwest, driving from bakery job to bakery job, and back—Cox Bakeries, with thirty-two stores in the heartland, had hired him to relieve their managers. How he was on the road while Darla worked as a bookkeeper/receptionist at a hospital in Minot, North Dakota. How he took a job with Myers Bakery in Minneapolis, so that Darla could finish the last two years of college. How Darla finished school and they decided to move to Alaska.

When they reached the point where Flothe had to turn over the tape, Galyan managed to get him to talk about his time in the Anamosa State Reformatory in Iowa. He also talked about his speech disorder. One of the counselors at the prison, Hansen explained, managed to get him speech therapy at the University of Iowa. There he had spent hours and hours sitting in a closet, looking in a mirror to watch himself stutter.

By the time he left, he said, his speech was quite a bit better. He had learned to live with his stuttering, he said, by learning to relax. He said he used to be a very nervous person but had mellowed out with age. To Flothe and Galyan, he still looked very nervous. This time he had a reason to be.

16

The question of how the search of the bakery should proceed was soon answered. The troopers returned and told the employees to clear out so that a search of the premises could begin. Smith got the key from one of the employees. That way they could lock up when they left and take the key to Darla.

As the search warrant noted, the troopers were looking for several things of evidentiary value. Bullington and Smith would go through every square inch of the bakery.

Special Agent John Douglas of the FBI had told Flothe to be on the lookout for mementos, which he believed were still being retained by Hansen. The bakery seemed a logical place to hide them. He spent many hours there, it was in close proximity to the area where the missing individuals were last seen, and items stored there were less likely to be inadvertently found by his family.

They also wanted to seize business and insurance records that might be kept at the business. Each time he had met a dancer, he had paid cash. Maybe he cashed a bakery check on or about the days when the victims turned up missing. The same bank statements might account for the presence or absence of Darla on those same dates. Or they might show any contacts Hansen had had with John Henning, as well as the nature of their relationship and the bias or interest involved in the provision of the alibi.

The insurance records, meanwhile, might corroborate the statement of the black dancer. If Hansen had smashed the driver's window of his truck with his fist during that incident, he would have had to fix it. Flothe expected Hansen had filed a claim with his insurance company, asserting that a prowler had broken into his truck or, better yet, that he had accidentally broken the window himself. By claiming that it was an accident he avoided the necessity of calling the police, whom he no doubt wanted to avoid after what had happened.

Smith and Bullington did seize business and banking records at the bakery. They spent hours and hours, though, going through the rest of the shop, looking for anything that might link him to the murders. They had no luck. The place was clean.

At the Hansen home, meanwhile, it had taken longer than expected to get everyone out of the house. Darla had been teaching and her students had to be sent home. And Bob's mother was visiting, so Darla had to find a place for her to stay. It was nearly an hour after the troopers had arrived before Darla was backing the family Subaru out of the driveway, her shocked mother-in-law at her side.

Because Darla's reaction was one of benign bewilderment, Haugsven sensed she could be trusted to cooperate. There was a pain visible in this woman, but a pain that bore no malice. Darla promised she would drive to trooper headquarters for an interview after she transported Bob's mom to a friend's house. Haugsven believed her. The way was cleared for a thorough search of Bob Hansen's family residence.

Troopers had reasoned from the very beginning that the search of the Hansen home might be the most strenuous and time-consuming. There was no guarantee he kept mementos there, but even if he didn't there were plenty of other things to look for. Things like rifles. Handguns. Handcuffs. Chains. Surgical gloves. Ace bandages. A bear-skin rug. Moose antlers on the roof (already confirmed). Fiber samples. Hair samples. Towels or other items the victim might have used. Newspaper clippings. Bank statements. Fingerprints. Expended cartridges. .223 ammunition (same as the murder weapon). Soil samples on any shovel they might find at the residence. Makeup and disguises. The portable airplane seat Kitty Larson had described. Notes or business cards that might chronicle his assignations. And what the search warrant described as a "rape/murder kit," consisting of restraints, a blindfold, and other items used to immobilize the victims.

Even while the troopers waited outside the residence for the search to begin, they knew they faced a daunting task. Though not a mansion, the Hansen residence was by no means small. Snuggled into a birch and aspen forest, it took up more than thir-

teen hundred square feet per floor, and that didn't
include the large two-car garage that was attached
to the house. The ranch-style house was on a big
lot, too—almost an acre—and there was a possibility Hansen had buried stuff in the backyard.

Inside the residence, the troopers found a house
crammed with the accumulations of a lifetime. The
garage, like so many garages in America, had rarely
or never been used to store vehicles. Instead it was
packed top to bottom with "stuff." There were
skis, boots, poles, a ton of toys and games. There
was a go-cart and a three-wheeler ATV, its seat
cover missing, showing a bare patch of discolored
foam. And there were all sorts of equipment for
reloading ammunition, including a press and work
bench filled with materials. Here they might find
some .223 ammo.

The inside of the house was extremely neat and
showed Darla's love of the homey artifact. The
living room was typical of her style. There was
blue-and-tan thistle-patterned wallpaper on the wall
facing the double picture window, and a clock made
of a polished tree trunk hung at its center. To either
side of the red brick fireplace were bookshelves with
her collectibles—a statue of an Eskimo in traditional
costume, a carved sailing ship, some figurines, a
decorative cup, and some blown glass.

Above the mantle was an oil painting of a ste-
reotypical Alaskan scene, framed on either side by
some Eskimo masks. In the adjoining hall there
were pictures of the children, Darla's family, and
of Christ. There was no mistaking that this was a
religious household.

Robert Hansen in police custody after his arrest for the assault of a real-estate secretary in December 1971. *(Anchorage Times)*

Phebe Padgett,
Robert Hansen's first wife.
(Courtesy of
Ralph Hudek)

Robert Hansen's high
school yearbook
photograph, 1957.
(Courtesy of Ralph Hudek)

Darla Henrichsen,
Hansen's second wife.
(Courtesy of
Ralph Hudek)

Robert Hansen, the hunter, in December 1969. *(Anchorage Times)*

Robert Hansen's home on Old Harbor Road. (Leland E. Hale)

Hansen's trophy room in the basement of his house. (Alaska State Troopers)

The hidden cache of guns which tied Hansen to the murders. (Alaska State Troopers)

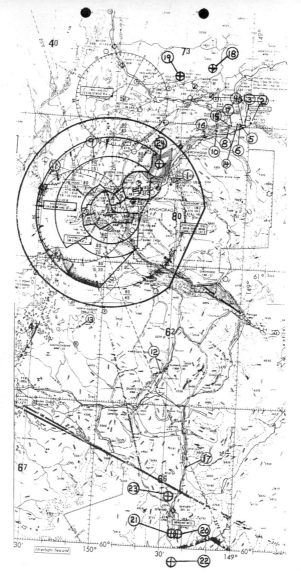

Sergeant Glenn Flothe's version of Robert Hansen's flight maps. Numbers 1-17 indicate locations that Hansen had marked on his map and where he admitted he had buried a body. Numbers 18-23 show additional sites that Hansen had marked on his map; he denied to officials that they indicated the presence of a body, however.

Hansen's plane, which he used to fly his victims to the isolated Knik River region. *(Anchorage Times)*

Alaskan troopers excavating for bodies and evidence at one of the grave-sites. *(Anchorage Times)*

(2) Sue Luna,
Old Knik bridge
parking lot, 5-30-82

Numbers, where listed, correspond with the body sites marked on Hansen's flight map. Also indicated are the burial locations, as well as the date the victim was last seen. (Courtesy of Alaska Public Safety Commission)

(4) Malai Larsen,
Old Knik bridge
parking lot, 6-?-81

(5) Lisa Futrell, Old Knik
bridge gravel pit, 9-7-80

(6) Tamara Pederson,
Knik River, 8-?-82

(9) DeLynn Frey,
Summit Lake, 9-10-83

(11) Angela Feddern,
Figure Eight Lake, 2-?-82

(13) Teresa Watson,
Scenic Lake, 4-29-83

(14) Sherry Morrow,
Knik River, 11-17-81

(15) Paula Goulding,
Knik River, 4-25-83

(16) "Eklutna Annie,"
Eklutna Lake Road,
mid- to late 1979

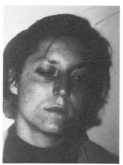

(17) Joanna Messina,
gravel pit near Seward,
5-19-80

(20) Megan Emerick,
Seward Bay, 7-7-83
(Denied by Hansen)

(21) Mary Thill,
Seward Bay, 7-5-73
(Denied by Hansen)

Roxanne Eastland,
unknown if body
recovered, 6-29-80

Celia "Beth" Van Zanten,
McHugh Creek, 12-22-71
(No proven connection
to Hansen)

Andrea Altiery,
unknown if body
recovered, 12-2-81

Sergeant Glenn Flothe, the Alaskan State Trooper who led the Hansen investigation. *(Anchorage Times)*

Frank Rothschild, the district attorney who argued for the maximum penalty after Robert Hansen had admitted his guilt. *(Anchorage Times)*

What the troopers soon noticed about the house, however, was the incredible amount of storage space. No wonder the place looked neat as a pin. There were closets everywhere. Above the bar was a long glass cupboard that held glasses and dishes. The kitchen was surrounded by blond cabinets, both overhead and at counter level. Just going through all this storage would keep the troopers busy. And they hadn't even started in the basement.

The basement figured to keep them the busiest. After all, it was reputedly Hansen's private torture chamber. There they might find Kitty Larson's fingerprints, or hair and fiber samples, or any number of items Hansen had used in raping and murdering the young women of Anchorage.

At first glance, however, it hardly looked like a torture chamber. The white linoleum, streaked with black, was utilitarian. The wood paneling was typical of many a finished basement. An old red couch was hunkered up against one wall, more accustomed to holding toys and pool cues than people.

Still, it was clear that the basement was more Bob's province than Darla's. Sure there was an Apple computer positioned along one wall, which Darla used for teaching. And at the other end of the room were a desk, five chairs, and a shelf of schoolbooks. But almost everything else was from Bob's world.

In the center of the large basement was a foosball game and a pool table. Along the walls were Bob's hunting trophies, the mounted heads of his world records, some of them reported stolen—but obviously not stolen. Along the south wall, moreover, was a large wooden storage closet. The locked doors held the promise of something important inside. When troopers opened it, they came across a cache of enough rifles and handguns to start a small armory. Altogether, the troopers expected to have a field day.

Meanwhile, as Hansen's interview eased into its second half hour, he was discussing his early years in Anchorage. He talked about his job at the Safeway on Ninth and Gambel and his wife's teaching job up on Government Hill. They had bought a duplex in Mountain View and sold it to buy a house almost three blocks due north.

"Everything went along pretty good there for a while," Galyan noted, "and then you got yourself in trouble there again."

"Um-hum."

"What happened then? You were involved in the theft of a chain saw?"

"Um-hum."

"Okay," Galyan said. "And ah . . ."

"Back in 1971," Flothe interjected, "there was an incident involving a young receptionist over there in Spenard. You were on your way, supposedly, to the base, or out to the airport to go bowhunting."

"Uh-huh."

"And apparently for some reason you got diverted over to this young lady's driveway," Flothe continued.

"That's true."

"What happened, Bob?" Galyan asked.

"Well, ah . . ." There was a long pause while

Hansen gathered his thoughts. He seemed to be thinking: Where are these questions leading?

"Everything seemed to be going fine for you," Galyan said. "You moved to a new state, you got a job, money, a new wife, everything was just going along great. And then you got involved with this young woman. What happened?"

"Well, I guess, more or less ah, um . . ." Hansen muttered. "I don't know what to say. I guess it may have been just an urge. I don't know if you want to call it that or not. Ah, it happened. I'm sorry it happened but it did happen, I can't, you know, dispute that."

This was not a cooperative Bob Hansen the troopers were hearing. He was acting like he wanted to cooperate, Flothe realized, but really he was being evasive and noncommittal. They had to press him harder, Flothe figured. And keep the pressure on.

"Does this incident have anything to do with what Dr. McManmon discussed in court at your sentencing?" Flothe asked.

"I don't know. I can't remember what—"

"Manic-depressive problems, a mental state that you would probably go into, and apparently it's an ongoing problem, according to the doctor," Flothe said, gesturing quietly with his hands. Hansen let out a deep sigh.

"Was the doctor totally out of line on that?" Flothe asked.

"Well . . ." Hansen paused again. "Yeah." He looked earnest.

Galyan decided it was time to move on to something else. "And after that particular incident," Galyan noted, "then you got yourself in trouble with a chain saw, am I correct?"

"Um-hum," Hansen mumbled.

"If I ask you an honest question, will you give me an honest answer?" Galyan asked.

"Sure try."

"Why didn't you just go buy one?"

"There ain't—ain't nobody in the world that's asked . . . asked that question more . . . more . . ."

"Than yourself?" Galyan filled in.

"Well, no, I—no one has kicked myself more for not doing it that way. Ah, I guess I, ah . . ."

Galyan now noticed something: Hansen kept looking over at the tape recorder as they talked. He had already noticed how nervous he seemed. That was to be expected. But Hansen couldn't keep his eyes off the tape recorder.

"Is that bothering you, Bob?" Galyan asked.

"I got a little bell in the back of my mind that's going off here," he said. The bell told him that he had a dilemma: By talking to them, he hoped to clear things up; but by talking to them he might also be giving them something they could use against him. Besides, he told them, he'd been warned by attorneys that he should "never under no circumstances ever talk to any police official without an attorney present."

"Well if you remember, now, that's up to you," Galyan said.

"Hum, I—I realize that. I know. I know," Hansen responded intensely.

"We don't lie to you, and at any time you can—"

"I know. I know," Hansen said again, almost impatient.

"—have one."

The look on Hansen's face said he had reached a decision, at least for the moment. Suddenly he circled back to the subject they'd just been discussing, a return so swift as to be nearly disorienting. But if Galyan and Flothe had learned one thing so far, it was that they should let the man keep talking.

"Yeah, okay," Hansen said, as though to dismiss Galyan. "Getting back to your question here— you asked if the doctors were way off-base? Ah, they were not off-base with what I told them, but what I told them at the time may not have been one hundred percent, you know, true."

"And you're actually going to hurt yourself by not being—" Galyan started to say.

Hansen cut him off. "I realize that, yes. Now. But at the time I didn't realize that, and once you start something like that you more or less feel that you've got to go through with it."

It was a stunning revelation: Hansen had lied to his psychiatrists. Why? To reduce his responsibility for the acts he'd committed? Or just to pull the wool over their eyes, to see if he could get away with it? Was all this just a game to him? Quick on the uptake, Galyan asked Bob if he'd taken some corrective measures once he realized he'd made a mistake.

"No," Bob said. "By the time I realized this—

here, you know, it was more or less all done with and, ah, like the old saying, you know, 'Let sleeping dogs lay.' "

Galyan kept after Bob about his psychiatric history but it was little use. He'd submerged all the memories that troubled him and replaced them with a standardized response. He insisted that he'd gone along with the program. Told them he'd taken his medication until everything stopped during his incarceration. Told them that if he'd just bought the chain saw in the first place, he'd never have had these problems.

They didn't get much further than that, so Galyan moved on to the topic of Robyn Patterson. It was a way to introduce Bob's continuing history of problems with the women of Anchorage. Hansen seemed to shrug it off.

"She was a prostitute," he said of Patterson, as though this designation in and of itself was enough to dispose of the matter. When he had finished explaining himself, he reduced the matter of her kidnapping and sexual assault to nothing more than a dispute over money. It was an old saw.

"She quoted me one price," he said of the incident, "and then she wanted an awful lot more money. And I told her, 'Hey, we agreed on one price, and that's what it's going to be.' And she argued about that and so forth and I said 'bullshit,' you know. 'We are going back to Anchorage, and I'm going to pay you the price.' And I give her the money and I let her out, and I guess her dad is a state trooper or something like this.

Anyway, she ran to her daddy or something or other. . . . ''

"Obviously, she told a whole different story," Galyan said.

"Huh?" Hansen asked.

"Obviously she tells a whole different story," Galyan repeated.

"Prob-probably does," Hansen admitted. "But that's the way it was."

Hansen denied everything that even remotely implicated him in the Robyn Patterson attack. He even denied destroying the incriminating piece of paper he had managed to steal back from the jail guards, the one with Robyn's name on it in his handwriting.

The denials had only just begun. Galyan brought up the 1975 incident when he had allegedly bound, kidnapped, and raped a woman from the Kit Kat Club. Hansen said he hadn't forced her to do anything. "And again," he said, "it was strictly for money."

Then Galyan brought up the 1979 assault and attempted kidnapping of the black topless dancer in Anchorage. That, too, Hansen said, was a dispute over money.

Exasperated, Galyan asked, "Haven't you learned by now, Bob, that hookers and street girls and whatever are not going to play it cool with you?"

"You're kidding," Hansen replied.

"You know, they've got a commodity that you want, that you can't get," Galyan said. "Only they have it and only they can give it to you, and they are going to get as much for it as they can and their word is no good. And why, with a nice wife at home, would you be down there on the streets digging around with these girls anyway? Is there a problem there?''

"Uh-uh. No. There's no problem at all whatsoever at home, although I mentioned to you, both the times there I wanted oral sex, okay?''

"You seem to be a little uncomfortable talking about—'' Galyan started to say.

"All right.''

"—oral sex.''

"Uh, well, it's just something that—I guess maybe it's an old-fashioned idea or whatever, but it's something that I would never, under no circumstances, ever want my wife to perform, okay?''

"Uh-huh,'' Galyan acknowledged.

"And, uh, this is what I wanted there. And you know, you hear so many guys talking about, 'Oh boy, this gal here or that gal there will give you a good blow job,' or whatever, and I guess it was just more or less out of curiosity. I would not want anything like that from my wife. I would want just more or less what you would call straight sex with my wife.''

Bob Hansen was persisting in his old theme: How can you take the word of a prostitute against that of a respectable businessman and family man? Every run-in with prostitutes had been a dispute over money. It was always a case of Bob defending himself against the mercenary women of the streets.

More disturbing, Flothe noticed, was that he had a very deeply etched moral standard that divided women into saints or whores. And when he was with women he didn't put in the saint category, things had a way of going awry.

"You've had a lot of incidents that have gone sour," Galyan pointed out. "Let me ask you a question to see if I'm too far out of the ball park. You tell me—and let's face it, you know, all three of us are men in this room, so—don't you think that sometimes we do things that we really can't stop ourselves from doing?"

"Oh, I don't agree with that."

"You think you could've prevented your—"

"Well, anyone that has a conscience, that's done something wrong, your conscience will tell you what's wrong."

"But we go ahead and do things that we know are against our moral teachings. Even though we know that it's wrong, we go ahead and do it anyway." Hansen was shaking his head in disagreement.

"You don't agree with that?" Galyan asked. "You think you have total control over all your actions all the time?"

"Yeah."

"Whether to do something, even though you know it's wrong or not?"

"Yeah. Everybody, whether they want to admit it, knows entirely what's right and wrong."

17

Neither Haugsven nor Von Clasen nor Maxine Farrell much relished the interview with Darla. Even in their brief meeting with her earlier that morning, they sensed that she had already suffered because of Bob Hansen. And though she was a tall, big-boned woman, what emerged in the interview was a soft-spoken woman who was gentle and somewhat shy. She was a willing talker, with nothing to reveal.

There was a certain ineffable quality about her, as though she had always been more serious than everyone else. There was also the sense that something had finally, after all these years, been drained out of her. She looked weary, harried.

When the interview was finished Haugsven, Von Clasen, and Farrell were collectively convinced that Darla Hansen knew nothing of her husband's crimes. How eerie that seemed: To live with a man, to share his bed, to bear him children and cook his meals, to love him no matter what he did, and not know that for twelve years he had been a cold-blooded killer.

They did not tell her that her husband was suspected of murder, since they were not at liberty to talk. They wondered: How will she handle the news when she finally learns the purpose of all this activity? How would anyone handle it? How many have to face the prospect of learning, after twenty years of marriage, that their life-mate has committed unspeakable crimes?

The troopers had been talking to Bob Hansen for an hour and a half, but they still were not near to getting him to confess to the murders. They talked instead of Hansen's psychiatric record.

Their suspect was clearly angry that they had copies of his records, especially after Galyan started asking questions about his compulsive stealing. His impression, he told Galyan, had been that what passed between him and his psychiatrist would remain confidential.

"I didn't know that these records could be gotten," he said, nearly spitting the words.

"Let me explain something to you first," Galyan offered. "These are only court testimonies that we have. We do not have—"

"These are before the judge," Flothe added.

"Um, okay," Hansen said, as he now overflowed with anger. "Look this up in your damn records then. I stated to him," he said, looking at Galyan, "and I'm gonna state to you now, when I was a young boy I worked at my dad's shop. I would get maybe thirty-five to forty-five cents. When I got to be a junior or senior, I wouldn't even get a dollar. Nothing was never really denied me that I needed, clothing or whatever, but as far as spending money I guess it more or less grew up with me that you don't spend money, and to this day I hate to spend money.

"Now I've read the stuff about this-here, too," Hansen continued, "and Dr. McManmon explained to me the same thing that you said just a while ago. I can't remember which one of you said it, but that people would go into the store—it was you," he said, looking at Galyan again, "that said something about a girl would go into the store, and have thirty dollars in her pocket, and steal a tube of lipstick, okay? I've done the same damn thing. Go in the store with money in my pocket and not want to spend the money, that I would take something.

"And yes, it was something that I didn't need really, and I'd think, Bob, you had money for this-here and you should not have stolen it. And I took the damn thing back in and put it back on the shelf, all right? And it made me feel good when I had done it."

"Okay," Galyan acknowledged.

"All right," Hansen responded.

"I can relate to that," Galyan said, almost perfunctorily. "Okay, you don't have to tell me if you don't want to, Bob, but have you completely quit taking things from the store, or in the past year or so have you, ah, taken anything?"

"When I was incarcerated, I had enough time to sit and think. The reason I'm working is to make money so I can go ahead and buy these things that I need, like my family needs, without having—I can walk out of the store feeling good that I'm not taking something, okay? And it's a good feeling for me, and that's the way it is. . . .

"And it makes me feel good to walk out of the store knowing that, hey, there ain't going to be somebody coming up behind me, grabbing my arm, and saying, 'Hey, where's the receipt for this-here?' Now I can walk around the store. As a matter of fact, you know, it makes me feel good to go in and buy something, and that's just totally different than—"

"Than before, when you would take something?" Galyan helped out.

"Right."

"But this has not been an overnight-type thing. It's been a long time coming to reach this point, hasn't it?" Galyan said.

"Yes."

"And how did you accomplish that, or reach the point where you no longer felt compelled to take something? Was that through the assistance of the psychiatrist?"

"No," Hansen replied firmly. "I just went through a system that I just got damned scared of doing it. I just kept tellin' myself, 'Bob, you've got to have priorities in your life.' I've put not only myself in trouble but I've done it to my family, too, and my wife. I've put her through an awful lot of grief, and I don't want to do that anymore, okay? My children went through an awful lot of grief, and I don't want them to go through that, okay?

"I hated, hated like hell," he continued, "when my wife—like I did not want her to bring my children out to Eagle River to see me when they brought me back from Juneau. But she was sayin', 'Bob, the children are asking all the time, "Where's Daddy, where's Daddy? Has he left us, don't he want us around anymore?"'

"And now I thought about that for hours and hours and days, and I finally come to the conclusion—of course, there was some kids that had come up to my children and said, 'Hey boy, your daddy's a jailbird,' and they had been makin' fun of 'em, and the kids came home cryin'—and so I said, 'Darla, bring 'em out and let's get this out in the open and let's deal with it.'"

"Did your family handle it very well?" Galyan asked.

"Well, yeah," Hansen responded. "yet my son doesn't, even today. Maybe it's just myself overreacting, but if we take a drive by Eagle River, at the turnoff going into the Eagle River jail, he'll look at that, and he'll look down. Or if we go duck hunting or something like that up there in the flats, and I fly him out there, why, a time or two I made the mistake of flying across Eagle River jail there with him in the airplane. And I looked around and there was almost tears comin' out of his eyes, and he said, 'Daddy,' he said, 'please don't go back there again.'

"You know, now when I take him, I make damn sure not to bring those memories back to him, okay? You might say I'm runnin' away from it, I'm not. If you want to call it that, okay, but it's part of my life that I'm very ashamed of. If I could turn the switch someplace and redo it, you damn well better believe it would never happen again. I can't undo the past. All I can do is—when I got out of this damn jail, I told myself, hey, you know, I promised myself or to my family to not put them through that again.''

With Hansen's speechifying temporarily at an end, Galyan decided to get back to business.

"There are so many separate and yet similar incidents that have happened,'' Galyan pointed out. "And each one of these girls has related a similar story. And each time you have been positively identified, so there's no doubt that you were involved there. And by your admissions you took some of these girls out or picked 'em up, or you gave them money for sex or whatever.'' Galyan looked at Hansen like he expected him to say something intelligent.

"Um-hum. I did. Now, I'm not denying that.''

"But yet starting from plumb back till 1971 right up until almost current, there have been different girls that have come to the police, who have said, 'Look, a person later identified as Bob Hansen did this to me. He bound me, he threatened me with a gun, threatened to kill anybody else, he did in fact rape me.' Some of them have admitted that they are prostitutes, that they charged you money, that you didn't take the money back away from them, but you did bind them, you did threaten them, and you did force your will upon them.

"I think the bottom line here, Bob, is that how can all these different girls—that have never met or even seen each other—in over a period of what we talked about—twelve or thirteen years—all repeat the same story to us, and there not be some validity somewhere? Do you understood where I'm coming from?''

"Yes, I do." Hansen suddenly looked contrite again, though he was by no means confessing to anything.

"Okay. When I take a half-dozen to twelve reports up there, over a twelve-year span, and each one of these people tell me the same thing happened to them, I've got to start believing that there's a pattern there, and that somewhere along the line, Bob, you haven't told me the whole truth. Okay? There's only two reasons why people don't tell me the truth. They're either fearful or they're embarrassed.''

"Well, I am embarrassed about this, yes. . . . ''

"But we're all grown men here, you know. We've been around the world a little bit, there should be nothing to be embarrassed about. Society accepts all forms of sexual activity. Prostitution, everybody knows it exists. It's been around for a long time, and we should be able to sit here and discuss these things. You know we shouldn't be too embarrassed, because we are all adults.

"But I'm talking about numerous—case after case after case, over a period of twelve years—and these girls are all telling me the same thing happened. Now you're telling me every one of these girls has lied just to get you in trouble, and they all, in their own minds, made up the same story? Bob, you're lying to me. Now tell me the truth here. I think there's a problem.''

At this point Hansen wanted to make sure the police didn't mean to prosecute him on these old cases. When Galyan said no, he asked, "So, ah, where is all this coming from?"

"Okay. One, as I told you, I'd like to understand you, I'd like to know who I'm talking to. Number two, the whole point is to show you that a pattern has been established here, that a sequence of events over a long period of time has occurred, and they are similar. Glenn, do you have something?"

Flothe was almost chomping on the bit. He was getting tired of Hansen's evasions. He now produced a photograph of Paula Goulding. He considered it part of his FBI bag of tricks.

"There's something going terribly wrong with this young lady here," Flothe began. "A .223 shell casing was found at her grave site, fired from your weapon. Something went terribly wrong. You asked why we're asking why, what went wrong? You didn't intend to hurt the receptionist; you didn't intend to hurt the black dancer. I don't believe you intended to hurt her," he said, pointing to Goulding's photo with his eyes. "She was shot and killed."

"Well, not by me," Hansen responded with snap-turtle precision.

"Well, how do you explain the shell casing from your weapon at the grave site? We have a team of investigators at your residence right now with a search warrant, and we're just determined to ask— why? We are asking why something went terribly wrong."

"You guys are telling me that I shot this person?" Hansen asked, incredulous.

"That's correct," Flothe replied.

"Well, you're wrong. I didn't shoot anybody. I would not hurt anybody. That's true."

"Well, how do you explain the circumstances, then? It's my understanding that you've been hunting out in that area before—Eklutna River. . . . " Flothe noted.

"Oh, yeah. I've been going over to Eklutna River for years."

"Well then," Flothe wanted to know, "how was it that we find a shell casing out in the Eklutna area from one of your weapons? Do you know what the FBI laboratory does? I'm sure that it's been explained to you how they make comparisons, how they make matches, for every shell casing from the Knik River. And the one from the grave site is from your weapon. From my understanding, we know for a fact that you've been out there hunting before. Now is there a correlation between a shell casing being there and you hunting, or . . . ?"

"Well, I didn't do that, ah . . ."

"Then explain to me how your shell casing got out there," Flothe demanded.

"I probably have shell casings all—halfway across Alaska."

"Explain a .223-caliber shell casing."

"I have a .223."

"Where's that one?" Flothe wanted to know.

"Home someplace."

18

The search of Hansen's house was not going as planned. The troopers were methodical in their approach, all right, but they hadn't found anything that would convict a man of murder. Behind the headboard of the water bed he shared with his wife they found an aviation map. Nothing too startling about that—the man was a pilot.

Elsewhere in the house they found what appeared to be a disguise kit, complete with phony mustache, skin adhesive, and a bottle of fingernail polish. They also found some Ace bandages, like the one found on Sherry Morrow's body up on the Knik. Most revealing, behind some dirty clothes in a cabinet they found a sack full of cash, complete with bakery receipts. As the search continued they found other sacks, also filled with cash. Hansen was an embezzler. It was hard to say who would be more excited—Flothe or the IRS.

Although all this plainly could help build a case against Hansen, it still wasn't much. No one from the DA's office would take it as evidence of murder, nor should they. What they hadn't found was more important.

They hadn't found any of the mementos, for instance—not the gold arrowhead necklace that had belonged to Sherry Morrow, not the gold nugget jewelry they'd also expected to find. Nor had they found any stash of women's clothing or newspaper articles about the crimes. Worse yet, there was no sign of the murder weapon, although they found a treasure trove of weapons, many of which they suspected were stolen.

In the living room closet they found a Ted Williams twenty-gauge shotgun. In the garage they found a .270 bolt-action rifle, a Browning .22 rifle, a Browning .22 semiautomatic rifle, a Colt Match .22 semiautomatic pistol, and a Colt Python .357 revolver. In the hidden cabinet in the family room they found, among other items, a Ruger .243 pistol and a Savage rifle. There was also an old .35 Remington with slide-pump action, a Remington automatic shotgun, a Remington Wing Master shotgun, a twelve-gauge shotgun, and an Ithaca twenty-gauge shotgun.

None of these weapons came even close to matching the .223 shell casing they'd found in the Knik River graves. They had expected to find a semiautomatic rifle of that caliber—where was it? They hadn't even found the Thompson Contender pistol that Officer Baker of APD had seen during the initial investigation of the Larson case.

Flothe was bluffing when he told Hansen the FBI had matched the Knik River shells to his weapon. Had Hansen seen through it? He sure hadn't broken down, if that's what they had wanted him to do.

As the morning stretched on to noon, the troopers at Hansen's home became more and more worried. Was it possible he had destroyed important evidence? Had he spotted the surveillance and ditched everything they'd hoped to find? The importance of finding the murder weapon, for example, could not be overestimated. If they could find it, and if a shell fired from it matched the shell casings at the Knik, then the troopers were a long way toward proving Hansen was the responsible party.

Two hours passed, but they seemed longer. Galyan and Flothe were by now bearing in on an area of considerable concern: establishing the fact that Hansen had been on the stretch of the Knik where the bodies were found. Hansen freely admitted that he'd been there.

"I don't deny I've been up and down the Knik River from one end to the other many, many times," Hansen admitted. "I've set traps up and down that river, my gosh, for years and years and years. I've gone out there rabbit-hunting with many, many people. I've shot bow out there many times. I've set bear stands out there. I've target-practiced up and down the river. They've got some beautiful sandbars out there. It's the most beautiful place in the world to practice your takeoffs, landings, short field work. . . ."

"What weapons have you fired out there, Bob?" Flothe asked.

".243, .270, .223, .338, .22, shotguns—you can just about name it and I've shot it out there."

Under questioning Hansen said he had been up on the Knik that fall, duck-hunting with his son.

He also said he'd been there during the summer. Where had he fired his .223 during that time? Flothe asked. On a map Hansen pointed to a big, flat territory to the west of the old Knik River bridge.

"There's some islands here," he said, pointing to the same spot. "Green islands in through here. I've gone on the banks there and shot into those banks along here many, many times. At some spots up there I've gone and put stuff in the river, you know, and flown over and tried to shoot at them to practice for wolf hunting. . . ."

"Oh, you've shot from the air?" Flothe asked, only half believing.

"Yeah."

"You've shot from the air," Flothe said again, sardonically. "I didn't realize you've done that. I have a more specific map of this area here. Hold it down. This is an aerial photograph. There's a bunch of little numbers on here and I can—I can explain some things to you afterwards, but let's do this in relation to the map you have in your hand now. Can you help me out?"

"By number three here?" Hansen said, pointing to the aerial map. "I've shot along these banks in here many times, because it's a good place to shoot, because you've got some good flat banks in here."

"Uh-huh," Flothe acknowledged.

"You can throw balloons in the water, and when you shoot you can see where your bullets are striking."

"This is from the aircraft flying over?" Flothe asked, still dubious.

"Yes. In the wintertime I shoot wolves an awful lot."

"Describe your .223 to me," Flothe said suddenly. "I am not over at the house now. Describe it to me."

"Just a normal .223. The old—there's only one model that I know of."

"Well, there's quite a few different models. There's, you know, there's M-16s, which are fully automatic," Flothe pointed out. "There's AR-15s . . ."

"Mini-14s . . ." Galyan added.

"14," Hansen responded, indicating that was the model he was familiar with.

"Okay, the Mini-14. And this is the one you're talking about?" Flothe asked. "You practiced dry runs, like shooting wolves, is that what you're talking about?"

"The reason I'm practicing here is to shoot wolves."

"And you've hunted in that area?" Flothe asked.

"Oh, yes. Here. You can see this-here river here, how flat it is. We put balloons out there. If you hit one, of course, it bursts. If not, you can see."

Both Flothe and Galyan had trouble suppressing their skepticism. Here was a man accused of murder, a man who now had to suspect that his shell casings were on the Knik, and he was trying to wriggle out of it by suggesting that he'd been up there shooting at balloons while flying a plane.

After several minutes of listening to him explain it, of listening to him talk about all the places he'd hunted, and whom he had hunted with, Galyan decided to bore in again. "Glenn," he asked Flothe, "do you have that picture of Sherry?"

"Um-hum," Flothe responded. But he had an agenda of his own. "Do you have a problem with your knee?" he asked Hansen.

"Do I have a problem with my knee?"

"Yeah, a problem with your knee, your leg?"

"I got cartilages torn out of both knees. I used to play quite a bit of softball and I tore up the cartilage in my knees."

"What do you use an Ace bandage for?" Flothe asked.

"To have with me, mainly; if I throw either knee out, boy they are so doggone sore I can hardly get them straightened out. But if I can wrap them real tight, I can still motivate with them, you know. I have Ace bandages around home by the jillion."

As Hansen talked Flothe retrieved the photograph of Sherry Morrow. When he found it he propped it up in front of Hansen. He wanted him to keep looking at her until he saw her.

"Who is that?" Hansen asked.

"That leads me to Sherry Morrow," Galyan said. "She was found in a shallow grave down in the Knik. With an Ace bandage wrapped around her arms, or what was left of them. There was a .223 shell casing found in the grave."

"Yeah."

"The shell casing in the grave of Sherry's was identical in extractor markings and fire pin markings to the shell casing we found in Paula Goulding's grave," Galyan continued.

"The shell casing is in the grave," Flothe added.

"It is not lying on top of the ground where it would fall like flying over in an aircraft or firing in the area. It is in the grave with the body."

"Um."

"And that shell casing is from the same gun that the shell casing from Paula's is from," Galyan said. "See where we're coming from?"

"Um-hum."

"Do you know where that puts you, Bob?" Galyan asked.

"You're saying that's out of my gun? Bullshit. It's not."

"But we need some explanations. . . . " Galyan said.

"I never shot these people," Hansen insisted. "I never intentionally hurt anybody in my life, and that's the truth."

"You're not telling me the truth, Bob," Galyan said in his most forthright manner. "You're making yourself look worse all the time."

"Look, I can't help that. I'm telling you the truth right now."

"You're not telling the truth."

"Yes, I am."

"I don't want to hear it, 'cause you just keep making yourself look like more the hardened criminal type," Galyan said.

"Where did you meet this girl?" Flothe asked, directing attention to the photo of Sherry Morrow. "Where did you meet her?"

"Ah, I've never met her."

"You have never met this girl before in your

whole entire life? You have never had sex with her?''

"No, I sure haven't.''

"How about this girl here—Miss Goulding?'' Flothe asked, pointing at her photograph. "Did you ever have physical contact with her at all, between yourself and her person, have sex with her and talk to her, ever meet her in a bar?''

"Does she work in a bar?''

"Both these girls do.''

"It's possible I seen 'em in the bars.''

"Think about it. Look at the girls, and see if you recall having any contact, physical contact, where the hair would fall onto your clothing, the hair would be into your clothing. . . . ''

"No. I have never had any contact with these girls,'' Hansen said with finality.

"So there's no way your hair could be in their clothing, or on their person?'' Galyan asked.

"That's right.''

"And their hair could not be in your vehicle or your house, or anyplace else, is that correct?''

"That's right?''

"That includes any other girls you've ever been with?'' Flothe asked.

"Now—what do you mean by that? I don't know what you're talking about. Explain to me, please.''

"You mentioned a minute ago you don't pick up girls all the time. How often do you pick up girls? How often do you have this urge?''

"I can see right now everything I say you people are going to try to turn around. Look, I have never seen those girls. As far as going out and picking girls up all the time, I don't do it. I ain't got time to do it.''

During Bob Hansen's interview Flothe was in and out of the room, communicating with the troopers at Hansen's house. He was naturally very much concerned about what might be found in the residence—it was one of the three pillars upon which their case against Hansen stood.

Now the whole edifice seemed shaky. Flothe and Galyan weren't getting anywhere with Hansen. The alibi witness still hadn't been found. And very little linking him to the crimes had been found at the house on Old Harbor Drive.

The bold gamble seemed to be failing spectacularly. At least he was still talking to them, not asking for a lawyer yet. But if something was going to break it appeared it would have to be Hansen.

Flothe had two tacks to follow. First, he had just received a package of evidence from the search of the suspect's house. He would confront him with that very evidence. He would also make a pointed inquiry about the kinds of guns Bob Hansen owned—and where he kept them. If there was one message coming from the Hansen home, it was this: Find out where he hid the .223.

Back in the interview room, Flothe casually plopped an odd assortment of novelty store items on the table. The ante had just been upped. ''What do you use this disguise kit for?'' Flothe asked. ''Mustaches and all that stuff?''

''I was going to try to see if it would work,'' Hansen deadpanned. ''I'm just curious.''

"Disguise for what reason?" Flothe demanded. "Enhance your appearance, or . . . ?"

"Well, I'm not the most handsome guy in the world," Hansen said. "I thought it would be easier—as a matter of fact, I even tried to grow one for a while. I could never . . . I make . . . could never grow one."

"Fingernail polish?" Flothe asked.

"Fingernail polish?"

"Is your wife aware that you have this stuff?"

"I don't know if she knows I have the fingernail polish."

"Mustache?"

"Huh. I just more or less wanted to see what I would look like with one on. And I tried to put one on one time and they give me some goop to smear on my lip and stick it on with and, ah, I put it on for five minutes and itched so goddamn much that I never tried it again. I tried to grow one here. As a matter of fact I grew one for about six or eight months or something. I got a funny lip—that one grows out and this one comes out and twirls one way and one wants to twirl down. . . . "

"List the weapons that you own," Flothe said, rapidly shifting gears. "Describe them to me—all of them. You're a gun collector. I'm sure you'll know each and every one of your weapons. You're an avid hunter."

"Okay. To start, I got a .270 model, pre-'64 model, okay? I got ah, ah, Ruger #1. That's a single-shot."

"Can you describe where these weapons are? Each weapon as you describe them."

"All right. They're in my gun case in the—well, not a case. I got one wall where it's—it's built out and you can take off the panels. You can get into it, okay?"

For the next several minutes Hansen described in great detail almost every gun and rifle he owned. He even mentioned the .22 single-shot he'd bought for his daughter when she took a firearms safety course, and how she won a trophy at one of the matches held by the sponsoring organization. The list of weapons seemed endless. But Hansen was holding something back.

"There's one gun we've talked about that you haven't described," Flothe finally pointed out.

"The .225," Hansen volunteered, getting the caliber wrong. "I think it's just down in that compartment down there, too. If I remember right. I can't remember where they're all sitting at."

"Do you have any at your cabin?" Flothe asked.

"Don't have a cabin."

"Isn't there a cabin that you usually fly to? A friend's cabin?"

"No," Hansen responded. So now Flothe knew. When Hansen had told the dancers he was taking them to his cabin, he was just saying it to try to put them at ease.

"What do you use the surgical gloves for?" Flothe continued.

"Surgical gloves?"

"Um-hum."

"Don't have any surgical gloves. I got some rubber gloves that I use when I am staining some horns. You know how you get some stain from the taxidermist and put the new stain on the horns? Why, that stuff, you get it on your hands—I got food color on there now—but boy, you get this stuff on and you got it for three weeks before you can get the damn stuff off your skin. Ah, that's the only gloves that are surgical or rubber-type gloves.''

In the next few minutes Flothe and Galyan punched and counterpunched their man with questions. It was time, they decided, to hit him with everything. They asked, for instance, about the burglary at his house, when all his prized hunting trophies were stolen.

Hansen was surprisingly forthright, telling the officers that his wife came home one day and found some of them in their backyard. He also told the officers that his insurance company had paid him about twelve thousand—and that he did not report the return of the items to the insurance company.

''Do you plan on paying them back?'' Flothe asked.

''Oh, yes.''

''You realize that you can turn the items over to the insurance company, because they actually belong to the insurance company,'' Galyan added.

''Well, whatever.''

Then they asked him about the cabin burglaries. Did he have a chain saw he'd taken out of a cabin in the Talkeetna area? Or weapons he'd taken from cabins that might have been unlocked or appeared abandoned? Did he have anything in his home that could have come from a cabin out there? Hansen denied having stolen anything. Flothe knew better. Troopers had already found what they thought was a robbery victim's Homelite chain saw in the shed behind Hansen's house. Beside it was another suspicious chain saw—and a portable generator. That wasn't all.

They found a CB radio in the garage, next to a GE radio. And a Sears battery-charger. And a forty-pound propane cylinder, by the loading bench. In the family room, moreover, they found a suspicious Sears radio-tape player. All these items fit the description of those reported stolen in the Talkeetna burglaries—they had already started to match the serial numbers.

There was no doubt that Hansen was lying to them, and both Galyan and Flothe let him know as much. They also told him that they couldn't figure him out, couldn't determine whether he was a man who needed help or a man who didn't want any.

"Surely you don't think that we went through all the time and money and the man-hours that it took to do the research on this—that we just did it for drill?" Galyan said.

"No, I . . ."

"It's serious, Bob."

"Yeah, it's serious. You damn right it's serious, but ah . . ."

"I don't see any remorse."

"The main thing that you're interested in is these girls. And I didn't do away with these girls, no."

Flothe's frustration was starting to show through. No matter what they confronted Hansen with, he covered it up with the most disingenuous explanations. Flothe cynically concluded Hansen probably would have denied he'd ever been born.

"You've definitely convinced me today," he said in exasperation, "that you don't have an IQ of 91, as indicated in some of these reports. You're a very intelligent man. *Very* intelligent man. Very manipulative man. You are, and you know it yourself. But you're a man that cannot face himself, and you're older than I am. You cannot even admit a little piece of guilt regarding anything. You have not shown any remorse to me at all today. No great sadness for what happened in the past. It's all a coincidence. Am I wrong?"

"No. No. I just—I don't know if you were in the room or not, and I told this gentleman here that I'm sorry for some of the things in my past that have happened. I wish they had never happened and I would do anything in the world if I could rectify that they had happened. But I can't change the past. . . . " A knock on the door came as welcome relief from this pageant of deception. It was the secretary, bringing news.

"Sergeant McCann wants to talk to you, sir," she told Sergeant Flothe.

"Okay," Flothe said, momentarily not knowing what to make of the information. Though he had been waiting for the call, it still caught him off-guard. He looked distracted as he walked to the phone, then cradled it tentatively when he picked up the receiver. Maybe that was because the last thing he wanted was more bad news.

19

It had been a long day for McCann and Stockard. Up at five, in the office by quarter to six, on the road by half-past. They began by driving to John Henning's shop at his home in Diamond Heights. The pretty young blonde who answered the door told them he wasn't home and didn't know when he would return. He was in King Salmon, a village at the apex of the rich fishing grounds of Bristol Bay. She said Joann Henning, his wife, wasn't home either, but was expected back at any time.

The troopers had no choice but to wait outside in their car. They waited and waited. Eventually they went back up to the house, wondering if there had been any word. There hadn't been.

The only thing McCann and Stockard could do was return to the Hansen residence. That's where they were needed. They reached the house slightly before one o'clock that afternoon. They could tell they were in the right place when they passed the dead-end sign: There was a line of trooper cars parked out front.

No sooner had they arrived, however, than they saw an orange Datsun go past the house and turn around. They were immediately out of their car. They brought the Datsun to a halt by standing in its path. The female driver rolled her window down.

"You're the one we're looking for," McCann said.

"Oh no, now just a minute here," the woman said, unbelieving.

"Well, aren't you Joann Henning?" McCann asked.

"Yeah," she responded.

"We were just at your house and we were looking for you," McCann said.

"Nah, I don't think so," Henning said, wondering where all this was leading.

"Would you step out of the car?" McCann asked politely.

"For what?" Henning wanted to know.

"We just want to talk to you."

Joann Henning complied. A grayish blonde in her early forties, she was surprisingly petite, since troopers knew her husband was a mountain of a man. She seemed only slightly nervous.

"You know what's happening here," McCann said flatly.

"Basically I know a little bit, vaguely, what's going on. I was told of some incident that happened this summer. But I was on vacation," Henning replied.

"So you know what's happening," McCann repeated.

"No," Henning said, "I really don't know. Everything I know is hearsay."

"Where's your husband, Mrs. Henning?" Mc-Cann asked.

"He's in King Salmon."

"Why don't you tell us what you know?" Mc-Cann suggested. Joann Henning was wary. Her body language was at once defiant and protective.

"I really don't know anything. All I know is hearsay," she repeated. "I am aware that there is a problem, that there is something going on, but until I really have an opportunity to talk to my husband I'm not going to tell you nuthin'. As far as I'm concerned that's confidential information until I get a chance to talk to John. Everything that's been told to me has been told by my husband, and it's hearsay."

The troopers were obviously disappointed with Joann Henning's verbal response, but her nervousness had in effect told them all they wanted to know. Now they needed an even more revealing story from John Henning himself.

"We've been trying to get ahold of your husband," McCann said. "We need to talk to him. You better go home and get him on the telephone and tell him the game is over." Joann Henning could tell that the trooper was dead serious. She left for home immediately.

It was not just a coincidence that Joann Henning had appeared at Hansen's in the first place. After returning home from a shopping trip earlier that morning, she found a family friend there. The friend was supposed to work on one of Bob Hansen's vehicles. But when he was turned away at the

bakery *and* at his house, he drove to the Hennings'
to see if they knew what was up.

"Would you go over to his house and check
what's going on?" the friend asked. "I can't get
no answers other than the fact that the bakery is
under investigation, the house is under investigation, and the vehicles are unavailable for servicing."

"Okay," Joann Henning said, almost coy. It
sounded serious, and she wanted to see how many
cop cars were at the Hansen's house.

She also knew more than she cared to admit.
Before leaving for King Salmon John had taken her
aside and told her that Bob had brought a prostitute
to his home, and hadn't been at the Hennings' having pizza as he had claimed to the police. As she
drove to the Hansen house she had a feeling that
this was what all the police action was all about.

After talking to the troopers, Joann Henning was
even more convinced that Bob's misadventure had
finally come home to him. She called her husband
immediately after she walked in the house. She
didn't mince words.

"You know that little problem your little buddy
friend Hansen had?" she said. "Well, I just found
out that it's quite a big problem. And you better
come home and address it before it turns into a
bigger problem."

Naturally enough, John Henning wanted an explanation. His wife readily supplied it. Still, she
could almost predict his reaction. This wasn't the
first time police had tried to get to him, or to other
family members, for that matter. Flothe made sev-

eral attempts to get John Henning to change his story. All had failed. This time, as every time, John's reaction was somewhat cynical.

"If they want me, they'll come get me," he said.

"What do you want me to do?" she asked.

"Go ahead and tell what you know," her husband replied.

That was the last thing Joann Henning would do. She felt John had to tell police what he knew. For her to say anything would be to oppose her husband. Besides, what happened if he never changed his story? No, she told herself, better let John do the talking. She had to protect her kids, and the ridiculous story her husband had given the cops. She tossed the ball back into her husband's lap.

"It's time for you to come up," she told him. "Nobody is worth your family, your kids, and yourself. I mean as far as I'm concerned this man is guilty, and there's no reason for you to have to lie about it no more."

John Henning refused to return voluntarily. He was in King Salmon to provide a living for his family, and by God that was what he would do. The police would have to subpoena him before he'd come back to Anchorage. Like it or not, Joann Henning was now in the middle of Bob Hansen's mess.

Back at Hansen's house, meanwhile, McCann and Stockard entered the premises to find everything turned upside down. A sense of blighted hopes pervaded the room.

McCann, on the other hand, could scarcely hide his excitement. He called Glenn Flothe immediately. Even as he spoke with Flothe, the joy of his discovery started to show through. Soon everyone on the scene knew they had their first break: The alibi witness was sure to roll over.

That seemed to give the searchers a second wind, a new determination to find the missing evidence. That new sense of urgency even infected Lieutenant Jent, who wanted to talk to Flothe immediately after McCann got off the phone.

"Hey, Glenn," Jent said, "have you asked Hansen about his weapons yet?"

"Yeah. He says his Mini-14 is in the cabinet built into the wall of his family room."

"No, it's not. We've already looked there. There's no sign of it."

"Well then, I'll ask him again. Can you hold?"

Back in the interview room, Flothe interrupted things to get in his question. He was almost absentminded in his inquiry, trying to seem offhand.

"Say, Bob," he said, "Where did you say your Mini-14 was?"

"In the family room. There's a gun case built into the wall."

"It's not there. We've already looked. Do you know anywhere else it might be?"

"Yeah," Hansen said, after a moment of collecting his thoughts. "It might be in my boat."

"Your boat?"

"Yeah. It's parked right next to my house."

Jent soon had the information he needed. But after he got off the phone he realized there was no way they could look for the gun in Hansen's boat without permission from Judge Carlson.

"Hey, Glenn," Jent said when he called Flothe back, "you know we're gonna have to get permission from the judge to let us look for the Mini-14 in the boat. The boat's not listed in the search warrant."

"You're right. You better call Judge Carlson."

"I'll get over there right now."

"Great. We gotta find that gun. Hansen ain't breaking."

"At least we got a break on Henning."

"Yeah," Flothe said, "but we can't make his wife testify against him."

"Don't worry. Once he knows we know, it's gonna be all over."

"Yeah," Flothe replied. "I'd still feel better if we found that damned Mini-14."

"We'll find it. If it's here, we'll find it. And I've got a feeling it's here. It's just well hidden."

All Flothe could do for the moment was hope that Jent was right. At least now they had more help on the scene. And maybe they would find the Mini-14 in the boat, although it seemed like a dumb place to hide anything. Then again, Flothe thought, Hansen could be lying. For Hansen, lying was a way of life.

After hours of questioning, Haugsven and company had reached the end of their repertoire. Darla Hansen could go. The troopers would call her when they'd finished the search, and someone also would bring her the keys to the bakery when they'd finished that search.

Darla still looked slightly mystified, or perplexed, or in a mild state of shock. What is all this about? she seemed to be asking with her eyes. No one was telling. Soon enough, she'll know soon enough, they thought, as they led her out of trooper headquarters. They had to wonder: Did she know her husband was in this same building even now, answering the questions of Galyan and Flothe just as she had answered questions of her own? Surely she suspected as much. But not once did she ask about it. Not once.

In the other part of the long, low building on Tudor Road, meanwhile, the interview of Bob Hansen continued. Galyan and Flothe were plodding onward, trying to get Bob to talk about his relations with prostitutes, trying to get him to link himself with his crimes.

"I think society as a whole downgrades prostitutes," Galyan told Hansen. "And because gals disappear from a bar, or someone takes them out and dumps them in a back alley somewhere, the whole world doesn't come to a screeching halt. Nobody really misses them, except maybe one or two close friends, right? The whole world doesn't mourn the passing of a prostitute that dies one way or the other, or even care how she dies.

"By the same token," he said, "what you find is that while growing up girls had a certain power over you. Most girls find that they have something that most of the boys want, and yet they dictate when you can see it, when you can touch it, when you can enjoy it sexually; anything pertaining to the sexuality of the female is dictated by them, and you're basically at their mercy. It's kind of nice when you get a little older, though, to be able to turn the tables around, and you dominate for a change, isn't it?''

"I can't seem to dominate, though," Hansen finally said, after a pause that had lasted a few seconds. It was a confession of inadequacy, born of a wish to appear innocent.

"How often do you get this urge and find yourself in a topless/bottomless-type bar?" Flothe asked. "How often do you find yourself wandering astray, as one might say?''

"Well, I haven't been in one for quite a long while now.''

"Does this seem to happen when your wife's out of town? Or when you're having problems at home?''

"I don't have no problems at home," Hansen said quickly. "I just, uh, like when I wrote a personal advertisement in . . . for the . . . [*Anchorage*] *Times* paper? Uh, look, you're talking about guilt feelings? Uh, I wrestled with that for a long, long time before I wrote that little piece in there. I wrote it, tore it up, wrote it again, and tore it up three or four times. . . . ''

"Um-hmmm," Flothe hummed.

"Morally, okay, I'll be the first to admit it was wrong. I should not have done—Being married, I should not have tried to make a date with these ladies, okay?''

"Do you feel guilt over that—between the relationship you had with your wife?''

"No, no, no . . . I felt a guilt that I am married and should not be, I say, going on while she's in Europe. . . .''

With Hansen each topic flowed into the next, stream-of-consciousness style. Soon he was talking about one of his bakery employees and how he'd taken her flying along the Knik River this past summer while his wife was out of town. How considerate of him to bring it up, Flothe thought. Maybe he could point out the spot where they'd landed. They had the maps right there on the table. . . .

Once Bob started looking at the map it was evident he knew the area quite well. He pointed to a spot in the river where there was a beaver colony. He pointed to another spot where there was a meat shack.

"Do you recall the big search that troopers had in this area here? It was in the newspapers and on TV?" Flothe asked.

"Yes."

"Were you out there before or after that search?"

"I haven't landed out there since that time. I've flown over it."

They had him—and they didn't. Galyan decided to try another tack. Their other choices were running out. This time he would offer Hansen help for his problem—before it was too late. But Hansen just sat there in his seat, a school kid trying not to listen to the lecture.

"From everything I've heard," Galyan finally told him, "you're not sincerely wanting to sit down and work at clearing up this problem. And I shudder to think what's going to happen when all this crap we found at your house comes back from the lab."

Still, nothing from Hansen. Galyan plunged

ahead, acting the role of school vice-principal, putting everything into a homey, country-store philosophy. You're a hardworking father figure who provides for his family, he told him, who's good at his profession. Who's made a success of himself. And then there's your other side, the side that's going to destroy everything you've built up over the years.

"Well, now, how could I say this?" Hansen ventured after Galyan's lecture had ended. "I appreciate what you say, but I mean—what do you want me to say? That I did something that I didn't do?"

"I don't want you to tell me anything that you didn't do."

"Well, he says I shot these girls out here. That I did not do. I've made a lot of mistakes in my life," Hansen replied, "but I never shot no one."

"Bob, I find that hard to believe, based on what we know at this point . . . and I find it hard to believe that some of these things didn't bother you later on."

"There is things I have done in my past that, no, I am not comfortable with."

"You keep referring to things in your past," Galyan said, "and I haven't the foggiest idea of what you're talking about, except that you allowed a girl to give you oral sex once."

"That's one of the main ones right there. Because I was being unfaithful to my wife. And every time I've even walked in to see a topless dancer, I shouldn't have been there in the first place. It's wrong, because it's something that I can't go home and say to my wife, 'Darla, I stopped down to the

Bush Company, or whatever, and went in and watched girls take off their clothes. And dance in front of me. I've even gone so far as to go down and give them five dollars for a doggone table dance. She come up and shaked her tits in front of my nose.' Ah, that, you know, is totally wrong.''

"I believe what those girls said," Galyan replied.

"Yeah. Do you want to convict me on that?''

"No. I just want to see if you got the courage to admit that she was telling the truth. I don't think you've got that kind of courage. Am I wrong?''

"Ah, sir, I think, ah, ah . . .''

"You know, I'm not going to do anything about those old reports back there, Bob. I can't even if I wanted to. And I don't really want to.''

"Well, I want to get that clarified in my mind. I would . . . I think . . . it's better. Because this is serious as hell.''

"Sure it is," Galyan agreed.

"And I think I had better not talk to you about those. I think I would like to talk to an attorney, and get him to tell me it's all right to talk to you.''

"Sure.''

"Ah, the matter about that—I didn't do that.''

"We shall see," Galyan said, looking at his watch. "The time is now 1:56. We'll discontinue the tape portion of the interview. Mr. Hansen has asked for an attorney.''

After Hansen contacted his attorney the troopers took him to a doctor to obtain blood and saliva samples. He was subdued as they drove to the doctor's office, as though he were enduring all this just to make the troopers happy.

Unlike other patients, he was taken right in to the doctor. The experience was designed to be coldly efficient and slightly humiliating. The needle in the arm, the wee bit of hair plucked from the head, the saliva sample collected in a small test tube—all were done solemnly, so that Hansen would know just how serious the troopers were. And then photographs were taken, front and side.

With that done, they were back in the car and on the way to see the judge. Inside the courthouse, Flothe learned that Judge Carlson had other business before he saw Bob Hansen. While they waited, Flothe stole a look at their suspect. He seemed to be bearing up pretty well. Of course he'd been through all this before. He was probably betting he'd beat them. Again.

In the judge's chambers, Bob Hansen was charged with rape and kidnapping in the Kitty Larson case. Hansen's obvious relief that he wasn't being charged with murder was Flothe's worry. For the present, though, it didn't matter. Hansen was going straight to jail. Judge Carlson set his bail at five hundred thousand dollars. At that level, they figured Hansen would stay put for a while.

But the search of Hansen's home had not turned up any important evidence. The Mini-14 was not in Hansen's boat. Nor were the mementos anywhere to be found.

When Flothe learned of their lack of success he was discouraged. The threads tying Hansen to the

murders were tenuous at best. Nothing they had
found so far linked him any more closely.

Now, more than ever, they had to find the Mini-
14. Deep down, however, Flothe was thinking the
unthinkable: Hansen had beaten them to the punch
and destroyed everything that would incriminate
him. This very minute, no doubt, Hansen was
smiling like a Cheshire cat.

As the hours dragged on and a dreary bleakness
settled over the Hansen home, the troopers on the
scene finally had covered every square inch of living space. The floors, the ceilings, the cabinets,
every recess and alcove had been picked clean.
There wasn't a thing.

All they had was enough to get him on some
cabin burglaries and an insurance fraud—and
maybe not even that.

It was Lieutenant Kasnick who volunteered to go
into the attic. The trooper was violently allergic to
almost everything, but soon he had disappeared
through the trapdoor, flashlight in hand, ready to
brave seven inches of fiberglass insulation, the most
irritating substance known to man.

The attic was cramped, and Kasnick soon found
himself on his hands and knees, crawling on the
beams above a sea of pink. This would not be fun.
And it would take forever.

The lieutenant had no choice but to start at one
side of the house and work his way across the elec-
trical wiring. He moved from one side to the other
in parallel lines that zigzagged from one cross beam
to the next. His plan was to start at the south side

of the house and work his way north, hobbling east
to west along each row.

The section nearest the perimeter of the house
was the worst. It was so narrow Kasnick had to lie
prone to shine the light into it. He found nothing.
Already he was starting to itch. He was starting to
sweat. The sweat only made the itching worse,
transporting the stuff to places he could not scratch.

No matter how bad it felt, though, he could not
stop his search. And fifteen feet east of the chimney, in a spot right over the garage, Kasnick stumbled across something.

Piled in a mound, he came across two or three
furs. Quickly, his heart pounding hard with expec-
tation, he pulled the hides apart, looking for the
mementos that had to lurk below. But even after a
black bear hide, sheepskin, and beaver hide had
been transported downstairs, and every inch of insulation along the chimney had been thoroughly
checked, there was no sign of the valuable evidence
they sought.

Reluctantly but doggedly, Kasnick got back on
his hands and knees, mentally marking each cross
beam as he went. Four. Five. Six. Seven. Nothing.
Eight. Still nothing. Row nine was his last chance.

Reaching the narrow, easternmost end, he hunkered down like a crab and thrust his head almost
flat against the insulation, pulling himself sideways
along the final margin of the house. Each inch was
another inch closer to despair, for the light showed
only the steady lines of pink fiberglass, uninter-
rupted, untouched, pristine. Kasnick felt increas-

ingly intense, and increasingly uncomfortable. He knew he had not missed a thing, but . . .

After probing thousands of square feet of attic, sometimes with his fingers alone, only a few feet remained. Kasnick reached his hand deep into the surrounding insulation and groped around. As he pushed on it it gave way, showing a hollowed-out cache. Suddenly it was Christmas morning.

In the corner was a Remington 552 rifle, .22-caliber. A Thompson Contender 7-mm single-shot pistol. An aviation map, with marks on it. Some jewelry, including a gold arrowhead necklace. A few newspaper clippings. A Winchester twelve-gauge shotgun. And best of all, a .223-caliber Mini-14: the murder weapon.

After more than fourteen hours, the troopers had finally found Hansen's stash. It was just as the FBI had predicted it would be. Flothe was ecstatic. So was everyone else. They all took turns gawking at the evidence, smiles bursting through. They had the son of a bitch. They finally had him. Or did they?

PART THREE

20

Now was the critical time in the investigation. After the adrenaline rush of the arrest came weariness and the pressure of the 120-day rule. Flothe had four months to put Hansen in front of a judge. If he failed, Hansen would go free without ever facing trial.

Flothe had two immediate concerns. Send the Mini-14 to the FBI for analysis. And keep an eye on Kitty Larson.

It was the FBI who could determine if the firing pin and extractor markings matched the spent shell casings found at the grave sites. Of course even a match would not make an ironclad case. The best evidence is a match between the weapon and the bullets taken from the victim. The bullets they'd found were shattered almost beyond recognition. It was a gap that a clever defense attorney no doubt could exploit. Flothe just had to believe that a match between the Mini-14 and the shell casings found in the graves would carry the day.

Flothe wanted someone to hand-carry the rifle to the FBI, four thousand miles away in Washington, D.C. It was a costly security measure, considering how much had been spent already, and the reception Flothe's request received was chilly. Someone suggested they send the rifle by Express Mail instead. "If we send it today, it'll be there tomorrow," somebody pointed out. Flothe protested, but to no avail.

Kitty Larson, meanwhile, was a critical link between Hansen's past and present. At that very minute she was working in a massage parlor run by her pimp. Flothe knew it was nothing but a brothel, but he could not simply snatch her up out of that environment, because she wasn't ready to leave it of her own volition.

Flothe knew it was crucial to establish a feeling of trust between them. Kitty had to know he wouldn't punish her but was willing to accept her faults. If he let her decide when the time was right, maybe she'd come to trust him enough to call him and say: "Glenn, I need your help. I've had enough."

Flothe decided to meet Kitty once a week for coffee. Just to talk. They would not talk about murder, or pimps, or the streets. They'd talk about the things that interested her, whatever they might be.

For their first post-arrest meeting Kitty came dressed in rabbit: rabbit-skin pants, rabbit-skin coat, rabbit-skin hat. She was wearing cheap jewelry and to Flothe's eye, looked like the whore she was. He tried to be complimentary.

"That's a pretty nice suit of clothes you have on," he said.

"Thanks," she replied. "My man bought 'em for me."

"Do you like nice clothes?" Flothe asked.

"Oh, yes," she said, smiling, her voice sounding dreamy. "If I'm ever rich, that's the first thing I'll buy. And then I'll buy a new car."

"What kind?" Flothe wondered.

"Oh, I don't know. A Camaro, or a Corvette, or . . ."

Suddenly Kitty Larson the prostitute reminded Flothe of his eleven-year-old daughter. Not because their lives were in any way alike, but because this street-wise young woman and his young daughter shared many of the same innocent longings. His daughter wanted nice clothes, too, wanted what was "in," wanted a Corvette. It was an intriguing parallel. Flothe decided to follow this line of conversation.

"What else would you do if you were rich?" he asked.

"Go to Disneyland and see Mickey Mouse and Donald Duck," she said, unabashedly.

"And what else?"

"Oh, I don't know. Buy a lot of stuffed toys and teddy bears. I really love stuffed animals. And you know what else I'd do?"

"What?"

"I know you won't believe this, but I've never even seen the Portage Glacier. Been up here all this time, and I still ain't seen it. That's what I'd love to do. And go to Fun World and slide down the water slides."

What Flothe learned in the next months was that Kitty was a little girl who'd never grown up. He also sensed that, despite her harsh life on the streets, she was very sensitive, a person who had a sense of right and wrong. And although Kitty was uneducated, she had a lot of street smarts. She was also very articulate and had an excellent memory. Flothe found her to be the best witness he'd ever had.

As the sergeant got to know her better and she started to trust him more, he learned just why she had never grown up.

"I started running away from home when I was twelve," she told him. "Started hanging out on the street. And then I met this guy—he was a pimp—and he took me in. Bought me nice clothes, which I'd never had before. I mean, we didn't have shit when I was a kid. And he gave me nice jewelry. And we drove around in a Lincoln Continental."

"That must have been all right."

"It was okay. But it's all a front, you know? It's for show."

"Did you stay with this guy very long?" Flothe asked.

"Long enough to become his main lady," she said, smiling again. "I remember once . . . I was about fifteen. And I was all dressed up in furs. He let me drive his Lincoln. That was a trip."

"I bet."

The barriers between them started to fall. Kitty told Flothe about things she was doing, though she was smart enough not to tell him the things he could arrest her for. In that developing relationship, Glenn Flothe became something of a father figure to her. He supported Kitty like a father, scolded her like a father. He had a lot to worry about.

Kitty's pimp sometimes took her and his other women to one of the after-hours clubs in town. He made them take their clothes off and stand on a bar or a table, like meat at an auction. The customers took their pick of the women and had sex with them on the spot. If the women resisted the pimp beat them or took away their status as his "main lady."

Flothe took these revelations as a sign that he needed to make plans to arrest Kitty and get her off the street. He desperately needed her help if he was going to keep Hansen in jail. The last thing he wanted was for her to be busted in a raid on an after-hours joint. Still, he resisted the impulse to bring her in. He sensed that Kitty understood her importance, even if she wasn't always able to control her own behavior.

Only days after Flothe mailed Hansen's rifle, the FBI laboratory in Washington, D.C., called. "The rifle hasn't arrived. Did you send it?"

"Yeah," Flothe said. "I sent it yesterday. Maybe it'll get there on Monday."

Flothe called the FBI on Monday morning. The rifle still wasn't there. Flothe contacted the Post Office, and put in a tracer. They had to find that rifle. Days passed, without word. He called the Post Office again.

"It's lost," they told him.

Lost? The crucial piece of evidence, the only piece of evidence that could directly link Hansen to the murders on the Knik, was lost? And all because they'd decided they couldn't afford to buy a trooper a plane ticket?

Flothe could hardly believe it. That piece of evidence they'd worked months to find, and, damn it, they'd found it. But now? Who knew where it was? It was more than Flothe could take.

As far as he was concerned there was only one fact that mattered here: Hansen had murdered over and over and over. Now, with his rifle lost somewhere between Anchorage and Washington, D.C., there was a chance he'd be able to pick up where he left off. Using an entirely new weapon.

Misery loves company, as the cliché goes. In that mood Flothe decided to pay the first of what would be several visits with Darla Hansen. He was concerned that, with Bob's arrest, the bakery would go under. That could devastate the family.

"How will you support yourself?" he asked her.

"I've always supported the children," she replied.

"You must have gotten some support from Bob," Flothe responded.

"Well, I pay the house payments and I buy the food, and I buy the kids' clothes for school," she said in a bland monotone.

"What about the money from the bakery?" Flothe asked.

"The bakery is Bob's," she said simply.

As they continued to talk the subject turned to Bob's arrest and the allegations made against him. It was a sensitive issue. Flothe couldn't talk openly, because a judge had placed restrictions on what could be said about the case. Only what was said in open court could be publicly revealed. Flothe did the best he could.

"Are you sure it's him?" she asked. "Could you give me a little more to convince me?"

"We've done an extensive investigation over the past few months," Flothe told her. "And everything points to your husband."

"Well, I guess if he's the one he should be in jail," she said, her voice plain and uninflected. She looked well in control of her life.

"Why did you live with him all these years?" Flothe asked, wanting to pierce her armor and find out how she really felt.

"Well," she replied, "so the kids would have a father."

"You know, Darla," Flothe continued, "when we searched the house we turned up item upon item that was stolen. Didn't you ever wonder where all this stuff was coming from?"

"Well, I kind of suspected that maybe he was taking things, but . . ."

"Yes?"

"I didn't think there was anything I could do about it. And if I did something about it, he'd go to jail again. I felt I had to keep the family together."

Flothe was amazed by Darla Hansen. Despite everything that had happened she wasn't enraged, didn't scream, didn't raise her voice at him. She didn't cry, wasn't aghast, didn't appear emotionally distraught. She didn't appear to be suffering from lack of sleep or depression. Throughout it all her voice never wavered from its bland monotone. And she seemed incredibly accepting of her husband, no matter what he'd done.

After his meeting Flothe found himself thinking back to the interview of her husband at trooper headquarters. He remembered thinking that Bob's relationship with his wife couldn't have been all that terrific. There was no way she was into all the sexual antics that Bob was.

After six days, the missing rifle was found on a loading deck in Chicago. The rifle was sent to Washington, D.C., immediately. True to their word, the FBI finished the lab work quickly. "You've got a match," the FBI agent told Flothe. "The shell casings you found at the grave sites were fired from this rifle. The firing pin, the extractor markings—everything's identical."

On November 20, *Anchorage Daily News* writer Sheila Toomey wrote that trooper investigators had reportedly "linked a bullet from at least one of the victims to a gun found hidden in the attic insulation of a suspect's home" and were preparing the case for a grand jury.

The unidentified "suspect" was Robert Hansen. Flothe wanted to take the evidence linking Hansen's rifle with the shell casings before a grand jury so he could get murder charges brought against the man.

In addition Flothe had John Henning served with a subpoena to appear before the grand jury. "Let's see if he lies now," Flothe told himself. Maybe the potential of a perjury charge would serve as a wakeup call.

Nonetheless, the thinking at the DA's office was that, even with the link between the murder weapon and the shell casings found at the grave sites, they still didn't have enough to indict Hansen on murder. If they did indict him it would be a risky proposition. There were several reasons for this.

First, just because they had the murder weapon didn't automatically make Hansen the murderer. Just because they'd linked the rifle to the shell casings at the grave sites didn't make him a murderer, either. He could have been flying with somebody else, for example, and that "somebody else" could have been the trigger man.

Related to this assessment was the feeling that the case still wasn't tight enough. That meant that Flothe had more work to do, including trying to track down people who could identify the jewelry found in Hansen's attic stash.

That was the source of the second problem. Even if they tracked down people who could identify the jewelry, would the IDs be specific or hold up under cross-examination? There were also questions about the search warrant—regarding not only its legality but its timeliness. Given the uniqueness of the search warrant and the grounds upon which it was granted—particularly the "criminal history" of the suspect—it was felt that this aspect of the case alone might provide grounds for an automatic appeal.

When these reservations were combined, the prosecution decided it was better to stick to the charges for which Hansen had been indicted. The murder charges were a gamble they could lose. *There would be no murder indictment.*

That decision didn't affect John Henning's appearance before the grand jury, of course. The troopers served him the subpoena in King Salmon and accompanied him back to Anchorage to testify. When his wife went to meet him at the airport she saw a man whose face looked paralyzed on one side, as if he'd had a stroke or something. Spittle was dribbling from the corner of his mouth. A doctor told him it was a nervous reaction to stress. His attorney, meanwhile, told him to tell the truth to the grand jury.

In his testimony, John Henning admitted that he'd lied to the police about what had happened on June 13, 1983. He'd done it, he said, to protect his friend. Even so, privately he felt that he hadn't done anything wrong. As far as his wife could tell, he didn't feel Bob Hansen had done anything wrong either. From Flothe's point of view, however, what was essential was that John Henning had rolled over. Finally.

21

With the seriousness of the Hansen case now evident to nearly everyone, no one was surprised when the DA's office assigned one of its heavy hitters to head the prosecution. Assistant District Attorney Frank Rothschild was regarded by many as one of the best and brightest.

Affable, articulate, evenhanded, highly intelligent, Rothschild knew how to put a good case together. He also had experience with highly publicized murder cases, including one in which the murderer had tried to dispose of his victim's remains by burning them in the fireplace. Flothe, and other troopers, felt he was just the man for this case.

As November became December, Rothschild was faced with the first of several pre-trial challenges by Hansen's defense attorney, Fred Dewey. In an impromptu December 8 hearing in Superior Court Judge Ralph Moody's office, Dewey asked that the judge seal court papers and close court hearings to the press. The defense attorney wondered how his client could get a fair trial for theft ''if the newspapers are trying to connect him with an uncharged group of murders?'' A discussion of the evidence in open court, Dewey said, could prejudice his client's ability to receive a fair trial, and might necessitate moving the trial to another town. Dewey also indicated that the defense planned to challenge the legality of the search warrant that had led to the evidence seized from the Hansen home.

Rothschild pointedly disagreed with Dewey's assertions. ''I have been involved in much more sensational cases,'' Rothschild said, alluding to the Lowry ''fireplace murder.'' ''With all of that publicity, we were able to pick a jury without any problem.''

Judge Moody agreed with Rothschild. ''Anchorage is now a big enough town to yield twelve jurors who have not been tainted by pre-trial publicity,'' he said. ''Even in the most sensational case.''

The judge also rejected Dewey's request for secrecy. It was inappropriate, he said. He added that it was his judgment that closing doors and files ''would cause more speculation than keeping them open.''

It was a minor battle, only peripherally associated with the war, but it was a victory for the prosecution and they'd take it.

One thing Glenn Flothe had learned about the women of the night, meanwhile, was that they could be unpredictable. He didn't figure Kitty Larson would be any different. The problem was: How could he keep his eye on her all the time?

In his weekly routine of picking her up at the Gentleman's Retreat massage parlor, he came to meet another woman who worked there. The woman believed that Kitty was doing the right thing by cooperating with the police. This was rare enough to deserve notice: Most of these women would rather not cooperate with cops on anything, even when they were themselves the victims.

As it turned out this woman was having some problems of her own—her family was trying to take her child away. That was something Flothe could do little to help with. Then when some money was stolen from the massage parlor, the pimp who ran the place accused the woman's roommate of theft and threatened to beat them both up. Flothe did a little investigating, found out who had really taken the money, and set the APD on the perpetrator. That took the heat off, because the APD came back and told the pimp they knew who did it.

Only a little while later Flothe learned that Kitty's pimp had received a half-pound shipment of cocaine. It was time, he decided, to have a little talk with Kitty's friend. Before one of their weekly meetings he took Kitty's associate aside.

"Look, I need your help to protect Kitty," Flothe told her. "I need your help because I can't watch her all the time. If anything happens to her, would you call me?"

"Yeah," the friend said. "I sure will."

Back at the car Flothe found Kitty sitting in the front seat and his partner, Lyle Haugsven, sitting in the back. As they drove to the coffee shop, Haugsven seemed anxious. He kept looking at Flothe expectantly. Finally he leaned over the front seat.

"Have you asked her yet?" he said.

"Asked her about what?" Flothe asked.

"You know, about Hansen's dick."

"Why don't you ask her yourself?" Flothe suggested, a smile crossing his face.

"Say, Kitty," Haugsven screwed up the courage to ask, "did you notice anything about Hansen's penis?"

"I don't really remember."

A more important matter concerned Kitty's consent to a pre-trial interview with Hansen's attorney. Fred Dewey had been pushing real hard on it. Troopers knew he wanted to discredit her as a witness against Bob Hansen. Kitty was smart enough to figure that out, too, and for that reason was reluctant to cooperate.

"Hansen's attorney has really been nagging at us for you to give them an interview," Flothe told her.

"I know, but . . ."

"What if I just give them your phone number at Gentleman's Retreat?" he said, knowing that that very day Fred Dewey had filed a motion to postpone the trial because he wanted to do more research on Kitty.

"Yeah, that's okay," Kitty said without enthusiasm. Flothe sensed that the pressure was getting to her, though he wasn't entirely sure of its source. Maybe, he thought, she's getting cold feet about cooperating with the police. Maybe she just doesn't want to go to court, and undergo the agony of cross-examination.

Whatever it was, he just had to hope that she'd hold up a little while longer. Because at the moment, she was everything.

The hearing on the defense motion to postpone the trial was scheduled for Wednesday, January 10, 1984. The weekend before the hearing Pat Doogan again flew down from Fairbanks to discuss the case with Flothe. It was more than a friendly visit.

Hansen's attorney had accused Frank Rothschild of deliberately withholding information from the defense, and Flothe wanted to make sure he had everything in order before meeting with Rothschild. Doogan was the most logical person to call for help, because he had been on the case from the beginning.

There was an avalanche of case materials to review, some old, some new. Flothe showed Doogan the business cards from the two missing dancers, evidence found in the search of Hansen's home. He told his friend that he'd shown the gold arrowhead necklace found at Hansen's home to the man who'd given it to her. Not only had he positively identified the piece but he'd told Flothe the name of the jeweler who'd made it. The jeweler also positively identified the piece.

And then they looked at the maps they'd found at Hansen's house. One had been behind the headboard of his bed. The other had been in the attic with the rest of the mementos.

Up until this time Flothe had been going a mile a minute. He'd spent little time being reflective. The maps represented nothing more than documents Hansen had used for hunting. Yet while examining the maps with Pat Doogan, he noted twenty-four X marks. Were these favorite hunting spots—or something else?

The answer that suddenly dawned on him was almost too grotesque to be believed. "Oh, my God," Flothe said, a chill coming over him. "What has this man done?" At that moment he realized that each X marked a body.

The room was abruptly still. Although Flothe had put together a long list of missing women and potential victims, until that moment he hadn't really known how seriously to take it. After all, the most they had on Hansen were the murders of Sherry Morrow and Paula Goulding, and even the links to those murders were tenuous.

Now he knew they would be up on the Knik River that summer, digging up bodies at every X. Ten of the twenty-four marks were concentrated along a seven-mile strip of the river bank.

Back at his office the next day, Flothe started to pull some case files. The first was on Joanna Messina, one of the many cases that comprised the huge chart taped to the wall of Flothe's office. A quick review of the case showed that the body had been found on the Kenai Peninsula. Hansen's map had several Xs marked on the Kenai Peninsula. Flothe called in Chuck Miller, the man who had investigated the Messina case.

"Chuck, why don't you show me where Joanna Messina was buried?" Flothe said, giving him one of the maps for reference.

Miller walked over and scrutinized the map closely. "Okay," he said. "Now here's Seward. And here's the railroad tracks. And up here—oh, you've already got it marked, Glenn. There's an X right there."

"I didn't mark that, Chuck," Flothe told him. "Robert Hansen did. You see, that's his map that we got out of his house."

At that point Miller too realized that the other marks on the maps were also bodies. Besides Joanna Messina there was one for "Eklutna Annie," whose remains had been found up near the power lines at the village of Eklutna, north of Anchorage. One for Sherry Morrow. One for Paula Goulding. And twenty others, four of which were either in Seward Bay or farther out in Resurrection Bay, into which Seward Bay feeds.

The two men looked at each other gravely. They weren't just dealing with a serial murderer. Robert Hansen was the worst killer in the history of Alaska.

22

The hearing on the postponement of the trial was scheduled for 1:30 before Superior Court Judge Seaborn Buckalew. In court papers Fred Dewey noted that Kitty Larson had an extensive arrest history, and requested that the trial be postponed from mid-February to May 1, 1984.

"My client has not been charged with murder," Dewey told the judge. "He has been charged with kidnapping and rape. And a key factor in this case is going to be the background of the woman who says she was raped. In fact the state's present case rests entirely on the credibility of the alleged victim. She is their case. But in order to defend my client I need time to investigate her extensive history of arrests for prostitution in Portland, Oregon, San Francisco, and Los Angeles."

Dewey then repeated his earlier charges that the state had been withholding information from the defense. "For all these reasons," he concluded, "I would request that the trial be postponed."

Then it was Frank Rothschild's turn. He had already filed a six-page rejoinder to Fred Dewey's allegations of incomplete discovery, detailing precisely what the police had found. "I am here to deny Mr. Dewey's accusations," he told the judge. "Mr. Dewey is really on a fishing expedition to get information pertaining to the murder investigation."

Judge Buckalew did not waste much time in contemplation. The next day he denied the motion to postpone the trial.

When Glenn Flothe realized that the maps showed the presence of bodies Hansen had left in the bush, he also came to another realization. Hansen had about thirty weapons at his house, but under the terms of the search warrant they could seize only five of those weapons, including the .357 magnum used in the Larson case and the .223-caliber Mini-14 they thought had been used in the Morrow and Goulding murders. Yet any of the remaining weapons in his house could have been used to kill one or another of the victims. How many guns had he used in his murder spree? They just didn't know.

With this in mind Flothe went to the DA's office. He wanted a search warrant authorizing him to seize all the other weapons and related ammunition from the Hansen residence. Both Vic Krumm and Frank Rothschild were in court on other matters, so Voitlander helped him prepare the preliminary documents.

At four, Flothe and Haugsven met with Krumm and Rothschild and went before Judge Carlson to request another search warrant for the Hansen residence. Flothe brought the maps with him, since they supplied the basis for his request.

"This is what we have, Your Honor," Flothe said. "We found these two maps at Hansen's residence and they are identical. Both of them are marked with Xs, Your Honor, and we have found bodies at four of these marks already. We feel that the bodies we've already found verify the map's authenticity regarding grave sites. But, Your Honor, we weren't able to seize all the weapons at Hansen's house when we searched it, because the previous search warrant limited what we could seize."

"If other bodies should be found at these other locations marked on Hansen's map," DA Krumm interjected, "the weapons and ammunition in Hansen's house would have to be seized for purposes of comparison."

"And the reason we want to search for weapons now," Flothe said, "is because he can call his wife, or anybody, and they can go in the house and remove these weapons. And come spring, Your Honor, we won't have these weapons to compare with the bodies we expect to find."

Flothe knew they were making a pretty big supposition. They were, in essence, telling the judge that there were people in all the graves that the map supposedly marked out. And on top of that they were telling him the guns in Hansen's house could help connect him to all these murders. In effect they were telling the judge that Bob Hansen was no longer the suspect in just a couple of murders, but ten times that many.

Judge Carlson approved the search warrant. At 7:30 that evening Sgt. Flothe, Sgt. Haugsven, Sgt. Stogsdill, and Trooper Von Clasen served the search warrant at the Hansen residence. Darla Hansen was present the entire time, during which they seized more weapons, ammunition, and reloading equipment. When the search finally ended at ten, the troopers felt that they had just removed half the National Guard armory from his house.

For Flothe, the beauty of serving the second search warrant against Hansen was that it kept the pressure on. The sergeant knew from Hansen's past that he'd never gone to trial on any of the crimes for which he'd been charged. When the time for his trials had come, Hansen copped a plea. Flothe hoped that by dumping and dumping on him they'd be able to work the same effect. It was, he hoped, like pouring water on a drowning man. And with the omnibus hearing getting closer and closer, Flothe wanted to keep the pressure on.

Hansen learned of this police activity the next day, when his attorney told him that the search warrant had been served at his home. Hansen had to know, at that point, that the police had his maps and understood what they meant. The search warrant spelled out the link between the maps, the bodies they expected to find at those sites, and the weapons they'd seized from his house.

Hansen had to figure that, come spring, after the ice and snow had melted, troopers would be searching for bodies along the Knik. The troopers told the judge there was a good chance they'd find some. However, Robert Hansen was the only one who knew for sure whether there were bodies along that picturesque and isolated river.

As expected, Hansen's defense attorney filed a

detailed motion challenging the legality of the
search warrant. Fred Dewey asked the Superior
Court to reject evidence seized in the October 27
search of Hansen's property. He also asked that the
trial be moved to "a location not readily influenced
by the print and electronic media of Anchorage."
According to Dewey, "Extensive publicity linking
Robert Hansen with the missing dancer investigation has made it impossible to seat an impartial
jury in Anchorage."

Dewey accused police of resurrecting the rape
accusation—four months after dropping it for lack
of evidence—as a pretext for obtaining the search
warrant. By October, he charged, Hansen had become a suspect in the case of the disappearing
dancers. But police had no evidence against him
and could not have gotten a search warrant in that
case.

The warrant that was finally issued, Dewey
wrote, was illegally broad and allowed police to
"rummage about" in Hansen's home, plane, and
vehicles. Dewey also noted that when police
searched Hansen's property the June rape accusation was too old to provide legitimate probable
cause for a search. Therefore, he said, all evidence
found in the various searches should be ruled in-
admissible in court.

Dewey's motion also made a pointed attack on
the FBI profiling techniques, which argued that
Hansen fit the profile of a serial murderer. Dewey
argued that the inclusion of the FBI serial killer
profile, and the comments of Dr. Rothrock to the
effect that Hansen "might be involved with the

missing dancers,'' improperly influenced Superior Court Judge Victor Carlson to approve ''an illegal search.''

Dewey also took issue with the list of Hansen's past convictions cited in the search warrant. He noted that such references are not considered legal grounds for issuing search warrants.

Taken together, it was enough to cause the prosecution plenty of worry. All the second-guessing done by the DA each step of the way had finally been borne out.

Only Frank Rothschild seemed unimpressed with Dewey's suppression motion, even though he knew that a success for the defense here would mean the murder case against Robert Hansen was a goner. Flothe was sufficiently worried about the motion's chances of success that he made an appointment to meet with APD vice cop Gentile that very evening.

''You got trouble, eh, Flothe?'' Gentile said when they met.

''Hansen's attorney is trying to get the evidence thrown out.''

''You got trouble.''

''There's somebody I need you to help me find.''

''Shoot.''

''I need to find a prostitute by the name of Gina Williams. I have some information that Hansen raped her in 1972. I need to find her.''

''Need some more witnesses, huh? Well, let's see what we can find.''

Again Flothe trekked into the streets of Anchorage with Gentile as his guide. Gentile drove his car up by the Sheraton Hotel. They got out and walked from there.

It was cold as permafrost, the sky dark as a black curtain. Even the neon looked frozen as it struggled against the icy evening. Streetwalkers huddled in doorways, dressed in furs and trying to keep their bare legs away from blistering gusts of wind. They shared cigarettes between them, blowing icicle ropes of smoke into the glow of street lamps.

The lucky ones, Flothe knew, caught a trick right away, and snuggled into the warmth of someone's automobile. The unlucky ones made a tortuous pilgrimage from the street to the beckoning lights of a nearby café and back, their every move under the dispassionate eye of a pimp. Yet even on a night as cold as this the women sauntered lasciviously along the streets, with as many of their wares on display as the Arctic chill would allow.

During the next few hours Flothe and Gentile hit every street corner and bar on the strip. It was all promises and no prospects, as though the street had swallowed Gina up and would not disgorge her. The street people had a secret society of sorts. "Tomorrow" was not a concept that interested them. *Now* was what mattered, and the only way to find Gina Williams was to find someone who knew where she was right now. But when Flothe finally dragged his numb body home, all he had was tomorrow.

The suppression hearing wasn't scheduled until February 1. The state still hadn't responded to Dewey's charges, although a response was expected by January 27. For Flothe that meant that the waiting game continued, as forces beyond his control waged a struggle of their own. Meanwhile many little things kept him busy.

On January 18 he contacted Kitty Larson at the Gentleman's Retreat. Accompanied by Trooper Von Clasen, he served her with a subpoena for the Hansen trial. Kitty didn't quite know what to make of it. It almost seemed like a breach of trust. She had no way of knowing that Flothe was simply trying to cover his ass.

Five days later the FBI returned most of the evidence troopers had gathered during their investigation. The only item remaining at the FBI laboratory was the .223-caliber Mini-14.

That same day Flothe got a call from the mother of one of the missing dancers. There was not much Flothe could tell her, since the search for bodies would have to wait until spring. On the plus side, however, she did have her daughter's dental records, and agreed to send them to trooper headquarters in his care. So it was that Flothe started a collection of dental records from women who'd been reported missing and were suspected victims of Robert Hansen.

On the 25th Flothe and Haugsven interviewed a former associate of Hansen, who volunteered that he might have some information useful to the investigation. Wanting anything they could get, they agreed to talk to him.

"I think Hansen might have been involved in the disappearance of some women down in Seward," the man told them.

"Why do you think that?" Flothe asked.

"Because of some newspaper articles I read at the time," he said. "And because at one time Hansen asked me if I knew any girls in Seward he could party with."

"When was this?" Haugsven asked.

"Back in the early seventies. I think Bob was on parole, or staying in a halfway house."

On January 31—just the day before the scheduled suppression hearing—Rothschild filed another round of papers in Superior Court. In it he summarized the forty-eight-page affidavit Flothe had presented to Judge Carlson in support of his request for a search warrant. The information in the affidavit, when taken together, established a solid justification for the search warrant, Rothschild said. Hansen's history suggested a pattern that "evolved into picking up dancers and prostitutes, abducting them at gunpoint, and flying them off into the wilds where they were murdered and buried," Rothschild noted.

Rothschild also noted that the judge had properly considered Hansen's criminal record and the FBI's opinion that he fit the profile of a serial murderer in issuing the search warrant. Those facts, Rothschild said, are "just the type of information on which a reasonable judge can base a belief that a crime has been committed," particularly when faced by a serial killer.

Defense attorney Dewey had earlier suggested that use of the FBI profile was a gimmick, one that essentially gave police free rein in their search of Hansen's house. Even in the June rape case, Dewey argued, police had had no right to assume Hansen would be foolish enough to keep evidence around his house for four months when there was a risk it could be used to link him to a serious felony charge. Yet Rothschild had a pointed rejoinder to Dewey's complaint that the search warrant was not issued in a timely manner.

Rothschild argued that Hansen himself had caused the delay when he trumped up a phony alibi that temporarily threw police off the track. "No criminal defendant should be allowed to take advantage of his own wrongdoing—creating a smoke screen and then whining when it takes time to blow the smoke away and discover the truth," Rothschild said.

In another development, the suppression hearing itself was postponed until the following week because Rothschild wanted another judge. A hearing on that matter was scheduled for February 7 before Judge Lewis, who was expected to rule on whether Judge Seaborn Buckalew would be the judge to rule on the legality of the search. There was no question now that things were getting interesting, even as the spotlight shifted from the police to the prosecution.

Behind the scenes Flothe conducted an interview with Hansen's friend John Sumrall, trying to get information about where the two of them had hunted together.

Sumrall was quite cooperative. Yes, he told Flothe, the two of them had often hunted the sandbars along the Knik River. And yes, they'd taken target practice there. They'd also hunted in the area around Jim Creek, which eventually flowed into the Knik River along its northeast margin.

Those weren't the only places, Sumrall said. They'd also hunted in the Chugach, the Kenai Peninsula, and among the hundreds of little lakes that dotted the Susitna River basin. In fact they'd hunted in a wide arc that extended about one hundred and fifty miles from Anchorage in any direction.

During the interview, Sumrall also told Flothe about a Ruger #1 pistol that Hansen had given him as a present. Suspecting it was stolen, Flothe requested the serial number of the weapon. Sumrall promised to get back to him with that information. Before he left, however, he wanted to know if Flothe really felt his friend was responsible for killing the dancers.

"Yes, I do," Flothe told him.

Sumrall shook his head vigorously. It just didn't seem like the type of thing Bob would do. Especially when he'd known him as long as he had.

Later that day, Sumrall called Flothe back and gave him the serial number on the Ruger. Flothe immediately ran the serial number through the computer. Sure enough, the weapon was stolen. Soon Flothe was back on the phone to Sumrall. "Could you bring the weapon into trooper headquarters?" he asked. "The weapon's stolen." There was a moment of silence before Sumrall answered. "Yes," he said, "I'll bring it in."

On February 3 Kitty Larson moved out of the Gentleman's Retreat without telling Flothe. It was a cause for concern, but not worry, since she still worked there. Then, three days later, Flothe got a call from his inside informant.

"Kitty doesn't work here anymore," she said. "And I don't know where she is."

Glenn Flothe panicked. The trial was only weeks away. The suppression hearing had not yet taken place. The result was not at all assured. And now Kitty Larson had disappeared. How could she do this to him?

Flothe had no choice but to start hitting the streets. He figured, it being winter, that she was working either in another massage parlor or in a topless club. That was more than an educated guess on Flothe's part, because the informant also had told him, "I think this other pimp came by and got her," she told him. "But don't ask me where he took her."

The possibility existed that the pimp had taken her out of the area—a contingency Flothe had not prepared for. He had been ready to arrest her, and maybe he should have, although it would have broken the bond of trust between them. But this disappearing act left Flothe feeling foolish and betrayed.

The very next day Flothe got word that Kitty was now dancing in one of the topless places. Almost immediately Flothe was there looking for her. It was a real dive—one of the worst in Anchorage. It smelled of urine and stale beer. The men seemed bored and half-smashed. The women had seen better days; there were no show girls here.

"I'm looking for Kitty Larson," Flothe told the bouncer. "Is she here?"

"I dunno," he said blankly. "Ask the bartender," he suggested.

"I'm looking for Kitty Larson," Flothe asked the bartender. "Is she here?"

"I dunno," she said, sounding preoccupied. "Ask Veronica."

"Who's Veronica."

"The manager."

"Do you know where Veronica is?"

The bartender shrugged her shoulders. Flothe turned to one of the dancers instead. "I'm looking for Kitty Larson. . . ." The dancer walked away without acknowledging him. Flothe went looking for the manager.

Suddenly Kitty materialized from out of a back room and ran to Flothe. As she gave him a squeeze Flothe noticed she wasn't alone. Another woman hovered nearby as they talked. Flothe soon figured she was the pimp's main lady, there to keep an eye on Kitty.

"So you moved out of the Gentleman's Retreat?" Flothe asked.

"Yeah," Kitty said matter-of-factly.

"How come you didn't tell me?"

"I don't know," she said.

She wore a dancing outfit—a G-string and a top so thin her breasts were hanging out. She looked absolutely horrible. Her legs were skinny. Her skin was white and pasty. She had bruises up and down her legs, shins, and arms. There were also big scabs on her arms. She'd been picking them. Her hair was a mess. She was shaking. She looked like death warmed over, as far as Flothe was concerned. It wasn't hard to tell that she was strung out on cocaine.

"So where are you staying?" Flothe asked.

Kitty cast a sidelong glance at her guardian, then shrugged. She wouldn't tell him. She looked scared. He sensed that she wanted to go to the safe house he'd found her, but was too fearful to tell him so with the pimp's main lady standing by. He decided to leave things where they stood, banking on the trust they'd built in the past five months.

"Well, just be sure to stay in touch with me," he told her, trying to sound fatherly. "You had me pretty scared there when you just disappeared on me like that."

"Okay," she said, her voice trailing off.

"Promise?"

"Promise."

"Good. I'll come by and see you in a couple of days."

On his way back home Flothe figured out what the problem was. The pressure was starting to get to Kitty Larson. He knew she had been having a hard time, and Flothe had been bothered enough by her situation that he'd repeatedly asked her, "The pimp knows we're coming to scoop you up, doesn't he?" He'd been trying to approach the difficulty as sensitively as possible.

"Yeah," Kitty had always replied.

Despite Kitty's assurances, however, Flothe had a hard time believing that her relationship with the police was all right with the pimp. He knew she'd told him the police were interested in her because of the Hansen case, but still wondered why the pimp had let it continue so long. Then it hit him: As long as Sgt. Flothe of the Alaska State Troopers needed someone who was in the pimp's stable—and needed her desperately—then the pimp was confident the police wouldn't do anything to him, even if they were aware of his various activities.

Yet the pimp must have had an underlying fear that Flothe would gain her complete confidence, and Kitty would dump on him. That was the source of the pressure. That's why she'd moved out of the Gentleman's Retreat and in with the other pimp. Kitty wanted out.

She was paying a heavy price, though. She'd gone downhill drastically, and looked worse than he'd ever seen her. He resolved to visit her more often, just to see her through her ordeal. He had no choice. He really did need her desperately.

Later in the day Roy Tuberger called Flothe from the FBI lab in Quantico. "Hansen's blood is A-sector," he told him. "And that's the same as we found in the semen of the underwear from the rape victim."

All things considered, February 7 was an eventful day. Earlier in the day Flothe had met Frank Rothschild in court, where the DA requested that the assigned judge in the Larson case be preempted. Hansen's defense attorney, Fred Dewey, had law-clerked for the presiding judge, Rothschild argued, and that judge should be removed from the case. Rothschild's request was granted. The suppression hearing was rescheduled for the next day before Judge Henry Keene.

Wednesday, February 8, 1984

Of all the milestones in the Hansen case until now, none had loomed larger than the suppression hearing. It was the last hurdle to be cleared before Hansen's trial. If the defense won, they stood a good chance not only in the Larson case but with any future charges that might be brought against Hansen. Flothe awaited the hearing with trepidation. If it went Hansen's way, all the critics who had feared being associated with a major failure would prove to have been justified.

Flothe knew that they'd gone out on a limb by requesting the search warrant on such unusual grounds. Anyone who had to go through the Office of Special Prosecution and Appeals before going to a judge with his affidavit had to be acutely aware of that. Usually, getting a search warrant simply called for the police to detail each item they planned to seize. The items had to be connected to a specific crime. The reasons they believed each item would be found at the place they intended to search had to be explained. Once a search was under way, moreover, police could seize only those items specified in the search warrant and any items they found in plain view.

In the Hansen search warrant troopers had specified items they wanted to seize, but they also had searched for other items broadly defined as "mementos" and "implements of murder." The seizure of these last items was in part justified by reference to the FBI profile.

After hearing arguments on both sides, Judge

Keene ruled that the search of Hansen's home was proper. He said in his ruling that the physical evidence linking Hansen to the slayings of Sherry Morrow and Paula Goulding—the ammunition that had killed both women, an Ace bandage wrapped around Morrow's head and face, the fact that Hansen made frequent trips in his plane to the Knik River area—was enough in itself to justify the search warrant.

He added that the psychological profile put together by the FBI was not needed to justify the warrant, effectively turning back Dewey's argument that police should not be allowed to search a person's home simply because of his past record or because a psychiatrist says the person "looks like he could have committed a crime."

It was an important victory for the prosecution. The way was clear for murder charges to be brought against Bob Hansen. It was the next act in the continuing drama, the increase in pressure that might finally make Hansen to break.

When Major Gilmour came across Flothe in the men's room the day after Judge Keene's ruling, however, he noticed that his main man looked sad.

"How's it going?" Gilmour asked.

"Not too hot," Flothe replied. "There's some question about the four-month rule and how it applies to the time lines of taking the bastard to trial on the murders. The DA's telling me we'd better just go with the kidnapping and rape charges and see what the jury does with that."

Gilmour could feel for him. There was no way Flothe would be content getting Hansen on rape and kidnapping when a dozen or more murders hung over him. Gilmour decided to cheer him up.

"Tell his attorney and the DA that you think that's great," Gilmour said. "Because every time he serves one sentence you'll be waiting to indict him on the next one, and that he can never be sure he won't end up in the shit five or ten years from now. I mean, every time we find another body we'll bring him up on murder charges."

Warming to the theme of the social good that could come from stretching the case out, Gilmour went on, "Flothe, the best thing that could happen is for him to be in the joint for the rape and kidnapping of some pimp's girl. And when they get done with him in the joint he can come back and we can try him for murder, and with a little bit of luck Alaska will have reinstated the death penalty. Hell, with a case like Hansen's hanging fire, all the notoriety could get people stirred up so we could get the death penalty by referendum."

"Oh," Flothe said. Gilmour could tell he was uncomfortable and would be happy just to get out of there.

"Like I told you before," Gilmour said, "no one confesses on the street, and the man in jail has ten times the pressure on him."

It was time for Kitty to meet with the DA, and on the evening of the 10th Flothe made his way to the topless club. This sleazy dive was at this point their designated meeting point.

Once inside the dingy darkness of the club Flothe made his way to the bar and asked for the manager.

He'd learned his lesson. Always go directly to the top.

While he waited for the manager to appear, he watched a listless striptease by a past-her-prime dancer. Her every move seemed arthritic. He couldn't help but feel slightly amused.

"So you want to see Kitty Larson?" the manager asked when she reached Flothe's side. She was a busty, hard-looking woman in her early forties.

"Yeah, if you don't mind."

"I don't mind," she said. "Only she don't work here no more."

"What do you mean she doesn't work here anymore?"

"I mean she don't work here anymore. What do I have to do, spell it out for you?"

"Do you know where she went?" Flothe asked, with a tinge of horror in his voice.

"I got no idea. Sorry."

There was nothing Flothe could do but hit the streets. Kitty had to be somewhere. Didn't she? Maybe she'd gone back to the Gentleman's Retreat.

She wasn't there. No one had seen her. "Call me if you do," he said. Somehow he knew no one would call.

Flothe's next move was to find Gentile. He might know where Kitty had gone. Gentile didn't know anything, though. "Shit," Flothe said. "Tell me this isn't happening."

Flothe spent most of the night cruising the streets, exactly as Hansen had done for more than a decade. Every time he turned a corner he hoped to see her. Every time he saw a group of women he hoped she was among them. But it was no use. She was gone. "Jesus," he said, "how could she do this to me?"

By the time Flothe gave up his search it was morning. A new day was starting. The worst day of his life.

As Flothe tried to sleep, he could almost hear Hansen laughing.

Early Saturday morning Kitty Larson called Flothe at his office. It seemed urgent. She was speaking in a whisper. "I can't talk too loud," she said. "I just got out of bed and I'm in the bathroom. I went to the bathroom so I could talk on the phone. I need you to come pick me up."

"What's the address?" Flothe asked without hesitation.

"Over on Government Hill," Kitty said, then gave him the street address.

"Are you at your pimp's place?"

"Yeah."

"I'll be there in a half hour or less."

Before going to Government Hill to pick up Kitty, Flothe rounded up some reinforcements. He didn't expect any trouble, but wanted to make sure he didn't have any. When he got to the unprepossessing apartment building he had three plainclothes officers with him as backup.

Inside the building, the troopers marveled at the setup. The first floor was like an atrium, with a ceiling that opened to the floor above. In the center of the atrium was a pool table. There was a bar off in the corner. In every direction they looked there were doorways leading off to individual rooms.

It was a party house. People could party, and when it was time to have sex they went off to one of the many rooms, not only on the first floor but also on the second level, which was reached by a stairway snaking up one side of the atrium. It was the perfect layout.

They found the room number Kitty gave them and knocked. No answer. "She knows we're coming," Flothe muttered. He knocked again. He wasn't about to barge in. The guy might have a gun. A second later Kitty came to the door, holding a bathrobe to her chest for cover.

"Come with me," she said to Flothe, "I gotta talk to you real quick." She led him to the bathroom, which was the next door over. Kitty closed the door behind them.

"I gotta get out of here," she said. "Get me out right now."

As a precaution Flothe had already called the safe house. "I think Kitty's ready. Don't be surprised if we show up in the next hour." Kitty had already met the woman who lived there, and seemed to like her. Now Flothe had to find out if she was really ready.

"If you go to this place you're gonna have to do as they tell you. You can't be leaving and coming and going and visiting your girlfriends in the street and all that bullshit."

"I know."

"Where's your stuff?"

"It's in the room."

When they walked out of the bathroom, the pimp was standing outside in a pair of jockey shorts. He looked angry. Kitty had been heading to the room, but froze as he spoke.

"What's you doin' witch my lady?" he said.

"We're with the Alaska State Troopers," Flothe told him. "She wants to go and she's coming with us. Period."

Flothe darted a glance at Kitty from the corner of his eye, as though to give permission for her to go into the room and find her clothes. The pimp looked worried, but he didn't want any hassle and let her pass.

When she reemerged from the room she had the bathrobe on and was clutching a blouse and some pants. She headed for the bathroom to put them on.

Having dressed quickly, Kitty rushed back to the bedroom to gather up a bunch of odds and ends, including a worn and tattered teddy bear. When she was ready to go she had most of her worldly possessions stacked in a cardboard box the size of a case of beer.

"What about my clothes?" she suddenly remembered.

"We don't have time for your clothes," Flothe said.

Kitty nevertheless hurried back into the room, after thrusting the box onto Flothe. When she came back out she was carrying some of her clothing and a few pieces of tacky costume jewelry. She slipped on her rabbit jacket, draped the clothes over one arm, and looking slightly scruffy, put her free arm around Flothe's waist as they walked out. She seemed proud of her police escort.

The pimp, meanwhile, watched implacably as

Kitty left. She never looked back. The troopers drove her straight to the safe house.

Later that same day Flothe decided to write a letter to Robyn Patterson, asking if she would be willing to come testify against Hansen. Even though she was married now, had gone to college and started a new life, a letter soon came back saying that she, too, was willing to testify against Robert Hansen. It had been more than twelve years. She was thirty, a different person. But yes, she would do anything she could to put this man in jail. It was where he belonged and, as far as she was concerned, had belonged for some time.

There was at least one irony about the safe house where Kitty Larson was staying. It wasn't that it was a Christian family taking in a prostitute. It wasn't that Flothe got her to go there only after an escape from a pimp. What was ironic was that this Christian family went to the same church as Darla Hansen.

Under this family's influence Kitty started to clean up her act. She called her parents and let them know her whereabouts. She stopped wearing the multiple layers of makeup, the eyeliner dark as night and just as thick. She helped make dinner, helped with vacuuming the house and the laundry. She started to become a real person again, at least as far as Flothe was concerned. She was even going to town and shopping with the family.

It was during this period that Frank Rothschild met with Kitty to discuss her testimony. Flothe was glad it hadn't taken place sooner. He could hardly imagine what Rothschild would have thought had he seen her fresh out of the topless club, or at her pimp's place on Government Hill. But now they had her off the street. She was skookum and ready to testify. This thing might work after all.

Hansen was cracking inside the confines of a cell—Gilmour was right. On Thursday, February 16, Flothe got a call from Frank Rothschild. "I want you to come down here and meet with us," he said. "Right now, if possible."

"What's it about?" Flothe asked, sensing an undercurrent of triumph in Rothschild's voice.

"Hansen's attorney just called. Hansen says he wants to 'clear the decks.' Those were Dewey's exact words. 'He wants to clear the decks.' "

"We'll be right down," Flothe answered.

All the way downtown Flothe kept repeating the refrain in his head. "He wants to clear the decks, he wants to clear the decks." The moment of truth had finally come.

23

The clearing of the decks was tentatively scheduled for Friday, February 18, 1984. The prosecution was concerned about where the interview took place. Rothschild suggested it be held in the DA's office, where recording equipment could be hidden from view. It seemed a good idea, considering how Hansen had reacted to the visible tape recorder during his October 1983 interview. Flothe did not protest.

In preparation for this all-important meeting, Flothe met with Frank Rothschild the day before. When Rothschild asked, "What if Hansen doesn't want to tell us everything we want to know?" Flothe repeated what Gilmour had suggested: "If he balks, just tell him that, come summer, we'll charge him with murder every time we dig up another body."

For his part Flothe was prepared to bring detailed sectional maps of the areas where Hansen's flight maps indicated there were bodies. That way Hansen could help them narrow down the sites where bodies were buried.

Rothschild, meanwhile, would start to work on some kind of an agreement between the various parties. The accord between counsel would finally consist not only of an agreement between the defense and prosecution concerning Robert C. Hansen, but a stipulation of Hansen's rights and an involved waiver of those rights—all in all, a long and somewhat unusual document for what was to be a long and somewhat unusual proceeding.

Even as Flothe and Rothschild met, however, they got a call from Hansen's attorney. Hansen wanted to postpone the interview until the following Monday. He wanted to think about things over the weekend. In the meantime Dewey's office said they'd worked up an "agreement of understanding," which Rothschild said should reflect Hansen's willingness to give a full statement and his fullest cooperation. The defense seemed amenable to that suggestion. What else could they do?

Fred Dewey and Joe Evans, Hansen's attorneys, had spent considerable time trying to get Hansen off on the charges lodged against him. They had called the charges ridiculous. They had even tried to defend him against murders for which he hadn't been charged, so much did they believe that he had been falsely accused. They'd done all this not just because they were expected to but because they trusted Bob Hansen. Now it was evident he'd been lying to them all along. Like so many before them, they'd been taken in by Hansen's heartless guile.

By Monday Hansen had decided to go ahead with the interview. It was another forty-eight hours before they would start. The interview, which they now knew would be confession, was set for the conference room of the DA's office. It was a room much like any other of its type, except for a long conference table with microphones poking up along its length. Still, an air of claustrophobic expectancy gripped the room as everyone waited for Hansen to arrive from jail. Today was the day they would learn the gory details of Hansen's deadly sport. No one really knew what to expect.

When Hansen arrived, the nervous chatter of last-minute planning came to a halt. Frank Rothschild, the man who had played such a forceful role in addressing the legal issues in this case, was the first to speak to the group.

"Are we on record?" Rothschild asked.

"Yes, we are," Flothe answered.

"This is Frank Rothschild. Sergeant, what time is it now?"

"Eight-fifty A.M.," Flothe responded.

"I'm here in the District Attorney Conference Room," the Assistant DA announced, "along with Mr. Robert Hansen, his counsel Joe Evans and Fred Dewey. Victor Krumm, the District Attorney, is present, along with Sergeants Haugsven and Flothe. The tape recorder is on, sir. We have it in the adjoining room, and Lieutenant Jent of the Alaska State Troopers is running the equipment and no one else. We have only law enforcement people in the accompanying room, and these microphones are picking up everything that is going on," Rothschild said, in effect letting Hansen know that the news media weren't going to get a direct line on his confession.

The first order of business was the signing of the Agreement of Understanding between counsel regarding Robert C. Hansen. Vic Krumm signed on behalf of the State of Alaska. Hansen's signature came next, and then those of his attorneys.

In the next few minutes Rothschild painstakingly went over the remaining documents, including a rights form and a waiver of rights. Each step along the way he made sure that Hansen understood what was happening and gave his assent to the agreements that had been worked out among counsel: There was a lot at stake. Each time Hansen said "Yes," in a nearly inaudible voice, and signed off on the documents. Rothschild quickly moved to settle another issue.

"There was one additional point that came up a bit ago, that we said we would straighten out here on the record before we began," he said. "That related to the timing of all of this as far as the court is concerned, and you . . . I'm told you would like to have this taken care of on Monday rather than the end of the week, which is certainly fine. And also you were concerned about the transport and the newspaper, or the press with their cameras being outside."

Rothschild's comments were directed at Hansen, and it was Hansen who answered them.

"Also the reason for that is, of course," Hansen said, "I want to minimize, if at all possible, exposure that my children are going to receive on this." In speaking at length for the first time, it was noticeable that his voice was tight and his phrases clipped.

"And, uh, I would like, if at all possible—and I don't care if I have to be brought in three hours earlier, or three to five hours after it's all done with—but I would like to, if at all possible, minimize being taken across the big parking lot with all the TV cameras and so forth, as my children will be exposed to this, and my main purpose, of course, behind the whole thing is to minimize, in any way possible, the hurts and so forth that this is going to bring upon my family.''

Rothschild, with Flothe's concurrence, quickly moved to assure Hansen both that special transportation arrangements would be made and that everything would be done to protect his family. He then asked the defense counsel if Hansen was giving his voluntary assent to these proceedings.

''I believe that he has,'' Joe Evans told him.

That's what Rothschild wanted to hear. It kept the appellate court at bay. And if he seemed to ask the same question more than twice, he had to be forgiven. He was protecting their effort. That done to his satisfaction, it was time to begin.

''Mr. Hansen,'' he said, ''I assume that you have been giving this a lot of thought, and rather than our asking you a lot of questions perhaps you would just like to start wherever it is most comfortable, whether that's at the beginning or elsewhere, and tell us what it is you are going to tell us.''

Rothschild's caution was obvious. And there was a reason for it: He wanted to make sure this was a voluntary interview, with no hint that they were putting words in Hansen's mouth.

Hansen, though, responded, ''I think it would almost be easier for me, sir—it's awful hard for me to talk about these things—if you would ask the question that you want to ask and then I'll try to answer it the best I can," Hansen said.

"All right," Rothschild answered. "Why don't we start then with what will be freshest in mind, which is the cases that are pending now and from what happened in June of last year. Can you tell us how that all came about?"

There was a considerable pause. Hansen seemed stumped. "Uh, you want me, sir, to start when I first met this Kitty Larson the first time, or—"

"Uh-huh," Rothschild said.

"Or what? Okay. I'm sorry I don't remember the right dates and so forth. I'm going to have to be a little bit vague on that."

"Would it have been during the time when your wife and children were out of—" Rothschild asked.

"Yes," Hansen said. "My wife and family were down in Arkansas visiting her folks' place and I met Kitty the first time uptown."

Lieutenant Jent, who was watching all this in the next room, noticed that Hansen appeared slumped and docile, like he wanted to get it over with. There were no gestures as he spoke. He was even-mannered and calm. The overall effect was eerie.

Hansen went on to reveal that he had first met Kitty near the 76 station at Fifth and Gambel. He was driving down the street when he saw her. He stopped, they chatted, she gave him her phone number. He called her to make a date but she couldn't meet him. Then one night, after modifying an airplane seat at John Sumrall's house, he started for home but ended up headed for town. He

decided to stop by his bakery to make sure the
lights were off and everything was closed down.

"I drove by the bakery," he went on. "I didn't
even stop in, just drove down the highway and I
seen its lights off and so forth. And that put me
downtown. Well, I thought, 'I'll drive downtown
and see what's going on.' I turned at the corner of
Ingra and turned west down Fifth there. And, uh,
Kitty Larson was standing on the sidewalk."

Hansen paused, then asked for a pencil and pad.
He started to draw a crude map to show the spot
where their paths had crossed that night. "And I
pulled in through the parking lot there," he said,
moving the pencil across the page, "and she walked
back to the car."

"She got in," he said, "and we discussed going
to my house and so forth. We drove to my home in
Muldoon and uh . . ." There was a pause, a gathering of his thoughts. "There we went down in my
basement, down into my den. . . ." Hansen took
a deep breath. "I turned on the television set and
so forth and we sat there on the couch for a little
while. I fondled her a little bit. We sat there and
discussed—oh, we didn't discuss much, really—just
talked a little bit. Chitchat. And then, of course,
she was saying that she had to get back."

"I told her, 'No, I would like to stay down here
in the basement,' " Hansen continued almost non-
chalantly. "I told her that I would like to do it a
little bit different. I would like to have sex with her
on a large bear rug that I had there, uh, not a large
one, just a normal black bear rug I had there on
the floor and so forth. And that I would like to,

while I was having sex with her, put a pair of hand-cuffs on her. And, uh, she said no, she said she didn't object to where we had sex and so forth, but not in handcuffs. And at that time I guess I showed her a firearm and told her that she had to put them on."

"That's the first time," Hansen insisted. "I know she stated that I forced her in the car and so forth—that's not true. The first time there was any force used was in my home. It is true I had sex with her there on the bear rug and so forth in my home. And it is also true, which she said, about after the sex act there, uh, I took her back to—my basement is kind of divided into two sections—I took her over and I had her lay down on the couch and then I sat down on my couch, then she got up. I said, 'No, no, no, I want you to stay where you're at.' And there is some pillars in my basement. I had an eyebolt stuck into the pillar. Well, anyway, when Kitty moved around I slid the couch over by that eyebolt there. I went out in the garage there, and got a length of chain and put her to that eyebolt so she couldn't move."

Hansen sped on into his interview, moving to a discussion of what he had done after Kitty got away from him. What worried him, he said, was the fact that she was still in handcuffs. That might arouse suspicion and get the police involved. So he went directly home and cleaned house—removing the eyebolt from the pillar and puttying the hole, toss-ing the revolver into the false ceiling of his base-ment. Then he went to the bakery and called John Henning.

"It was me that approached John," Hansen said. "It wasn't John who approached me on that."

After meeting with Henning, Hansen said he drove home, where the police were waiting for him. They asked to search his car, plane, and house. Hansen knew it was a risk but agreed. There were a couple of close calls.

While the police were in his basement, one of the officers lifted up the panels in the ceiling to look for hidden evidence. "He spot-checked two or three places," Hansen said, "and he lifted up the ones on both sides of the one where I had the pistol laying. I doggone near died of a heart attack right there." The officer didn't find the pistol.

Out in the garage there was another close call, when the officers almost found the chain and the eyebolt he'd used to restrain Kitty in his basement. "I don't think I could swallow if I had to," Hansen said, but again he got away with it.

After allowing him to drive his own car to the airport, the police made a thorough search of his plane. "They were satisfied there was nothing in the airplane," he said, "so they went their way and allowed me to go . . . go, uh, mine."

Hansen again called his friend John Henning, who came by Hansen's place and drove him around while he ran some errands. Later Hansen called Teamster Legal Services and was assigned Fred Dewey, the lawyer who still represented him. It almost sounded like Hansen knew exactly what he was doing.

As the interview wore on and the questions kept

coming, a problem developed. Hansen still hadn't said word one about murder.

Instead he was striving to make everything seem so innocent. He even revealed that he'd taken some dancers into the bush and brought them back alive. But what about the other women who obviously hadn't survived? Why had their fate been so different? If no one else was going to ask, Flothe decided, he would. He waded right into Hansen's morass of evasions.

"What made you decide not to bring some of them back?" he asked, his voice trailing off gently. "What happened?"

"Well, uh . . ." Hansen said, hesitating. "Once out there, there was no need for any restraints or really anything else, any firearms or anything." There was another pause, and then a mumble. "They would take off and want to leave, you know," he said.

"Girls would take off and want to leave?" Vic Krumm asked. "Or you would take off and want to leave?"

"They would want to take off and leave, okay?" Hansen replied. "Uh, twice they got their hands on firearms that I had with me and I came pretty damn close to getting shot. There was no hurt created, if you want to call it that, as long as they didn't panic on me. As long as she would go along with what I wanted out there, okay, I would let her go home and that was it."

"And if they didn't?" Flothe asked.

"They . . . they stayed." It was the first cold-blooded statement of the morning, and there was a brief pause while everyone caught a breath. Vic Krumm was the first to fill the silence.

"What do you mean when you say, 'hurt created'?"

"Uh, okay, uh . . ." Hansen became contemplative and looked down at the table rather than face the eyes. "I'm sorry," he offered. "This is hard for me to talk about."

"Go ahead," Flothe suggested with the patience of a man who's already waited a long time. "Just take your time."

"Uh . . ."

"Can we talk about an incident in particular? I think that's a good way to start. Let's talk about the two that we have already found. What happened there?" Flothe asked. "Just tell us in your own words what happened."

"Well, in both cases—I don't know. The one—I made the mistake. Now if I completely controlled the situation, there was never any problem. I can come home with the person and that was the end of it. But if I didn't control the situation—they'd either try to do something to get the firearm or just plain take off and try to leave—and then it would become a deal. The first one that was found, I brought her back twice."

"What's her name?" Flothe asked.

"I'm sorry, gentlemen. I know you're going to ask me some names, and I can't put names on them."

"Describe where she worked and what she did," Flothe suggested, every bit the cop.

"Well, she was a dancer out at the Good Times.

Or that—yes, that's the one I'm referring to, gentlemen, is the first one that was found. You know which one that is,'' Hansen said, suddenly coy. "Well, I won't say I know, but I'm pretty sure she was the one that come from the Good Times out on Dimond. Am I right on that? Help me out.''

"Well, just describe—'' Flothe began to suggest, and then shifted gears in mid-sentence. "Maybe we can do this another way. How many girls have you not brought back since you came to Alaska? And let's start with the first one. If we're going to clear this up we're going to have to start somewhere, and I think that's a good place to start. And you know which one it is,'' Flothe said, throwing the ball back into Hansen's court.

There was a long silence, during which Flothe gave Hansen a look of fatherly patience. "You have all the time you need,'' he finally announced.

There was another long pause while Hansen gathered his thoughts. His eyes wandered through the room. He looked about to speak, then didn't. "Gentlemen, I'm trying to get them in the right sequence.''

"Bob, maybe I can help you,'' Lyle Haugsven said. "The first girl that was found was from the Wild Cherry.''

"I'm talking—I'm talking earlier than that,'' Flothe said.

"Yeah, I know,'' Haugsven replied.

"I'm talking back in the early seventies in Seward. Can we start with those and work up to the present, or would you rather start in the present and work back?'' Again there was a pause while Hansen contemplated his answer. Flothe, for his part, was curious as to what Hansen might have to say about the disappearance of young women into the glacial waters off Seward. Apparently Hansen wasn't taking the bait.

"Seward was not the start," he said.

"Where was the start, Bob?" Flothe immediately wanted to know.

"The start was the body that you found on the Eklutna power line."

That would have been "Eklutna Annie," whose badly decomposed body had been found near Lake Eklutna on July 17, 1980, by power line workers. She probably had been murdered in the summer of 1979. Flothe had difficulty believing that she was the first one, but let Hansen continue. They'd get the whole truth soon enough.

"I can't remember anything about her," Hansen said. "I'm sorry, I wish I could. I can remember one thing—I think she said she either lived or her folks lived in Kodiak. That's the only thing I can say for sure about her."

"Describe to me what happened. Where did you pick her up, where did you go, what did you do, and where did you subsequently leave her? We have lots of time. And we're going to have to take the time or else we can't clear these up," Flothe said, sounding more stern now.

"Yeah, okay," Hansen responded, impatient.

"So take your time," Flothe said.

"I'll try anyway, you know. . . . Gentlemen, I don't want to give the impression I'm trying to hedge on something," Hansen said. "I'm not. If you have stuff down on records that I can't keep in my head, you know. Uh, the first gal is a gal that I think was found by some power line employees, or something to this effect, they found up here by Eklutna.''

"How was she killed?'' Flothe wanted to know.

"By knife,'' Hansen said in a near inaudible whisper.

He started to draw a crude map, showing the trailer park and a restaurant at the turnoff. And then he drew the turn that went to the power line, near a spring or seep where Hansen wanted to park the truck because he had a bear stand nearby. But then things started to go badly.

"As I come around this here seep here, I got the damn thing stuck. And I come along with a bunch of ropes and so forth in the back of my pickup and I was going to try and pull the truck back up. I broke the rope two or three times there. There was no traction at all going backwards, so I had to come along the whole weight of the truck back up. And she was still sitting in the cab. She wasn't restrained in any way, shape, or form. I said, 'Hey, as soon as we get this damn thing unstuck, I've lost interest in this-here. We're going back home.' I can remember thinking to myself, Hey now, this is not the way I'm supposed to be doing this.

"Anyway, I got us going up the hill like that, with her helping me. The ground was getting a little firmer there and I thought I could back up just with the power of the truck then. As I was getting in and running the truck, instead of her sliding over I told her, 'Get out and I'll try and back it up so we can get the hell out of here.' She started running down the road. She didn't go back toward the highway or back toward the gravel road, she went the way that the truck was facing.''

"Toward the power lines?'' Frank Rothschild asked.

"Right. And I remember I slammed the thing in gear and shut off the key and ran after her. She was running down the road. . . . I caught up with her. We stopped and—matter of fact I grabbed her by the hair. Anyway, I grabbed her and she had a big knife in her purse. If I remember right it was a big black-handled buck knife. And she grabbed that out of her purse and swung around and I . . . I grabbed her hands and I tripped her down. She fell down and she started screaming at me, 'Don't kill me, don't kill me!' I said 'I'm not going to kill you.' I said we was on the way home. And she kept on yelling, 'No, no, you're going to kill me!' and so forth and, uh, then things just got all out of hand. I can remember she was laying facedown and, uh, I just stuck her.''

"Where?'' Frank Rothschild asked.

"In the back . . .''

"Did you leave her clothes on or take her clothes off?''

"She never had her clothes off. I never had sex with her.''

Then he started making personal revelations in an attempt to explain himself. He talked about his stuttering, his pimples, his anger at being the butt of all the jokes at school, especially among the girls.

"I didn't start to hate all women. As a matter of fact I would venture to say I started to fall in love with every one of them. Every one of them become so precious to me 'cause I wanted their friendship. I wanted them to like me so much.

"On top of the things that have happened, I'm not saying that I hate all women. I don't. Quite to the contrary. I guess in my own mind what I'm classifying is a good woman, not a prostitute. I'd do everything in my power, any way, shape, or form, to do anything for her and to see that no harm ever came to her.

"But I guess prostitutes are women I'm putting down as lower than myself. I don't know if I'm making sense or not. And you know, when this started to happen—when it happened the first time at Eklutna I went home and was literally sick to my stomach. As a matter of fact I was sick out there to my stomach. I can remember I sat and cried. I knew what I did was totally, totally wrong. It had come so close to happening before with Robyn Patterson. . . . "

"The daughter of the trooper?" Frank Rothschild asked.

"Right. There were other girls there, ah, it come so close to happening, but it hadn't."

"Because they hadn't tried to run?" Vic Krumm asked.

"Right. As long as they didn't run away, things went as I controlled it. I guess I wanted to control things. It made me feel masculine or powerful or in control of my life. And as long as things went fine, you know, that was it. But this time it went too far. My gosh, I can remember I never even drove downtown, I think, for six months. I can remember driving downtown and seeing a prostitute down there and my gosh, my whole body just tightened up. I didn't even want to go close to one.''

In almost the same breath, however, Hansen proceeded to describe how he played a game with the topless dancers. ''They had to pitch the ball before I could bat,'' he said. ''They had to approach me first, saying we could go out and have a good time or something like that. If they didn't say that, we weren't playing the game right.''

''Can you tell us when you started meeting women like this?'' Frank Rothschild asked. ''We know that Robyn Patterson was 1971. Had you been doing that for a number of years before then?''

''No,'' Hansen replied. ''That's just about when it started. . . . ''

What was interesting about that last revelation, of course, was that it led them dangerously close to the death of Melanie Michaels, who had frozen to death at McHugh Creek State Park just the week after Hansen had kidnapped and raped Robyn Patterson. It was still an unsolved case. Would it now become part of Hansen's confession?

As lunch approached, there were other revelations. ''The one thing that kept Bob Hansen in check at all was my wife,'' he told them, which explained why many of these incidents had occurred when his wife was out of town. Before long, however, he was rambling on about other things, following only his own logic.

''I have a thing about taking things,'' he told

them, "cause I just loved to see if I could get by with it. My gosh, I damn near ejaculate in my pants if I could walk into a store and take something and get out the dang door with it and not pay for it." He told an affecting story about how he had stolen baseball equipment for a softball team back when he lived in Minneapolis because it made him "a good guy." Soon he turned to his stealing escapades in Anchorage. "Hell," he bragged, "I stole more stuff in this damn town than Carter got little green pills."

Hansen then abruptly returned to the subject of Eklutna Annie. He started off by saying that, prior to this incident, things always had gone as planned. He brought them back alive.

"This time it didn't go right," he revealed. "And the sad part about it, you know, I found myself after a period of time back uptown looking again—like a moth that's drawn to a fire—I'm back again. It scared me, you know. I got to thinking, 'Oh my God, this can't go on anymore. What if it goes wrong again? I need help.' God, I've wanted help so damn much in my life," he said, looking around at every face in the room.

"But who do I go to for help?" he asked, his eyes tightening. "I sure in hell can't go in to somebody and tell them I killed somebody. I don't want to spend the rest of my life in jail any more than anybody else. I don't want to go back to jail again. I've been there. And who do I talk to?

"Well, there's an old saying," Hansen went on. "You can go talk to a minister and it's supposed to stay between him—and gentlemen, I don't know how many churches in this town—I've walked around the block 'til I damn near wore out the damn sidewalk. Twice I went as far—I don't know why I picked that-there church—as that big church right downtown here—I guess because it was the biggest one. And I thought, my God, there's got to be somebody here who can help. I went as far as walking in, and it's a Catholic church. I'm not a Catholic, but they got confession. I see all the time in the movies and everything where the guy don't even look at you. That was the guy I was going to talk to, but I got as far twice, even up the goddamn steps, and turned around. 'No, no, Bob, you can't do this now. Goddamn, now, you can't talk to him.'

"You can't go talk to a doctor. Boy, a psychiatrist was about the first no-no on the damn block. And how the hell do I talk to a friend about something like this? I can't talk to my wife about it. The one person I should be able to sit down and discuss anything with . . . but how in the hell do you tell your wife that you're going out, having sex fantasies and having sex with another woman, and worse than anything else, you killed one of them?

"Where in the hell do I go, you know? Ah, the judge in his wisdom stated when I first got in trouble that I was supposed to have psychiatric help the first time back there. Boy, you know, I would have. I knew I had a problem way back then. And doggone, way back in Iowa the judge said that I was supposed to have some help, and of course that never happened. That was a farce. The only one I ever talked to was before I got sentenced, not after.

"The only thing that happened was that I was

sitting there knowing—it's rough, gentlemen, to set so close to somebody that can help you, but knowing that you can't ask for help, because if you ask for the help, goddammit, you're going to get in more trouble. You know, this would be aside from this-here, but in the future, to keep someone else from sitting where I'm sitting right now, and what happened, have in mind—goddammit, leave the doctors alone," he said, his voice now becoming more strident.

"Really. Let them help somebody. Don't put restrictions on them. If I had had help back then, the first time, I probably wouldn't be here, and there would probably be some people alive today. Now I'm not putting all the blame on—I'm putting the blame on me, because I'm the one that went and done it."

"Do you want to break for a minute?" Vic Krumm asked.

"Could we stop for just a few minutes?" Fred Dewey replied.

After a short discussion Flothe said for the tape recorder, "The time now is 11:59. We'll take a break for lunch."

After they took a short break and ordered out for food, they went back to the interview while they waited for the food to arrive. Frank Rothschild continued by asking Hansen to "go to the next time you can remember when things didn't go as planned."

"All right," he said. "That was up on the Knik River, the first one you found up there."

That would have been Sherry Morrow, the topless dancer they had found with an Ace bandage around her head, buried in a shallow grave that made it look like she'd been executed. The woman whose gold arrowhead necklace had been found at Hansen's house.

"How did that all happen?" Rothschild asked him.

As Hansen related the story, he said he had probably picked her up in one of the downtown bars where she was a topless dancer. "There again, like so many others before her, if things hadn't gone wrong it would never have happened."

"What went wrong?" Rothschild asked.

"A combination of a few things. My stupidity, for one. I guess I was deceived too much in going out there. I got too relaxed. It's quite a drive out there."

Hansen hadn't used a plane at all but had driven Sherry there in his old brown Subaru, showed her a gun, and told her he'd bring her back that evening if things went exactly as he wanted them to. His plan was to take her to a lean-to in a remote spot along the Knik, which was accessible by a pitiful excuse for a road that dipped and twisted through stands of birch and degenerated into nasty mud holes along its length.

"The only thing is," Hansen revealed, "I got stuck before I got there and then all of a sudden she turned around—trying to scratch me in the eyes and fight and so forth—and it just went from bad to worse."

"Did she try to run, or was it just because she was fighting with you?" Rothschild asked.

"Well, she fought with me and she started running and I caught her again and I can't even remember how it happened, but somehow or other—I know I was sitting on my ass and she was just standing there screaming at me—and I just pointed my gun up toward her and pulled the trigger."

"Do you remember anything about what she looked like?" Rothschild asked. "Her size? Her hair? Was she bound in any way at this point? You said she was scratching you, which almost makes it seem like she wasn't bound. Do you remember that, anything about her?"

"Ah, going out there," Hansen said without pause, "I did not want her to see where she was going and so forth. I had a bandage around her head, an Ace bandage, so she couldn't see, and she was tied. I can't remember when I got out of the car. I know when it was all over I had bruises on my legs, one cut I think was from her kicking me. Whether she had her hands tied or not I can't tell you for sure."

"Do you remember an unusual necklace that she had?" Flothe asked, joining in. There was a pause, and Hansen looked at him inquiringly. "You're a bow-hunter," Flothe said.

"If you're referring to that fish necklace—or what . . . ?"

There was a chorus of no's. "The gold arrowhead necklace," Flothe said.

"Arrowhead necklace, whatever it was," Hansen said with a shrug. "Boy, you know . . ."

This time the pause was much longer. Hansen seemed to be searching every drawer of his memory. The cops and prosecutors gave each other quick glances, trying to see if anyone was going to jump in, but knowing everyone would wait until Hansen spoke.

"If . . ." Hansen started haltingly. "I can't tell you," he finally said. "I really can't. I know the first gal there on Eklutna Lake, or road, ah, I didn't take nothing there. Of course the first time it happened I was so damn panicked."

He looked around the room. "I know you gentlemen took, or found in my attic, a bag of jewelry." Suddenly someone outside the room let out a jolly laugh, then another, which served as bizarre counterpoint to what Hansen was saying. It seemed to distract him and he lost his train of thought completely.

"I know there's been at least three times I've taken some piece of jewelry from someone I've brought back for momentum [*sic*]. I took something off her, don't ask me why I took that or why I took something from any one of them. . . .

"I suppose I could have grabbed her and pulled her someplace. As a matter of fact I can even remember dropping the weapon there, and I ran back to the car and there in the truck was that little shovel—those little shovels, they're not a straight shovel, you can turn the handle so it goes down and tighten it up so you can dig like a hoe, you know. I was there digging like a mad fool, looking, hoping that there was nobody coming. And I just got her in below the ground and scooped stuff back on top of her and left. I never went back again."

"So where's the next spot?" Rothschild asked,

slightly perturbed. He'd caught the looks from Flothe and Haugsven, telling him Hansen had lied about not going back to the site of Sherry Morrow's murder: Paula Goulding's body had been found at the same spot less than a year later.

"That's below the railroad bridge near the new highway bridge across the Knik River. That one there was in the wintertime."

"Do you have a map that shows where the new one crosses?" Flothe asked. There was some fumbling around for maps and a brief lull in the questioning. Vic Krumm soon took up the slack.

"I want to ask you a question," he said to Hansen, "while we're getting this squared away for you. The Ace bandage that you had in the car, was that part of the plan ahead of time?"

"Yeah," Hansen replied almost cavalierly. "So she couldn't find her way back later on. I knew I was going back to that spot. It worked well. It went well for me before."

"Was it around her eyes?" Krumm asked. "If I understand what you're talking about?"

"Wrapped around her head like a turban, or around her face . . ."

"The pattern that you used with Kitty Larson— underneath a blanket, and that type of thing—is that the same kind of pattern that you developed over the course of time?" Krumm asked.

"No, it was far better if they sat in the front seat, sat on their knees facing the seat, that way they could be no problem at all."

With the maps in front of him Hansen pointed to the spot where he'd parked his car on a service road. He'd fondled the woman's breasts, and she had performed oral sex. Then she'd told him she wanted to go to the bathroom. He let her out then followed her, taking a gun with him.

The woman walked off a ways and, hearing her start to relieve herself, Hansen decided he would do the same. He put the gun on the hood of the car, walked off a few steps, and began to urinate. Then he heard the sound of footsteps on the gravel and turned just in time to see her reaching for the gun. He lunged for her, trying to get the gun away, trying to twist it out of her hand.

Finally he got the gun by the barrel and slammed it on the hood of the car. The gun fell away and Hansen pushed the woman to the front of the car. She came at him like a mother bear protecting her cubs, poking her fingers in his eyes. "I just picked up the gun again and shot her," he said.

"What did you do with her?" Frank Rothschild asked. "Did you bury her out there?"

"No. I carried her down the railroad tracks and she went in the river."

Everyone else in the room perked up: This was a murder of which the troopers had been unaware. But Hansen could remember little else. He didn't know if he took some of her jewelry, though he thought it was possible she was the one with the "fish necklace." He didn't know her name. He didn't know the time of year—it could have been late fall or early spring—but remembered that it was very cold.

"Was she a very big-breasted girl?" Haugsven asked.

"Very."

"And she had just been to Alaska a very short period of time?" Haugsven asked, looking for clues to the woman's identity.

"That I don't know," Hansen replied.

After a few more questions, Rothschild asked him if he was trying to teach these young women a lesson. It was like lobbing him a fat pitch: "I never had one of them that didn't say, 'Well, I've learned my lesson, this is the last time I'm going to do this. I'm just gonna dance and keep it straight from now on.' "

Vic Krumm asked Hansen if he took the money back after he killed his victims. "Oh, yeah," he said, "I'm too damn tight to let it lay."

Hansen also volunteered that he pretended to be from out of town when he met these women, and always arranged to meet them in a public place. In addition, although he was temporarily terrorized by his murders, after a while he ventured out onto the strip again, tentatively at first, just to see if anyone noticed. Soon he was back to thinking aloud about all the times when everything had gone well. The good times.

The troopers' hunch that Hansen had killed more women than they'd found had just been confirmed. They now knew there were at least five dead: He'd given them three already, and there were another two whom they'd also found. But all of a sudden Hansen launched into a whole new episode of murder.

"There was only one other time it went bad," Hansen claimed, "and that's down by Seward.

Maybe she was desperate. That one, I've had an awful lot of second thoughts about.''

Flothe and Haugsven knew at once that Hansen was talking about the ''Bear Lady.'' They'd already matched the spot where her body had been found with a mark on Hansen's map. They also knew that he'd conveniently forgotten to mention Paula Goulding, the woman whose body had been found not far from Sherry Morrow's. But they didn't point out the discrepancy. They were giving him rope.

According to Hansen he had met Joanna Messina on the docks in Seward. Their conversation was pleasant and Bob started to think she liked him. They went to dinner, and Joanna revealed that she was camped in a tent at the state campground and looking for work in the Seward cannery. Bob got to thinking he could talk her into spending the night with him in his camper.

''While I was sitting there talking she just came right out and said, 'I haven't even got money to get back. I'm up here camped. I haven't got a job. We could have a real nice time if you have any money.' And it just went from day to night. She was a prostitute, or she propositioned me anyway.''

''What did you decide to do when you realized she was coming on to you?'' Vic Krumm asked.

''Ah, I just said, 'Gee whiz, I got my pickup and camper out here, let's go.' ''

Hansen parked the camper at a remote spot and the two of them walked down to a nearby river. There Joanna propositioned him again. This time Bob got mad and stormed back to his camper. Joanna followed him, but when she got in Bob started to drive off. This time it was Joanna's turn to get mad. She accused him of getting her out there under false pretenses and started to scream at him.

"So I stopped the pickup and I said, 'Okay, come out, let's get in back then.' We got in back and I told her, 'Hey now, you fucking bitch, this is as far as it's going as far as the goddamn money goes. Here, this is all you're worth,' and I think it was something like five dollars or something like that I fucking threw in her face. Plus I said, 'That's all you're going to get, and if you don't like it that's too damn bad.' I told her she was a goddamn whore. That started the fight." They ended up outside the camper and, as Hansen put it, "That was it."

Again came the questions. Did she have any pets? "Yes, she had a dog." What happened to the dog? "I shot the dog." Did she tell you her name? "She probably did, of course, but as far as remembering, I can't." Did she tell you where she was from? "The only thing that I can remember, I think she said she was taking some nurse's training. Or something to do with medicine—dental assistant or nurse's training or something."

There was no question now that Hansen was talking about Joanna Messina. Everything corresponded: the dog, the nurse's training, the camping gear.

Pursuing another line of inquiry, Rothschild wanted to know if Hansen got the same rush from the women as he did when he stole something. "Well, there was a feeling when things were going right, there was a great sexual surge, but not the same feeling as when I was stealing something out of a store.''

Soon Bob was bragging about stealing guns and how it was harder to get the long guns. Next they showed him more maps, but nothing was gained from it. Finally someone came to the door of the conference room.

''Bob, the food is here, if you want to take a break,'' Haugsven announced.

''Sure could stand some,'' he replied.

''Yeah,'' Haugsven said, almost laconically. ''It's, ah, 2:03 right now, according to my watch.''

''We'll go ahead and discontinue the taping,'' Flothe said, looking in the direction of Lt. Jent.

''I talk—talked that much?'' Hansen said, incredulously.

''Time goes by, doesn't it?'' Vic Krumm said. The tape had finally stopped rolling for the day. During lunch, Hansen told them he was too tired to go on.

If anyone had thought that Hansen was going to give a straightforward confession, they had been sadly disabused of that notion. They had come to that vexing axiom: If a subject is lying but not lying all the time, everything he says is untrue, since there is no reliable way to tell when the person is lying and when he's telling the truth. To challenge Hansen they were going to have to find a way to attack the known, or strongly suspected, weaknesses in his story. That had to start, it seemed, with a full accounting of the number of victims.

24

On the second day of Hansen's confession, Frank Rothschild wasted little time. He had Hansen sign another waiver of his rights. He recapitulated the final minutes of the previous day's confession. Then came the pointed question.

"I'm wondering," Rothschild said, "if we can just go on, Mr. Hansen, with your describing some of these other times when things didn't go as you had planned and hoped with some of these prostitutes and dancers in town?"

"I'm sorry, sir," Hansen replied, "I don't quite understand what you're saying."

"All right," Rothschild said. "It seems that from what you've told us that you basically had an idea of picking up prostitutes and dancers in town and offering to pay them money. You pretty much had it planned out in your mind that you didn't want to harm anybody, but there were just times when things didn't go according to plan. You've told us about a few of those," Rothschild said patiently, "and I'm wondering about others."

"There is no others, sir, that didn't go right. Five times it didn't, but—"

Hansen stopped, realizing his mistake. He had mentioned only four the day before. Rothschild started to count them off, with Hansen's help. It took a fair amount of time to do so. Hansen kept stalling, taking them off the track into details.

"You mentioned when we started off that there were five times. What would be the fifth?" Rothschild asked.

Hansen seemed confused, and his eyes narrowed. He was obsessed with getting everything in the right order.

"Let's see, the first one was—up there—I'm really sorry, I'm really confused here. Okay, at the power line, first time, sir. Then we went out to the flats out there, where I'd been once before. There's one in there down the Knik River further, in between the second body that was found, ah, I guess would be the third. I don't know the sequence."

"Another somewhere on the Knik?" Rothschild asked.

"It's on the Knik River. Yes, sir."

"Well," Rothschild said, "we didn't talk about that yesterday. Why don't you tell us about that?"

"Yes, sir, we did," Hansen insisted. "It was— how do I explain it?"

"Would you like a map?"

"Yes, sir."

Flothe was the keeper of the maps, and unrolled one for the area where Paula Goulding's body had been found. Knowing that the spot was almost inaccessible, Rothschild asked a loaded question.

"Did you drive in there as well?" Rothschild wanted to know.

"No, sir."

"How did you get there?"

"We flew."

"So this was after you bought your airplane?" Rothschild asked.

"Yes, sir."

"What year did you buy your airplane?" Rothschild asked.

"I've only had this plane here about, ah . . . '82?"

And then they started talking about Paula Goulding. He even gave them a sample of his standard speech.

"I pull out the gun—I think the standard speech was, 'Look, you're a professional. You don't get excited, you know there is some risk to what you've been doing. If you do exactly what I tell you you're not going to get hurt. You're just going to count this off as a bad experience and be a little more careful next time who you are gonna proposition or go out with,' you know.

"I tried to act as tough as I could, to get them as scared as possible. Give that right away, even before I started talking at all. Reach over, you know, and hold that head back and put a gun in her face and get 'em to feel helpless, scared, right there. Then tell them to turn around and face the seat on their knees on the floorboard. That way they were down, they wouldn't start anything there. I'm sure—maybe it's not the same procedure for you—you always try to get control of the situation, so some things don't start going bad."

"Sounds like you had a good way to work it," Flothe commented.

"Maybe I've seen some cop shows on TV, I don't know, okay?" Hansen said, snickering slightly.

What Flothe was most curious about at this point was how Hansen had controlled these women when he had them in his plane. Hansen said he handcuffed them—and once he was off the ground, he didn't care if they screamed or what they did.

"You weren't nervous they were behind you?" Flothe asked.

"Well, I'm not saying I wasn't concerned about it, but it was, I thought, a hell of a lot safer than in the car. But I only used the airplane three times," Hansen explained, trying to end their confusion. "Probably the girl was more scared of being in the airplane than she was scared of me, I don't know."

"Scared of being in the airplane," Flothe said. "You mention that this area was pretty populated, but in the wintertime with skis you were somewhat unlimited as to where you could go. Your privacy was pretty much up to you. Or were you concerned about flying a long time? You mention three girls but I'm just wondering, with skis, you know, in the winter, you could go just about anywhere."

"I could," Hansen responded, "but wintertime wasn't the time to do it. Things were dormant in the wintertime. This was a summertime project. . . ."

In that instant they all saw the cold-blooded cruelty of the man. Yet Hansen passed off this casual utterance without a further thought, and spent the next half hour talking about anything he could think of as long as it wasn't the murder of Paula Goulding. At 10:30 Frank Rothschild called a break.

It was 11:00 before they got started again, and Hansen used the opportunity to deny that he had ever thrown any of the victims out of the plane. It wasn't until 11:30 that Hansen started talking about the Goulding murder in any detail, and then only obliquely.

Even though Hansen didn't know her by name, Flothe was fairly certain that Hansen was describing the Goulding murder. In the manner of investigators everywhere, Flothe tried to get Hansen to reveal something he could have known only by being there.

"I'm curious about one thing," he said. "This last girl that you talked about, where you had problems out there in the sandbar and the airplane flying over—that girl—what happened to her shirt or sweater or her garment? There was something unusual there that we saw that we're looking for an explanation for."

"Well, I know the last time I caught her, ah, I caught her by the back of her shirt and I know it ripped at least partway off. Then when I ripped it back down, she halfway stumbled to her knee, and then that's when she seen I had the rifle in my hand and she kept going on about that—'You're going to shoot me, you're going to kill me'—and I said, 'No, I'm not. I'm sorry I tore off your clothes.' It was hanging half off her shoulders and so forth. Then she started struggling again some more. I don't know if it got ripped more off during the struggle or—I know I lost some buttons in the confrontation there—I know her clothes were ripped, but they should have been on her.''

"That's what I was looking for,'' Flothe answered.

For the next hour Hansen dragged them through minutiae. He admitted being careless with his brass out at the murder sites, but said he was very careful where he met these women for their "dates.'' He always met them at public places like Wendy's, because he wanted to make sure they were coming alone. He wanted to make absolutely certain no one saw them together. He said he backed off if there was even the slightest risk of that occurring.

He also said he told the women different stories—on different occasions he was a doctor or lawyer or photographer—but he wore ordinary clothes so he would blend in with everyone else. He had turned to disguises, he said, because he was starting to get scared that someone would recognize him in one of the clubs. In fact Hansen talked about anything and everything except the other murders the troopers and the DA were certain he'd committed.

At 12:41 they took a break for lunch. At that point Hansen had still talked about only five of his murders. In four hours he'd added only one to the previous day's list. How much longer could this go on?

After lunch Vic Krumm started to hammer away.

"You told us a number of things yesterday,'' Krumm said, "that we know are not totally accurate, and we don't believe you've been totally candid. So far it's my impression that you've given us only the evidence on the two victims that we know for a fact are alive and willing to come forward and testify, as well as the five victims that we found.''

Krumm was mostly right: Hansen had talked about Kitty Larson and the black topless dancer, both living witnesses who had agreed to testify, and he had also talked about five murder victims, though troopers had found only four of them. It was a trivial detail, however, given the fact that Krumm was about to hit home with his real message.

''You told us yesterday that there were some bad times but that there were twenty-one good times, and that those twenty-one good times correlated to your flight chart. We have looked at your flight chart, and one of the things that Mr. Rothschild's been doing the last couple of days, in his inquiry of you, is asking you to explain whether or not the five places that you went . . . if they were all bad times, or if there were good times coupled with bad times. And on a number of those places you described to him that there were only bad times. Never any good times coupled with them. Your flight charts have the twenty-one little asterisks on them, including the five places where we found bodies that you've talked about, leading us to conclude that there may well be twenty-one girls out there.''

Hansen was beginning to twist nervously in his seat. So were his lawyers. What was the point of Krumm's speech?

"Now where we sit is this," Krumm told the gathering. "We are prepared, and will in fact go into court, as we indicated we would, on Monday, avoiding the publicity for you. But come springtime we're not going to let this sit. We're going to go out there and we're going to be looking for sixteen more graves. We're going to show you the flight charts this afternoon, and we're going to ask you if, in fact, there are bodies at one or more of those asterisks. To the extent that you tell us that there is a body there, we would like to, you know, pinpoint a little more closely where those are, so that we don't have to spend an inordinate amount of man-power looking for it.

"On the other hand," Krumm said, "if you tell us today that a certain asterisk does not have a body assigned, we're still going to look for that body. If we find that body we're going to charge you with murder, and every body we find we're going to charge you with murder. We won't be able to do that until summertime but we're going to do that. Now, you're the only one that knows how many people you killed." Krumm paused only briefly, letting the message seep in. He was about to make Hansen an offer he couldn't refuse.

"If you want to cooperate and get this out of the way," Krumm said, "I am prepared to simply charge you with the crimes you have now admitted to. We're going to show you pictures; we're going to talk to you about burglaries; and again, what I'm trying to do at this point is simply find out from you what you did and what you didn't do. If you didn't do it you simply have to tell me, because then we'll keep looking for somebody else. But if you did do it it's in your best interest to tell us, because this will close it out as far as we're concerned. I don't want you to confess to things you didn't do. That's the one thing you must not do, is confess to things you didn't do. Do you understand where we're coming from on this?''

"I think so,'' Hansen said after a pause, his voice choked, his whole being chastened. A look of panic had settled on his face. "I understand what you're saying, sir.'' He stole a glance at his attorneys. "But there's one more thing that you just mentioned there that I want to talk to these gentlemen about here.''

"That's fine,'' Krumm said.

"That's fine,'' Joe Evans said. "Let's go across the way here.''

Hansen's panic had spread. Hansen's attorneys didn't know what the hell was going on, and they looked betrayed. When they got to the meeting room across the hall Hansen's counselors could be heard yelling at him. It sounded like a dogfight. Hansen yelled right back. It was a while before calmer voices prevailed.

Eventually Joe Evans emerged from the conference room and held a huddle with Vic Krumm and Frank Rothschild before returning to his client. Soon Hansen reemerged. He was ready to talk. He understood the terms of the agreement. He was ready to clear things up, once and for all.

There was no question now that the hardest part was going to be locating the bodies. Hansen's maps encompassed hundreds of square miles of the Alaskan bush. And the maps weren't detailed, either. They were flight maps, not detailed sectionals.

The plan, therefore, was for Hansen to start with his flight maps and then go to the detailed sectionals for greater precision. If that didn't work, they had aerial photographs as backup. And if that didn't work they could fly him to the Knik River area, where most of the marks were concentrated, and have him point out the spots on the ground.

"Are we on record?" Vic Krumm asked as the group readied itself for the next phase of its ordeal.

"We're on record," Haugsven reported.

"The time now is 2:24 P.M." Flothe said.

"All right," Krumm announced. "Mr. Hansen, we're at the point where we'd like to show you the first item, which is a flight chart. Frank, could you just hand this to him? This is a flight chart that I believe we got out of his airplane."

"Do you recognize that?" Rothschild asked.

"Yes, um-hum," Hansen said.

"Those marks that are on that flight chart, do you know how many of those are on there, sir?" Krumm asked.

Hansen inhaled deeply and let out an audible sigh. Then he started to count, moving his lips as he did so. "I count, what, nineteen?" he said. "Am I wrong?"

"I believe there's twenty on the face there, and on the back side of that map I believe there's an additional mark," Flothe said.

Hansen started to count again, diligently. "Hmm," he said after a while, "I lost track on that count. . . . Seventeen that time."

"Let's just assume twenty-one, for purposes of discussion. The number doesn't mean a whole lot at the moment," Krumm said. And then he led Hansen through the list, pointing to spots on Hansen's flight map that Hansen had identified as burial sites in the past two days of his confession. But there were other marks, too, and that was what they wanted to know about.

"Can we have a meeting of the minds right now?" Krumm pointedly asked, trying to catch Hansen's eye. "How many women, sir, have you killed in Alaska?"

Hansen balked momentarily. He turned to Fred Dewey to make sure he would not be further incriminated by responding. Finally he said, "There's a lot of marks here. I'm going to be very honest: These marks represent something. They do—" Then he abruptly changed the subject. "Do you have another map of this-here?" he asked. "This map is not in detail. Do you have another map?"

This started a complicated process. Hansen's own maps were paraded before him, but none of them was detailed enough for him. Then they started bringing out the detailed sectionals, huge maps that would have to be taped together to take in the areas under discussion and that eventually would crowd out everything but the microphones on the conference table. Even with that, Hansen was hardly satisfied. He kept insisting he had a more detailed map at home, one that marked specific sites with greater precision.

In spite of Hansen's protestations, they stayed with the sectionals. He was going to point out spots on the sectionals and then they'd narrow it down on aerial photographs. "I can see this is going to run into an awful long time," Hansen said, pulling one of the maps closer to him. "All right. You take the old Palmer Highway, you drive north on here, and you've got Barnhart's Mill Road—goddamn, you know, I can't, even with this-here map I can't even put it exactly. . . . "

Hansen nevertheless did his best to describe the location, saying it was off the Knik at the end of the road, in an alder scrub next to a high embankment.

"Will you take us to that if we can't find it?" Krumm asked.

"When?" Hansen asked.

"If we leave, like, tomorrow or Saturday with a helicopter and go right out to these spots, we can mark them and next spring we can . . ." Flothe suggested tentatively.

"Well," Hansen replied, "if you give me the aerial photographs I can show them to you exactly."

"Well, we'll do that," Krumm said, "but, okay, assuming that we can't show exactly, would you at least give it some thought?"

"All right."

Hansen went back to the map and pointed to the spot where he thought a body might be. Hansen himself marked the spot with a green marking pen, the color meant to represent murders to which he was confessing but would not be charged with. "And this will be uncharged number one," Krumm said. "Okay."

He moved to the next map: one of the old Palmer Highway. He pointed to an area just off the old highway bridge and made three marks near a huge gravel pit.

"There's a total of three on this chart?" Vic Krumm asked.

"Three on this chart."

"Uncharged numbers two, three, and four," Rothschild announced, as he marked a crude little map Hansen had drawn as a visual aid.

Hansen was starting to get cold feet, however. Having all the maps marked and put in order made him nervous. He was overcome by a small bout of terror. "Where are we going to put this, gentlemen?" he asked, pointing at the sectional map and his drawing. And then he began a convoluted, fractured speech which was summed up by a single sentence: "Before we go any further here," Hansen declared, "I want something back on these-here, too."

Nobody from the prosecution was giving anything more to Hansen, so he was forced to go ahead without further assistance. What he had to say would best be described as a paranoid vision calculated to win sympathy.

"Some of these gals are girlfriends and in with organized crime. They were sent up here by organized crime. They're the girlfriends and so forth of The Brothers motorcycle gangs and so forth here in town. Now, nobody is gonna bullshit me into thinking this is not going to come back on my family. Now, what are you people gonna do? I know you're not going to put a State Trooper on my driveway.''

"Well, Bob, here's what's going to happen," Krumm broke in, trying to calm Hansen down. "I mean, as a practical matter—"

"When you put this in the paper, all these-here names . . ." Hansen said, his voice rising.

"Well, there won't be any names attached right now," Krumm indicated.

"Now, wait just a second now," Hansen interrupted. "Let's say I can account for all the goddamn dancers that are gone. That don't leave no doubt, does it? They're still gone. They can put a flyer out on me, no matter where I'm at, if they want to get me. And I don't really give a shit, you know. I am going to die in prison anyway. As a matter of fact it probably would be better for me if I die quick, *but* my family is here. Now what are you going to do about that?" Hansen's voice was charged with emotion.

"How recently have you talked to your wife, Bob? Do you know if she is planning on staying up here? Do you really know what her plans are?" Krumm wanted to know.

"If she would leave up here, that solves the problem right there. Okay, but you know I can go down here and I can pinpoint every frickin' one of them, and I'll be glad to do it, but you know I want something—the only thing I can do, sir, right now, is try to protect my family."

For the next three-quarters of an hour Hansen could not be moved from his fears for his wife and children. Their address had been printed in the newspapers. They'd lose money if Darla sold the house right away and moved out of state. He was afraid for his own life. "Even in the little confinement that I have had, there have been two different people that have come up to me, right there in—in one of the most confined modules over there—and said, 'Hey, you're dead. We heard the word that they will kill you.' "

Flothe changed the subject back to Bob's wife, but it didn't seem to do much good. He suggested several options Darla could pursue—going back to her maiden name, staying with friends until she got squared away—but it just served to confuse Hansen the more. It was suggested that it might take a while to identify the bodies, most of which hadn't been found, and that seemed to alleviate some of his fears.

"If you want me to go out in a helicopter tomorrow," Hansen finally offered, "I'll go out. You can put an X on the goddamn snow or a tree, wherever you want to dig in the spring. Is there any way possible to keep that part of it out until, let's say, till she leaves? Which I'll say will be for sure within six months."

Krumm tried to turn Hansen's fear of publicity against him, suggesting that unless he came clean with everything the papers would be filled with speculation. Hansen remained confused, wondering out loud what he could do to help eradicate the fears he had for his family.

Finally attorney Joe Evans called for a break so he could make some suggestions. At 3:28 P.M. Glenn Flothe announced that they were concluding the taping. Somehow Lieutenant Jent didn't get the message in time and the tape recorder caught a hushed conversation between Haugsven, Krumm, and Rothschild, who had assumed they were off the record.

"He's not even half done on the murders," Krumm whispered.

"He does know where every one of them is at," Haugsven added.

"Yeah, he does," Krumm said, "He's not even half done."

"No," Frank Rothschild said, "but he is a hell of a humanitarian for his family, isn't he?"

They finally did get back to the maps. Hansen identified number five (uncharged) as well as the fifth victim he was being charged with. They were ten yards or so apart, up on the Knik. Number six, he said, was nearby. Number seven, meanwhile, was up toward the Eagle River jail, killed right around the time he had been released in 1973.

"That's number seven, right?" Rothschild asked, trying to make sure he was keeping up.

"Yes," Krumm reminded him.

Hansen, meanwhile, pored over the maps. He did so without relish, having insisted earlier that it would be better if they just flew him up to the area by helicopter and assuring everyone that it would only take a half hour if they did it that way. Before long Hansen looked up with disgust and said: "The best thing you can do with these damn maps is burn them."

Number eight was a black girl from "a long time

ago," buried up by Summit Lake on the Seward Highway.

Pretty soon Rothschild was pointing to Seward and asking Hansen if he'd had anything to do with the disappearance of women from that town.

"Ah, out of Seward, gentlemen, I never had anything to do with any girls out of Seward."

"There was one missing in '73 and one in '75, and they disappeared while you were there," Flothe reminded Hansen.

"I heard about that. I mean, there was posters all over Seward and everything else about them. But that's not me. That's the truth."

But Hansen did spot another of his kills on the Kenai Peninsula. Number nine, near Scenic Lake. She was blond, he said, and quite thin.

Soon pictures of the victims—living and dead— were pulled out, though Hansen didn't recognize many of them. They went back to the maps. Number ten was on Figure Eight Lake, just east of the Susitna River.

In an idle moment Frank Rothschild asked an idle question. "Why did you keep the map?" he asked.

"Ah, it was kept for . . ." Hansen looked vacant, then caught himself. "One night I was sitting at home and, ah, there was some marks on the map that didn't have any correspondence to, ah, these girls. And I was looking at places that I had some bear stands, and for some reason or other I just started correlating where the people were to my bear stands, for some reason."

Number eleven was at Horseshoe Lake. Hansen pointed to some of the photographs on the table.

"DeLynn Frey?" Haugsven asked. "Did you remember a name for her? A nickname?"

"No. What did she have for a nickname?"

"Sugar," Haugsven said.

"That's possible."

What was interesting about this one, moreover, was that Hansen had used his plane, and he told them that the reason this woman ended up dead was because he broke a strut that held up one of the skis on his landing gear. The woman panicked, he said. But now Flothe also had an idea how Hansen had ended up with the distinctive skiprints that led to his being fingered in the cabin burglaries.

Flothe pointed to another mark on Hansen's map, near Lake Clunie and on the northern border of the military base. This one Hansen denied, saying he'd put the mark in the wrong place. Two more sites, up in the Matanuska Valley, were also denied. He also denied, again, that any of the marks in Seward and Resurrection Bays had anything to do with missing women. Were they getting close to the end of his string? Krumm was counting them all up.

"Bob," he said, "you've given us, at this point, sixteen girls. Are there any more on any of these maps?"

"No."

"How about taking a girl to McHugh Creek on the Seward Highway south of Anchorage, back in

'72? [*sic*]'' Flothe asked.* All the troopers present knew that this one was for Major Gilmour.

"Oh no, you're talking about the Michaels case. . . . "

"Uh-huh."

"No. I didn't have nothing to do with that, I didn't have nothing to do with that. I know, they asked me about the Michaels case when I was in trouble before that, uh, about the Patterson girl."

"Uh-huh?" Flothe said, noncommittal.

"But, uh, no, I didn't have nothing to do with that," Hansen said, his voice cracking at the end of the sentence, then trailing off.

Frank Rothschild changed the subject. "Are you guys going to get together tomorrow and take a little—if the weather's right—take a little ride?" he asked.

"I think that, perhaps, maybe we could take a quick break and resolve what we're going to do tomorrow, and get back on tape, maybe—because our boss is right next door here," Flothe said quickly, sounding slightly nervous but trying to appear cool.

They would not go on after taking a five-minute break, however. The chilling confession of Bob Hansen was finally at an end.

---

*The transcript of the confession says " '72"; the actual date was 1971.

25

Lieutenant Jent told Sgt. Flothe that it was perfectly all right for them to take the State Trooper helicopter up to the Knik River to look for burial sites, and when Flothe passed along the information to Krumm and Rothschild they decided to take Hansen up to the Knik the following day, a Friday. In the meantime they would make arrangements for Bob to see Darla Hansen, so the two of them could straighten out some of their domestic business.

Flothe barely slept a wink that night. In his mind Flothe imagined Hansen going for the control stick of the chopper and then saw them wheeling toward the ground as the pilot vainly tried to regain control. Hansen was laughing the laugh of the howling dead.

The trooper sergeant was convinced that taking Bob Hansen up to the Knik River in the State Troopers' Bell helicopter was a suicide mission. If they could get a bigger chopper, something like a Huey, he'd feel better, but there was no way the colonel was going to approve that. It would run something like five grand a day, and they'd already spent enough money on this case.

The next morning, however, when Flothe screwed up his courage to ask the colonel to rent a larger chopper, Kolovsky shrugged. "Of course," he said.

"That way," Flothe went on, "I could put a guy on either side of him, so he doesn't pull any funny business."

"Of course," Kolovsky repeated.

"And I can sit up front with the maps, with a bulkhead between Hansen and the pilot. . . . "

"Of course," Kolovsky said. "Anything you need, Glenn, anything you need. Oh, and by the way, congratulations." Then Kolovsky reached for a case at the front of his desk. "Have a cigar."

Saturday, February 25, 1984

Flothe finally got his helicopter. It was of military vintage, and just what he wanted. The pilot's compartment was separate, with a metal panel between the cabin and the passenger area. Flothe put Lieutenant Jent and Trooper Von Clasen on either side of Hansen and hooked him up to some headphones and a microphone.

Because of the eight marks along the Knik River, that's where they headed first. The first place Hansen took them was near the meat shack, in an area that was a long sandbar in summer. Paula Goulding had died there, Flothe remembered, and at least one other body was still waiting to be exhumed.

On the ground Hansen and Flothe donned snowshoes and headed toward a clump of alders. Jent and Von Clasen followed behind them with high-powered rifles, with orders to shoot if Hansen tried to get away.

Hansen bounded through the snow like a rabbit. He was a sight to behold: dressed in just a sweatsuit, his hands in handcuffs, knee-deep in powder snow. Flothe was having trouble keeping up with him, even though all he had to carry was a can of fluorescent spray paint to mark trees with.

"Hey, slow down!" he yelled at Hansen.

Hansen stopped and panted a little, sort of like a dog taking his master for a walk. And just like a dog, he was impatient to stay on the scent now that he had found it. Soon Hansen located the tree he was looking for among the cluster of alders. Immediately he was on his hands and knees, digging into the snow with his bare hands, oblivious to the handcuffs or the cold or anything else.

"No, no, that's all right," Flothe said when he finally caught up to him. "It's probably five or six feet deep. We'll just spray this tree here and come back during the spring."

Almost at once Hansen was whirling off to another nearby body. And then to another, where the digging ritual was reenacted. The last one was a surprise. It wasn't on his maps. Maybe he was wrong? Flothe marked the spot with the spray paint all the same.

And then they were in the air again, flying east to Jim Creek. From there he took them west toward the Susitna, to Horseshoe Lake and Figure Eight Lake, Hansen telling them he didn't know the lakes by name, only by shape. And they flew south, near Hiland Drive and the Eagle River jail. It was just starting to get dark as they headed home. Hansen had led the troopers to twelve bodies that day alone.

It wasn't until approximately 2:45 on Monday afternoon that Bob Hansen appeared before Judge Moody. Attorneys, law enforcement officers, members of the press, and friends and families of the victims packed the third-floor courtroom. When Vic Krumm announced that Hansen had admitted to the serial murders, Kitty Larson ran crying from the room. Others who had known the dead women also cried, some throughout the proceeding. Frank Rothschild, meanwhile, launched into the best courtroom speech of his career.

"Your Honor," Rothschild said, "before you sits a monster, an extreme aberration of a human being. A man who has walked among us for seventeen years, serving us donuts, Danish, and hot coffee, all with a pleasant smile. Mellow, mild-mannered, bespectacled Bob the baker. A family man. A man so cunning, so clever, that his friends and acquaintances are in shock at what he now admits to before this court. Not even his wife of nearly twenty years had any idea of his dark, evil side.

"He's a man," Rothschild continued, "who has manipulated his family, his friends, countless women, the police, and the courts of our state for the many years he has been here. He is, to be blunt, the most prolific mass murderer in modern Alaskan history. A man who purposely, coldly, plotted and planned the kidnap, the terrorizing, and the rape of scores of women who lived here in Anchorage, who admits to murdering seventeen women, seventeen young, helpless, frightened women, and then burying them in our wilderness.

"His crimes numb the mind. Hearing him tell of his crimes, which we did last week for ten to twelve hours, sapped the body of energy, it sapped the spirit. But the story must be told, for our community wants to know how it is that this man got away with these crimes all these years and how it is that we finally caught him. His manipulations are immense.

"And while he doesn't admit it," Rothschild suggested, "it's obvious from reading through and looking at where things started and where the women ended up, he hunted them down, Judge. He let them run a little bit and then he enjoyed a little hunt, just like with his big-game animals. He toyed with them, he wanted to scare them, he got a charge out of all of this. They weren't shot right where it all started: He let them run, he grabbed them and they'd claw a little bit, and he'd let them run a little more and played with them," Rothschild went on, letting his imagination run away with him.

"He doesn't look big and strong, but he is," Rothschild went on. "One time he called this his 'summertime project.' What a lovely word for his handiwork, a 'summertime project.' And he did admit that none of them went willingly. Even when he went through the map and talked about where all these women were and pointed out to us where they were, it was cold. He said, 'Well, there's one here and there's one there, and you'll find one next to this tree and one under that road.' They weren't human beings to him."

Rothschild told the judge of his fears that there were yet more bodies that Hansen hadn't told them about. "He is a compulsive liar," Rothschild said. "He gives us what he knows he has to give us and no more.

"He says he cares about his family," Rothschild said. "That's a fiction. His family was a prop so he could hide behind decency, to show 'I'm a family man.' And he's a baker and he makes money and it's all part of a game.

"So we have to ask ourselves, Can he be rehabilitated? We know that's a joke. It's too late. Will this deter others? People like this aren't going to get deterred, not that have the kind of problems this man has. We can sure isolate him, and we can sure tell all the people in our community and reaffirm their value system that this man will never see the light of day again. We can't put him to death, but truly that would be too easy for this man, Your Honor. It's really what he'd prefer at this point. It's better that we lock him up and make him live with this for each breath that he takes of prison air that he'll be breathing the rest of his life.

"He asked that we recommend—and we strongly recommend—that he be sent to the federal prison system. We ask the court to make that recommendation. He's asked for psychiatric counseling. We agree, if for no other reason than to try to make him aware of what a monster he is."

When it came time for sentence recommendations, Rothschild did not spare the rod. For the murder of Sherry Morrow, he asked for a ninety-nine-year term. For the murder of Paula Goulding, another ninety-nine-year term. For Joanna Messina, another ninety-nine-year term. For the kidnapping of Kitty Larson Rothschild asked for another ninety-nine year term, and then an additional thirty years for her rape, twenty-five years for five counts of felony weapons possession, and ten years for two theft indictments. That was a total of 461 years. Rothschild added a request for a life term for the murder of "Jane Doe," also known as Eklutna Annie.

It could have been worse. Hansen wasn't even charged in the rape and kidnapping of the black topless dancer, nor was he charged with the murder of the woman he threw off the railroad bridge on the Knik. The number of murder charges was down to four, Hansen's original number. It was still enough to put him away for a long time. And even that wasn't enough assurance for Frank Rothschild. "For these people that he has slain, for those lucky enough to have survived," Rothschild said, "Your Honor, we ask that you rid us of this beastly man forever."

Judge Ralph Moody had a difficult task before him. He stood at the apex of a system that had failed miserably in its assigned role, and he seemed responsible for explaining how it could have happened.

"It's hard to believe that humanity produces and sustains people who have the ability and the propensities to commit such enormous, such beastly, such indescribable crimes," Moody said. "There are no words which can adequately describe him. What we have seen here today, and what the defendant has admitted to in many respects, is a condemnation of society as a whole.

"We have let down not only the victims but many of our compatriots here in court, here in Alaska. The court system has failed. Knowing that he was a problem, probation officers, police officers, members of society themselves who would not come forward, I can't think of a bigger indictment of society than this. And we might as well face the music and resolve now and forevermore that we're not going to allow people like this to remain on the streets. If there ever was a case in which a man or defendant needed to be surveillanced for the rest of his life, it is this gentleman here, and it's been known for many years.

"But what did we do? We say he paid his debt to society when we give him sentencing, we depend on psychiatrists—and here again, we've got doctors and psychiatrists in this indictment, too, as well as all of you know, I'm sure, we're involved. I'm a judge and a lawyer, and so I place myself in the collective pot for criticism.

"Society had better take another look when you've got people like this. And there should be laws which allow you to supervise and keep some kind of control over people like this, the rest of their lives if it's necessary. Here we've turned a person loose several times, knowing that he had the propensity for what he did. There's absolutely no excuse for it, there's no justification in any sense for the cruelty he's shown.

"In these cases he took people who could least protect themselves, people from the standpoint of the lower point of society, but from the standpoint of the man were angels compared to what he had done. There just isn't much you can say of what happened here, of what this man has admitted to, of what he has placed upon society, and what society has to a great extent allowed to occur. I hope when we leave this courtroom today that I have to the best of my ability provided this man shall never walk the streets of America or any other place as a free man.''

Judge Moody did just that. He gave Hansen the maximum sentence on each count: 461 years, plus life. Still, there were grumblings even before Hansen was sentenced about reviving the death penalty in the State of Alaska.

The night the Hansen conviction came in, Glenn Flothe held a quiet celebration at one of Anchorage's finest restaurants. It would cost him three hundred dollars but it was worth every penny. His wife Cherry was with him. Kitty Larson was with him. And so were the two women who had watched over Kitty after she'd decided it was time to come in off the streets.

It was a gathering interwoven with emotion. Everyone spoke nervously, but with evident relief. Everyone except Kitty, who was subdued, pensive, and somewhat withdrawn through much of the evening. She was emotionally drained.

Flothe hoped Kitty had learned something from her experience. At dinner she looked scared straight, ready to trade her life on the streets for life in a Christian home. Flothe resolved to do everything he could to help her stay on the right path.

He promised himself not to let her down, now that her "usefulness" to the criminal justice system had been fulfilled. It wasn't long, however, before this sensitive young woman was back on the streets. That's where her friends were. That was her life.

26

Sergeant Flothe, Trooper Von Clasen, and an AST pilot flew the trooper helicopter to the grave sites marked along the Knik River. They wanted to see if they could begin the search for additional bodies. From the air it looked encouraging. Much of the snow cover had melted. On the ground, however, they discovered that the earth was still frozen. They would have to wait.

Two days later Flothe got a call from Darla Hansen. Something had been bothering her, a memory brought back by Bob's visit to look for stolen booty.

"After Bob was arrested," she told Flothe, "he asked me to remove some weapons from the backyard."

"Was that before his confession?" Flothe asked.

"Yes."

"Where did he say they were?"

"He led me to believe they were buried in the backyard."

Later that day the sergeant was back at Old Harbor Road, this time with a metal detector. He slowly swept the area in back of the house, while

Darla stood by nervously. They didn't find a thing, and Hansen had already denied throwing anything into a septic tank he said didn't exist.

In truth Flothe was hardly disappointed. He was glad for the chance to talk to Darla again. He wanted to see how she was coming along with her plans.

"Have you decided to stay on in Anchorage?" Flothe asked.

"All the neighbors have said they want us to stay," Darla revealed. "They've been really nice. And I'd rather live here. But it's been awfully hard on the kids."

"Uh-huh."

"I said we could move to the lower forty-eight. My family is down there. But the girl says she doesn't want to move, so I don't know."

"And how's your son?"

"He's okay. He's a lot younger."

As Flothe looked around him he saw a big backyard that made you feel you were in a small forest. If you loved Alaska, it would be a hard place to part with. Looking at Darla again, Flothe noticed she still had something to say. He wasn't sure she would say it.

"I don't know how you do it," Flothe told her. "You seem so strong."

"What can you do?" she replied. "Just die?"

There was nothing Flothe could say. All he could do was shrug his shoulders sympathetically. And then she started to talk about her husband.

"You know," Darla said, "I can kind of understand some of these things. . . . '' Her voice trailed off. "But things came easy for him. He was good at a lot of things. He was a good baker. A good pilot. Anything he wanted to do, he could do. But he had to cheat on things, and that I could never understand. You know what he told me once? That when he was in Boy Scouts he had to have the most merit badges. And he cheated on every one of them, even though his father was the Scout Master. He didn't have to cheat. But he did. He had to cheat on everything.''

At that moment, in Darla's forthright naiveté, Flothe once again saw the perfect wife for a killer. Still Flothe could not help but feel compassion for her. As he headed back to his car he said, "If there's anything you need—anything—if you get a single harassing phone call, or a single threatening note—just let us know. We're here to protect you, Mrs. Hansen. Whatever it takes, we'll do it.''

"Thanks,'' she said. "We're fine.''

While Flothe was talking to Darla Hansen, Troopers Bullington and Von Clasen flew out in the AST helicopter to check some grave sites located west of Wasilla, at Horseshoe Lake and Figure Eight Lake. There was still a great deal of snow cover, however, and excavation was not yet possible.

In the succeeding days the AST Tactical Dive Unit, consisting of Laddie Shaw, Sgt. Don Savage, and Trooper Mike Dekreon, conducted an underwater search of the Knik River beneath the railroad bridge in the vicinity of Mile 30.4 on the Glenn

Highway. The bottom search was conducted between the south three sections and the bank, using a straight line method in addition to individual search. The water depth averaged twelve to twenty inches, with a maximum depth of approximately four feet. On the bottom was a layer of silt over a layer of gravel/silt mix. The river was very clear, with only scattered debris.

They didn't find anything. What was really bothersome, moreover, was the fact that the tidal change in the previous year had been in excess of six feet, and the bottom gradient of the Knik River had changed dramatically. Sandbars had shifted. The composition of the bottom had changed. The decision was made to search the area again in late fall, after spring runoff had been completed.

In Juneau, the state capital, the Senate was being asked by Senator Fritz Pettyjohn to reconsider a capital punishment bill introduced in the last session of the legislature. Speaking of Bob Hansen, Pettyjohn asked his colleagues to "consider whether or not this gentleman would be the proper subject for Senate Bill 121. This is the kind of gentleman this bill is intended to reach," Pettyjohn continued, "someone who has committed an outrageous act that shocks the conscience of the entire community."

Pettyjohn's bill proposed to make murder in the first degree a capital felony, with terms ranging from twenty to ninety-nine years in prison, or a sentence of death. The bill still had opponents.

"I don't want the senator to think the bill was

introduced and didn't receive action,'' said Senator
Joe Josephson of Anchorage. ''We held hearings on
that bill in Anchorage and most of the testimony—
over thirty witnesses—was hostile to the proposition.''

The Senate adjourned without taking any action
on the measure.

Saturday, March 10, 1984

More than a month after his sentencing, Robert C.
Hansen was finally moved out of Anchorage. Lieutenant Jent and Sergeant Flothe accompanied him
to the federal intake prison at El Reno, Oklahoma,
for eventual transfer to the Lewisburg Federal Correctional Facility in Pennsylvania. They were hoping Hansen would elect to tell them about the other
murders they suspected he'd committed, in addition
to those he had already confessed to. But Hansen
wasn't interested in talking about the past. ''I can't
see anything in it for me,'' he told them. ''What's
done is done. It's behind me now. I've still got the
rest of my life ahead of me.''

What Hansen wanted to talk about was the future. It looked rosy to him, considering. ''What am
I?'' he asked rhetorically. ''Forty-five? I ought to
live until I'm eighty. I still have half my life to live,
even if I have to live it in prison.''

''What are you going to do with your life?'' Jent
asked.

''They said they're going to retrain me,'' Hansen
said. ''I want to become a writer. What I plan to

do is get experience by writing humorous stories. Then I'll write my own story.''

Jent was convinced that Hansen eventually would write a book about his killings. Two publishers already had contacted him.

27

The smell of fetid death became the signature for the spoiled fruits of Hansen's Arctic summers. The stench of decaying human flesh was sickeningly sweet, and could turn a stomach inside out. The knees wanted to buckle, but the legs wanted to run away. Flothe and his fellow troopers knew they were in for some hard duty.

Not until the end of April, however, had the ground thawed enough to permit an effective search. The first breakthrough came on Monday, April 23, when Trooper Wayne Von Clasen, checking grave sites at the Knik River bridge, found a suitcase and a purse at a spot Hansen had marked as grave number six. Hansen had told them a purse was buried at this spot, and Von Clasen was using a probe to test the hardness of the ground when he found it. The contents were well preserved, and the plastic case itself was soon identified as one belonging to Tamara Pederson, one of the missing dancers.

The next day at 10:30, Jent, Kasnick, Flothe, and Von Clasen dug up the first body, at Hansen grave site number two. They were concentrating on places in the sun, and this one was near Jim Creek, east of the old Knik River bridge, on the north side of the river. Making sure not to disturb the body, they used hand shovels and ice chippers to remove it from the river bank. What they found was a badly decomposed body consisting of bones, some flesh, hair, and bits of clothing. Very slowly they slid the remains into a body bag, being cautious not to jostle it too much.

It was a busy day. About a mile and a half west they found another body, this near the parking area of the old Knik bridge. It was recovered about 1:00, and was distinguished from the first body by the fact that it was wrapped in a plastic bag. The troopers took that as evidence the murder had happened elsewhere, and the corpse was transported to the river bank for burial. Lt. Jent also thought the body was nude, but couldn't be sure because it was so badly decomposed.

What was uncanny, though, was the fact that the troopers didn't have to dig more than one hole for each body. Hansen had been right on target, a remarkable feat, considering that some bodies had been there for at least two years.

The next day was even busier than the day before. It was a bright blue day, the mountains snow-capped and magnificent, when the troopers returned to the parking area near the old Knik River bridge, searching for Hansen grave site number three.

Because Hansen couldn't quite remember where he'd buried this body, the troopers had to probe carefully. They began by raking various spots near

the marks Hansen had given them. At each spot
they dug a small test hole. They were trying to
think like a killer. Their efforts were rewarded by
piles of moose nuggets, rusting beer cans, the remains of a dead dog.

To make things interesting, someone was watching them work: Sheila Toomey of the *Anchorage
Daily News*. They noticed she was trying to evade
the scent from the grave they'd opened the previous
day. She went off to the left. Then back to the right.
Then she stepped back. Everywhere she went, it
followed her. The death stench stuck to everything.
Even as the reporter tried to escape, she took the
smell with her. It was on her shoes, on her hands,
in her hair.

The troopers, meanwhile, talked as they worked,
as was their habit. It helped them put their minds
on something else. Finally tired of coming up
empty-handed, however, the troopers decided to
split into two teams and move on. That way they
could cover more area.

Using a four-by-four, Troopers Von Clasen and
Haugsven checked grave site number eight, on the
island south of the place where Paula Goulding's
body had been found. The body was supposed to
be buried in the sandbar but, not sure of its exact
location, the troopers didn't find it.

Flothe and Kasnick, meanwhile, took the AST
helicopter to check grave site number seven, which
was next to the Goulding grave. The ground was
frozen eight to ten inches deep and, uncertain of
the body's exact location, the two of them decided
to return later.

From there Kasnick and Flothe flew to Horse-shoe Lake, east of the Susitna River, where Hansen had marked grave number nine. They found a body not more than fifty feet from the flag left by Hansen. One of three bodies Hansen said he hadn't buried, it was on top of the ground, lying facedown and prone. The body was fully clothed. Although somewhat damaged by small animals and mostly skeletal, the jaw was in one piece. There was hope the body could be identified through the dozen sets of dental records Flothe already had collected.

Back at trooper headquarters, Flothe found several messages waiting for him. The first of them was news about the preliminary autopsy reports on the bodies they'd found the day before. The identities were still unknown, but they had some partial descriptions.

One of the bodies was that of a woman in her twenties, 5'5" with blond or strawberry-blond hair. She was wearing jeans, a long-sleeved black-and-white sweater, a white zippered jacket with colored trim, high heels, and a cheap gold necklace. The second woman was about 5'3" and had brown or auburn hair. She was, as Jent had suspected, completely nude. She had been shot just once.

Thursday, April 26, 1984

Working zealously so they could quickly put the worries of the victims' friends and relatives to rest, Flothe and Von Clasen were at it again promptly the next morning. Using the AST helicopter they flew north to Figure Eight Lake, Hansen grave site number eleven. Located just east of the Susitna River was another spot where Hansen said he'd left a body on the ground. That's where they found it, lying beneath a flag placed there by Hansen himself.

What they found were pieces of clothing and bone resting on the still frozen earth. They couldn't dig out the pants, which were bonded to the soil beneath them, without destroying the evidence. Again they had to wait for it to thaw further.

The jawbone of the victim was found on top of the ground, near the pants and separated from the rest of the body. It was clear much dental work had been done on the teeth. They were a good candidate for identification. Flothe picked up the jawbone and took it back to the chopper. They'd take it back to Anchorage and compare it with their dental records.

The next stop was Scenic Lake, almost directly due south across Cook Inlet, on the Kenai Peninsula. It was Hansen grave site number thirteen and this one, Hansen had said, was on the ground but covered by some brush. At this site they found a small rib bone and a torn red blouse, both of which they seized. There was also ''bear sign'' noted around the body. Unfortunately the ground was frozen. They couldn't remove it yet. While there Flothe and Von Clasen looked for the victim's purse, but there was still ice along the edge of the lake where it was allegedly located.

Back at headquarters, the jawbone seized at Figure Eight Lake was immediately compared with dental records. The dental X rays were positively identified as those of Angela Feddern, reported missing in February 1983 by Joe Majors, owner and operator of Murphy's Law, a bar featuring nude female dancers. In a way the troopers got lucky on this one. The incident had been reported to them, but no APD report was ever filed. Looking at the Trooper Incident Report, however, Flothe learned that Feddern had been working as an avenue prostitute and allegedly had had a date with a doctor when she disappeared.

In Seattle Angela's mother, Mary Radford, soon learned that her daughter's body had been found. "I was prepared for it," she told the Associated Press. "I knew something was wrong when she stopped calling last year. In a way, there's some relief. You wonder what happened to them until you know for sure."

Asked what she thought of Hansen's plea-bargained sentence, Mrs. Radford turned bitter. "I don't see why he should be alive and they dead," she said.

Mrs. Radford also acknowledged that her daughter had chosen to be a prostitute, knowing it was a rough life. "That was the life she chose," she said. "Angie just couldn't find it in herself to go out and get a thinking job. She did the best she could."

Friday, April 27, 1984

By Friday Dr. Rogers had used dental records to identify the first body troopers had found, the one in the old Knik River bridge parking lot. She was

Sue Luna, one of the first women Flothe had asked about. He remembered that her sister had reported her missing, and looking at the records, found the date to be May 30, 1982. Almost two years before, to the day. She was a woman who had been offered three hundred dollars for sex, little knowing that her date would kill her and take his three hundred back.

That Sunday, moreover, off-duty Palmer Police Officer Al Moreau found another body while walking along the Knik River with a friend. A knee bone and a tattered piece of blue jean material had protruded through the sand and caught his eye. "I figured it was a body," he said. "It was probably the worst smell I had ever smelled in my life."

Moreau called the troopers and stuck around to help them dig up the remains. "All night I kept seeing the same thing," Moreau said. "Picking up the legs and putting her in the body bag. She was cold, real cold."

What was noteworthy about the discovery was its nearness to Hansen grave site number six. And it was across a sandbar from where troopers had earlier found the lavender purse and blue suitcase belonging to still missing Tamara Pederson. Was it she? An autopsy disclosed the victim had been shot twice with a large-caliber bullet that appeared to match those from a gun used by Hansen in some of the other murders.

By the middle of the next week Dr. Rogers had once more used dental records to identify the body. It was indeed Tamara Pederson. She had been twenty-one when she disappeared from the Wild

Cherry nightclub in August 1982. The discovery of her body brought to six the number of bodies troopers had found during the week. Altogether they had accounted for ten of the seventeen women Hansen had admitted killing.

Mr. Pederson, Tamara's adopted stepfather, met with Flothe on Wednesday, May 2, and again the next day, when Flothe flew him to Tamara's grave site at his request. It was a grim pilgrimage to a spot that had retained its serene beauty despite the carnage. While on the scene, Flothe used an infrared heat-detecting video camera he'd borrowed from the Alyeska Pipeline Company to see if he could find more bodies at Hansen grave sites number one and three. The results were negative.

Later that same week Flothe checked on an alleged grave site on Eagle River Road, one that had been called in by a concerned citizen. Although no mark on Hansen's aviation maps corresponded to this location, it was still worth checking out. Maybe Hansen had missed one. As it turned out the site was just a natural ground formation; no grave was found, and no items were recovered.

The search for bodies had become an all-consuming task for Flothe and the troopers who worked with him. At one site they dug test holes. Although they couldn't find a body, the ground had at least thawed and become suitable for digging.

Back on the Knik, troopers Von Clasen and Bullington went to a gravel pit on the northwest side of the old Knik River bridge. There, with the help of the heavy equipment operator who owned the gravel pit, they dug up a body believed to be that

of Lisa Futrell. The body was found in an embankment beneath six inches of leaves and soil, her body
parallel to and under a log. It was on its back, the
head pointing north.

In mid-May troopers found a deteriorated paper
bag buried near Hansen grave site number eight
across from the Goulding grave. Inside they found
a bloodstained woman's dress jacket, bloodstained
Levis, shoes, nylons, and Buck hunting knife, and
a purse containing makeup, lipstick, a Bic lighter,
a spoon, and a hypodermic syringe, but no identification. They dug test holes about thirty-five feet
on each side of the bag, but without results.

Later that day they resumed their search at Hansen grave site number seven, which was next to the
Goulding grave. They dug for about five hours, using staggered test holes and seven people, but to
no avail. It was a strikeout kind of day: They used
a metal detector at the Pederson grave, with negative results. Troopers Von Clasen and Bullington
weren't having any luck at Hansen grave site number three at the old Knik River bridge parking area,
although they were using a Cat to hasten the job.

As the summer days grew longer, Flothe started
to have other concerns. It explained why he was
pushing to get this grisly task finished quickly. "It's
important that we get out there soon," the sergeant
told a reporter from the *Anchorage Times.* "The
buried bodies are pretty well protected, but the ones
on the ground are not. They could be carried away
by animals, and we'd never recover them."

What that meant was that troopers were temporarily suspending their search at Hansen grave site

number seven, where the sack of blood-stained clothing was found. Instead they concentrated their efforts on the above-ground bodies, all of which had been found but were impossible to move without destroying evidence.

By the middle of the month they'd identified another of the bodies from the old Knik River bridge parking lot as that of Malai Larsen. The body found on the ground at Summit Lake was tentatively identified as that of DeLynn Frey. The body found on the ground at Scenic Lake was tentatively identified as that of Teresa Watson. By the end of June, moreover, Lisa Futrell's body had been positively identified. Alaska's short summer was almost at an end.

Flothe knew he would never find some of the victims. The woman tossed off the Knik River railroad bridge was one. And then there were the bodies marked on Hansen's map, the ones at Resurrection Bay, although Hansen denied that the marks showed the presence of victims.

Flothe also knew there were some murders to which Hansen would never confess: If the victim wasn't a prostitute, then Hansen's claim was that he hadn't killed her. He could handle killing prostitutes, apparently, but not the murder of the girl next door. It was doubly disheartening, therefore, to talk to Vincent Thill, father-in-law of Mary Thill, a young woman who had disappeared from the docks near Seward on July 5, 1975. She had never been involved in prostitution in her life.

"Hansen was known to be in the Seward area that Fourth of July," Flothe told Thill. "The same year your daughter-in-law was reported missing. We also found some aviation maps at Hansen's house, and so far there's been a pretty good match between the marks on the maps and the grave sites of the women he killed. And there are several marks in Resurrection Bay, down near Seward, which leads us to believe that Mary might have been one of Hansen's victims. He has, however, denied that allegation.''

Two days later Flothe took another difficult call, this from Mona Altiery in Hawaii.

''Has my daughter's body been found?'' she asked.

''I'm sorry,'' he replied. ''It hasn't.''

''Well, could you send her jewelry to me?'' she asked. ''Primarily the fish necklace and ring is what I'm interested in.''

''No problem, Mrs. Altiery.''

At summer's end eleven bodies had been found, putting the total at twelve of those who had been accounted for, if the woman thrown off the Knik railroad bridge was counted in. It was all the consolation anyone could hope for, because there would always be those others whose identities would never be known, nameless victims of Bob Hansen's blood lust, abandoned forever in the drifting sands of the Knik. The known dead were:

Joanna Messina, found July 8, 1980, at a gravel pit near Seward.
''Eklutna Annie,'' found July 17, 1980, at Eklutna Lake Road.
Sherry Morrow, found September 12, 1982, at the Knik River.

Paula Goulding, found September 2, 1983, at the Knik River.

Sue Luna, found April 24, 1984, at the old Knik River bridge parking lot.

Malai Larsen, found April 24, 1984, at the old Knik River bridge parking lot.

DeLynn Frey, found April 25, 1984, at Summit Lake.

Angela Feddern, found April 26, 1984, at Figure Eight Lake.

Teresa Watson, found April 26, 1984, at Scenic Lake.

Tamara Pederson, found April 29, 1984, at the Knik River.

Lisa Futrell, found May 9, 1984, at the old Knik River bridge gravel pit.

Epilogue

Those were real women Bob Hansen killed, real families who wept, and real graves that had been dug, and yet with time even graves go unnoticed. All that endures are traces of memory. Some of them odd. Some of them oddly affecting.

There were many memories for Glenn Flothe. The first thing he spoke of when he thought about Hansen was his sense that the man had no feelings about lying, and his need to build himself up.

"If you shot two polar bears," Flothe recalled, "then Hansen shot two hundred. He was the greatest hunter that ever walked the face of the earth." Flothe laughed about that part, but still had deep respect for Hansen's skill in the bush.

He was also reminded of the jail house story that there were probably men among Hansen's victims. Flothe thought of a man in Seward who had flatass disappeared. All troopers had ever found of him was his truck.

Most of all, Flothe remembered what Major Gilmour had called Hansen. "A chicken-killer," Gilmour had said. Too afraid to kill himself. Too willing to kill somebody else.

But time does move on. Other cases must be brought to justice. The cast of characters brought on stage for the Hansen drama, meanwhile, would soon drift out of the theater.

Kitty Larson, the star witness who had never had to say a word, returned briefly to Seattle to visit her parents before resuming her life in the streets and massage parlors.

The other dancers went back to business, trying to put the terrible memory of Robert Hansen behind them. Some of them had been his customers. The lucky ones were those who thought there was something odd about a man who offered them three hundred dollars to go to lunch. Within a couple of years, however, a new crop of dancers would hit Anchorage, and they would know nothing of Bad Bob Hansen or the serial murders that had so recently decimated their ranks. They were like a new crop of chickens, waiting to be plucked.

Darla Hansen, meanwhile, moved herself and her kids to Rogers, Arkansas, where they could be near her parents and family.

Col. Kolovosky, on the other hand, lost his job to a change in the governor's office. Kolovosky was the odd man out. He decided to retire.

Kolovosky's successor for a brief while was Major Walter Gilmour. It was a holding action. It was time for a changing of the guard. Soon Gilmour also retired.

Glenn Flothe represented part of that change. He was transferred to the Soldotna Trooper Post, down near Kenai and Homer on the Kenai Peninsula. He soon made Detachment Commander. And soon he was reminded that many of the people he had looked to for inspiration had left the force or retired. Men like Chuck Miller, Joe Hoffbeck, Sam Bernard, Walter Gilmour, and Rollie Port—all of them were gone. It was a big gap to fill.

Dr. Rogers, meanwhile, the man who had done the autopsies on Hansen's victims, was taking things a step further by suggesting that Bob Hansen might be the man responsible for the Green River murders in Seattle. As far as he, and some others, were concerned, nothing investigators had done in Seattle had eliminated the Anchorage baker as a prime suspect. And what was spooky was that the Green River murders stopped at about the same time Hansen was arrested in Alaska.

The cause of all this trouble, Robert Hansen, was determined to stay unpredictable to the very end. After a couple of years in jail, for instance, he told the troopers he'd let them know the identity of his accomplices in crime if they'd let him come to Alaska. It was interesting bait, and the troopers took it seriously enough to question at least one of Hansen's friends, but nothing came of it.

Another surprise came in 1988, when the results of a lawsuit by Alaska convicts made it possible for Hansen to request a transfer to a newly finished maximum security prison near Seward, Alaska. Bob Hansen requested a transfer, despite his earlier fears at being jailed in Alaska, and was transferred to the state prison near Juneau.

In the spring of 1990, Hansen pulled another surprise. Corrections officers in Juneau discovered that Hansen had planned an escape: They found stamps and an aviation map of southeast Alaska hidden in his cell. They surmised that he planned to steal a plane after escaping and use the stamps for cash. Hansen was immediately transferred to the maximum security prison near Seward, where he is still incarcerated at this writing.